AF323225

PARADIGMS OF PEACE

A Pragmatist Introduction to the Contribution
to Peace of Paradigms of Social Science

PARADIGMS OF PEACE

A Pragmatist Introduction to the Contribution to Peace of Paradigms of Social Science

Timo Kivimäki
University of Bath, UK

Imperial College Press

Published by

Imperial College Press
57 Shelton Street
Covent Garden
London WC2H 9HE

Distributed by

World Scientific Publishing Co. Pte. Ltd.
5 Toh Tuck Link, Singapore 596224
USA office: 27 Warren Street, Suite 401-402, Hackensack, NJ 07601
UK office: 57 Shelton Street, Covent Garden, London WC2H 9HE

Library of Congress Cataloging-in-Publication Data
Names: Kivimäki, Timo, author.
Title: Paradigms of peace : a pragmatist introduction to the contribution to
    peace of paradigms of social science / Timo Kivimäki.
Description: New Jersey : Imperial College Press, [2016] |
    Includes bibliographical references.
Identifiers: LCCN 2015047344 | ISBN 9781783269433 (hc : alk. paper)
Subjects: LCSH: Peace. | Peace-building. | Constructivism (Philosophy)
Classification: LCC JZ5538 .K59 2016 | DDC 303.6/6--dc23
LC record available at http://lccn.loc.gov/2015047344

British Library Cataloguing-in-Publication Data
A catalogue record for this book is available from the British Library.

Desk Editors: Suraj Kumar/Mary Simpson

Typeset by Stallion Press
Email: enquiries@stallionpress.com

Printed in Singapore

Contents

Preface

This book is partly motivated by the realization that peace research has failed to follow and utilize the progress made in social sciences. The mainstream of peace research is still very traditional and the main journals in peace research are still bastions of positivism. Most of the post-positivist, new and innovative ideas in the study of peace and conflicts come from security studies. Yet, security studies approaches peace and conflict from a normatively repulsive, partisan perspective. It is interested in someone's security rather than being focused on peaceful relationships. Security can be achieved by destroying enemies, while for peace, destruction is never the answer. This is why peace research is still important, but it needs to embrace the progress in social science, including in security studies. This book is a study that seeks a way how peace research could utilize the discoveries in social sciences. It develops an agenda for pragmatic peace research — peace research that can be an instrument of peace and that also creates interpretations that constitute peaceful social realities. Consequently, this study walks the reader through the main discoveries in social sciences picking up lessons for peace research. This makes it useful for advanced students of peace research and the related disciplines.

I have written this book also to correct the common misunderstanding according to which only traditionalist approaches to peace and conflicts can be used in practice. At the same time, we often think that more contemporary approaches are innovative and philosophically more advanced, but that we cannot really use them in practice for anything else but critique. This, many think, is because the everyday understanding of peace and conflicts is still too far from these philosophically more advanced approaches to social sciences. My disagreements with these views made me write this book. I think, for example, that discoveries of securitization, structural violence, positive peace and the denaturalization of racist, militarist or partisan language and practices have made a huge change in the way we construct the social realities of peace and war. They have been crucial for a more peaceful future. In the formulation of an agenda for peace research, I have approached traditionalist as well as more contemporary discoveries in social sciences from a pragmatist point of view. I have tried to see how different progressive steps can be utilized for peace research and how they can be useful in the construction of more peaceful social realities. This way I have tried to also link the more contemporary ways of thinking of societies to pragmatic value for peace.

I started writing this book after leaving the intellectually inspiring, but politically and institutionally oppressive environment of the University of Copenhagen and after returning to the University of Helsinki. I continue to be inspired by the innovative critical work of the Copenhagen School — Ole Wæver, Lene Hansen, and Anna Leader — but this book was even more affected by the Critical Realist environment of the University of Helsinki. In addition to the above-mentioned pioneers of the Copenhagen School, I owe a great debt to Heikki Patomäki, Riikka Kuusisto and Teivo Teivainen. My discussions with Heikki Patomäki on theory, research, and world politics made my short stay at the University of Helsinki worthwhile, and gave me the inspiration to write this book. Furthermore, I owe a great debt to my new intellectual home, the University of Bath, whose open and inspiring environment made it possible for me to finish writing this book. For encouragement, advice and comments related to some of the final difficulties in this book, I am grateful for Anna Bull, Bill Durodie, Brett Edwards, David Galbreath, Leslie Wehner and Bryan Wong. Finally, I am grateful for the opportunity to develop some of the ideas that I write about in this book in the Conflict Research Society. I am especially grateful for the comments, encouragement and advice from Gordon Burt, Judith Large, Hugh Miall and Chris Mitchell.

About the Author

Dr. Kivimäki is Professor of International Relations with particular expertise in peace and conflict studies at the University of Bath. Previously, he has held professorships at the University of Helsinki, University of Lapland, and at the University of Copenhagen. Professor Kivimäki has also been Director of the Nordic Institute of Asian Studies (Copenhagen) and the Institute of Development Studies of the University of Helsinki.

In addition to purely academic work, Professor Kivimäki has been a frequent consultant to the Finnish, Danish, Dutch, Russian, Malaysian, Indonesian, and Swedish governments, as well as to several UN and EU organizations on conflict and terrorism. He was the co-initiator of the West Kalimantan peace process, led by Indonesia's Vice President, Jusuf Kalla and advisor to President Martti Ahtisaari, who was the mediator in the Aceh Peace Talks.

Professor Kivimäki's latest book, The Long Peace of East Asia (Farnham: Ashgate, 2014) offers a constructivist explanation to the relative peace of East Asia since 1979. Kivimäki's book, *Can Peace Research Make Peace. Lessons in Academic Diplomacy* (Farnham: Ashgate, 2012), was nominated for the prestigious Best Book Prize by the Conflict Research Society in year 2014. Kivimäki's recent articles on peace and conflict topics were published in the Chinese Journal of International Relations, Pacific Focus, the Pacific Review, International Relations of the Asia Pacific, Journal of Peace Research, Asian Security, and the Middle East Policy.

Chapter 1
Introduction

Paradigms in this book mean approaches to research, or research programs that like theories have some views about reality (ontology), but unlike theories, these views about reality have important implications concerning what we can know and what we should study (epistemology), as well as how this knowledge relates to reality and how it can be used for our projects (praxeology). The positivist paradigm, for example, has a view of reality according to which even social reality is ultimately materially constituted, and thus it is possible for a scholar to know social realities just as she knows realities of natural sciences (epistemology), and thus she can also manipulate social realities as an engineer manipulates physical reality (praxeology).

Most theories can be placed into paradigms on the basis of what they claim of reality, what kind of knowledge they seek and sometimes implicitly how this knowledge is to be used. Pragmatism in this study is called a *philosophy* or a *meta-theory*, which is an approach to the assessment of theories or paradigms. Instead of claiming something about reality, this meta-theory contains value judgments that will be presented and argued for in Chapter 2. These value judgments are then used to assess how valuable the different paradigms and the theories presented with the paradigms are.

This volume is a study and a textbook that presents five paradigms of social sciences as logical progressive steps in the field of peace and conflict studies. It is intended to facilitate learning for advanced students and scholars of peace studies and international relations by presenting the premises and the historical development of critical, pragmatic perspectives to problems of peace and war. The book contains text boxes that explain the key concepts, especially those that the literature of peace research uses with confusingly different meanings.

This book is not written in a traditional educational material style, giving shallow, neutral overviews of all and everything and without committing itself to any theoretical positions. Instead, it is written as a study that employs a meta-theory that guides the assessment of the merits of different social science approaches to peace in a novel way, suggesting completely new ways of looking at peace and the theory of peace and war. It presents strong arguments as well as various scholarly positions arguing against their alternatives. Thus, instead of just repeating the arguments of the five paradigmatic steps — positivism, anti-determinism, symbolic interactionism, social constructivism, and critical theory — this book assumes a pragmatist meta-theoretical criteria for the assessment of theoretical paradigms and shows, by means of numerous real-life examples what happens to peace research and peace and conflicts when each of these steps are taken, and what could happen if the wisdom of these paradigmatic approaches is not accepted.

The meta-theoretical pragmatism of the book is appealing as it takes its rationale from real life rather than emerging from inside an existing or newly invented "-ism". In this way the book avoids the tautology of first presenting a philosophical meta-theory with criteria for theories and then showing the merits of the meta-theory by using its own criteria.

As a pragmatist analysis of approaches to peace and conflict research, this book poses the pertinent question "What should we know and consider as real in order to end wars?" and follows that question into the depths of philosophy of social sciences and theories of peace and conflict. Yet, true to the ideals of pragmatism the theories presented in this book are kept in touch with praxis by presenting a variety of examples in which the theory materializes in conflict situations. If a theory cannot be related to real-life examples, it does not relate to real-life itself and thus it is useless. And usefulness for the real-life problem of conflicts and violence is what this book is all about. Instead of considering relevance as *one* of the objectives of peace research, this research program serves praxis and nothing else.

Pragmatism in this book takes off from the idea of classical pragmatists, Peirce, James, and Dewey. However, the book updates the pragmatist meta-theoretical program by offering a constructivist twist to classical pragmatism. Knowledge, theories, concepts, and paradigms will not only be assessed for their instrumental value for peace action. Instead, ideas are also assessed for the peacefulness of the realities they themselves constitute. The pragmatic meta-theory that will be used for the assessment of ideas, theories, and paradigms will be built in Chapter 2. After that, the book walks the reader through some of the main developments and paradigmatic changes in social sciences in the past 50 years. All through the process theories and paradigms will be assessed for their value for peace and peace research. The assessment of paradigms will start from positivist peace research, which from the pragmatist perspective offers a way for "peace engineering", i.e. fixing conflict relations much the same way as engineers fix bridges. From there the journey continues, through many revolutionary innovations to approaches that are available for peace research, but rarely used. These intellectual starting point and the newer innovations treated in this book are:

1. *Positivism: Social engineering of peace.* The book takes a standard positivistic peace research as the point of departure for its analysis, and develops positivistic peace and conflict research from the point of view of pragmatism. While later showing many of the problems of this approach, this section of the book will also acknowledge the merits of the traditionalist approaches to peace research.

2. *Anti-determinism: Inventing the social science of peace.* As the next step, the book complements the empiricist classical pragmatist ideas, common for much of mainstream peace research, with the idea of alternative futures that people have for themselves as individuals, groups and as human beings. In addition to what we can

empirically observe, there is the reality of possibilities that never materialized, but which are nevertheless real as a possibility (Kurki, 2008; Patomäki & Wight, 2000). While some of these possibilities are based on coincidences, some are due to the opportunities for purposive actors to choose between alternative futures. The discovery of a purposive subject, the free will, has implications for peace research and pragmatist modeling of conflict and peace that classical pragmatists could not imagine. Following the implications of possible futures available for purposive actors as opportunities fundamentally changes the way in which science is made by separating social sciences from natural sciences: people decide to go to war, while water cannot decide to boil, it just reacts to conditions that make it boil. The book follows phenomenalism, hermeneutics and various post-positivist approaches by suggesting that deterministic treatment of conditions around human beings shrinks the "human" side of people (Gadamer, 1989; Heidegger, 1962; Arendt, 1970) and deprives us of our freedom if we think that our choices are nothing but reactions either to our instincts or to our environment (Fromm, 1973).

3. *Interpretationism: The discovery of the value of perceptions and interpretations.* The discovery of the meanings that actors involved in conflict give to their environment, the actions of their enemies or their own actions further separates natural sciences from social sciences: water does not have a reason behind its boiling, while for a fighter an act of violence can be revenge, the enforcement of law, a fight against terrorism or any number of things that a scholar of conflicts has to be able to reconstruct in order to understand the actions of the fighter. Meanings and interpretations also broaden our understanding of the reality as in addition to empirically observed opportunities and potentials also the world of meanings is real. In order to advise peace actors on how conflict situations can be transformed, how conflicts can be resolved and how violence can be managed, peace researchers need to problematize and interpret the meanings that people give to different policies and elements of their environment. It is important to understand how conflicting parties tick, but also to

know how conflict situations can be reinterpreted (critical meaning-giving) and framed in a way that is more conducive for peace (Blumer, 1969; Charon, 1995).

4. *Social constructivism: From transformation by innovative peace action to transformation by ideas.* Interpretationism easily leads to the discovery of "institutional facts" (Searle, 1976) and social constructs that exist as interpretations, conventions, and mindsets of conflicting parties and societies. Collective agents in conflict, including nations or races, or political groups exist only in the imagination of the fighters while their actions, such as revenge, religious war, appeasement, pre-negotiation, and mediation exist as action categories only because people have a common understanding of their meaning, and sometimes because they have a name in the dictionary (Dessler, 1999; Hopf, 1998; Wendt, 1998). The fact that these meanings actually create or constitute social realities, further distances neo-pragmatic, post-positivist peace research from the empiricism that classical pragmatists saw as the common scientific approach both for social and natural sciences (James, 1977).

5. *Critical perspectives: The denaturalization of violent constructions.* The fact that conflicting parties, just like classical pragmatists, failed to realize the social origin of many of the constituting elements of war and peace often leads to situations where people are unable to change social structures. The relevance of ethnic origin as an identifier in conflict, the fact that offenses need to be avenged, and the fact that national interest is the foundation of a state's foreign policy is often taken as a natural given, while in reality, in order to resolve conflicts, one needs to be careful with "realities" and "natural" phenomena in wars. From the point of view of pragmatist knowledge production, the idea of constructivism automatically leads to the need to reveal naturalized constructs so that, it would be possible for a peace researcher to see all the opportunities for the deconstruction of knowledge that is harmful for peace or unfair and violent for part of the population. It is, therefore, the task of neo-pragmatist peace research to reveal and denaturalize harmful social constructs, which as "false

consciousness" legitimize direct and structural violence (Booth, 1991; Krause & Williams, 1997; Marx, 1990).

In addition to assessing different ways of doing peace research and indicating the progress peace research could follow, this book also applies the progress of paradigms it explicates in an analysis of the current mega-trends in the development of peace and order in the world. By reviewing the long history of violence available in the analyses by Anthony Giddens, Norbert Elias, Charles Tilly, Mohammed Ayoob, Mary Kaldor, Steven Pinker, and Frances Fukuyama the book reveals the long-term mega-trend the world is facing with its transformation from a national state-based order into an order beyond such a basis (Ayoob, 1991; Elias, 1939, 1982; Fukuyama, 2000, 2011; Kaldor, 1999; Pinker, 2011; Tilly, 1990, 1993). While revealing the opportunities involved in the emergence of a cosmopolitan solidarity towards all civilians regardless of their nationality and the expansion of security communities, the book will also show that this transition from national to cosmopolitan order has two challenges that cause the rise of what could be called Cosmopolitan Protection Wars that result in more than half of all conflict-related fatalities in the world.

The first of the two challenges to the cosmopolitan agenda is the asymmetry between cosmopolitan loyalties and nationalist agency in the protection of global civilians: the willingness to protect globally, but the unwillingness to allow global participation in the production of global security. The second is the asynchrony of the global south and the global north in the preparedness for cosmopolitanism in security affairs. Asymmetry and asynchrony will be the main challenges to peace research and peace activism in the forthcoming decades if not centuries.

Chapter 2
Classical and Constructivist Pragmatism

Pragmatism, at its core, is a philosophy according to which the correspondence between true claims and the reality they refer to is based on practicality. A sentence should be considered true if it advises us in a manner that help us to deal with the reality it refers to in a way that serve our purposes. We know something if that knowledge helps us to deal better with the something we know about. According to pragmatists then, our interests about the target of our knowledge are relevant to our knowledge. A soldier could probably say that he knows what a rifle is if he knows how to use it, while for a scholar who studies metallic molecules knowledge about a rifle would be something entirely different.

Since peace research starts with an interest in the prevention of violence and war, knowledge of a social situation would then relate to this interest. First, in this book we seek knowledge that could help us find ways to prevent the causes of conflicts and promote preconditions for peace. Such knowledge would reveal the conditions of peace and war and the mechanisms in which they relate to peace and war. Such knowledge could help us identify all the linkages in the causal chain from a condition to war or peace. Later in this book, once we have assumed a somewhat different idea of the relationship between knowledge and social realities, we will also think whether something should be considered to be real from the point of view of how different theoretical truth regimes constitute peaceful or violent social realities.

2.1. Classical Pragmatic Peace Research

Classical pragmatism is a philosophical program normally associated with William James, Charles S. Peirce, and John Dewey. The philosophical attraction of pragmatism lies in the idea that it does not create a tautological, cyclical system of reasoning that eventually justifies itself. Instead, pragmatism acknowledges the primacy of being and life that eventually offers the criterion for knowledge. Placing philosophy above life and common knowledge was seen by classical pragmatists as the very reason for the isolation of philosophy and the sciences that followed philosophy, from real-life. This for Dewey and James was the very reason why philosophy and science have often dealt with some higher truths that had no value for the humanity (Dewey, 1993, p. 2; James, 1913, pp. 12–17).

The criterion of knowledge is found in real-life rather than in the axioms of philosophy and science invented for itself to follow. We want something in life and thus we search for ways to relate ourselves to the reality that surrounds us to get what we want. Pragmatism seeks knowledge as something that serves life and the purposes of people who are investigators of knowledge, and the criterion of knowledge is its usefulness for the purposes of the investigator, which in science is the universal investigator. This does not mean that philosophy would not ponder and offer arguments for questions concerning what we should aim at, and what our purposes should be. In this respect knowledge interacts with purposes. Scholarship is not purely instrumental to politics, but criticizes politics and political purposes. Dewey emphasized that the relationship between knowledge and purposes is not mechanistic, but reflective. Preferences change sometimes as a result of scholarly investigation (Dewey, 1993, p. xv). But ultimately, purposeful life sets criteria for knowledge: Knowledge is a practical approach to realities around people. Knowledge is wisdom "a better sense for the better kind of life to be led" (Dewey, 1993, p. 1). "New opinion is considered true exactly as much as it satisfies the needs of the one judging it, and as much as it requires the melting of the previous experience and previous beliefs" (James, 1913, p. 44, translation by the author). This formulation by James is useful as an example of the instrumentalist attitude of pragmatism toward knowledge and theory.

However, this book will not follow James' relativist formulation, which suggests that the truth value of a sentence depends on the purposes of *the one judging the sentence* (and not on the purposes of humanity). Furthermore, here James talks about truth, rather than knowledge and this is somewhat problematic for pragmatists. Elsewhere, James emphasizes that truth is not important for the judgment of a sentence, as the entire concept somehow refers to a correspondence relationship between a sentence and a reality outside, which pragmatism rejects. For pragmatism, it is important to consider whether we should consider different things real or not. This we can judge on the basis of the practical value of considering something real. If we think as Dayak warriors in the Dayak–Madurese ethnic war in West Kalimantan, Indonesia in 1997–1998, and believe that spells are real and that they make us invulnerable, we will not need to be careful about bullets. Once we are then hit by them we (or the survivors around us) will see that we should not have believed in spells of invulnerability against bullets. Yet, the hardness of bullets is just a meaning that is in our heads, and thus to say that there is a correspondence between the hardness of a bullet as an idea and the bullet itself, is not accurate. For pragmatism, the concept of truth is not really useful, and thus we will do as James did (James, 1977), abandon it and focus on what we *should* consider real and what not. And the criterion for such judgment is the test of practice. In this way pragmatism does not have a foundation in theory but in practice.

It is useful to consider pragmatism as a philosophy that acknowledges the reality outside the consciousness of the philosopher or observer. Yet, as discussed in connection to James' denial of truth, the connection between a subject and the object is not that of correspondence. The reality does not express itself automatically, there is no automatic correspondence between reality and our consciousness. James followed this line as far as denying the existence of consciousness (James, 1910), but for the purpose of this book, it would be better to consider that the pragmatism that this book represents recognizes the assumption of reality as useful, but that our relationship to it is defined by our interests. We see objects in war as weapons and define them as things that can shoot and kill and thus meaning is given to guns by our purpose of killing or preventing killings. Only through our purposes do these objects acquire their meaning as weapons.

Peirce puts this in a philosophically more elegant manner. According to him "The *hardness* of an object can of course be felt, but the meaning of this predicate concerns not the qualitative immediacy of feeling but its implied bearing on conduct." It concerns how objects under this description *would act* on things other than themselves. What is true of predicates like hardness here is true of all other "intellectual concepts": they "essentially carry some implication concerning the general behavior either of some conscious being or of some inanimate object, and so convey more, not merely than any feeling, but more too, than any existential fact, namely, the 'would-acts', 'would-dos' of habitual behavior" (Peirce, 1931, p. 467). "To say that an object is *hard* is, thus, to imply something about how it would act; what we mean by this term is, at least in the context of inquiry, inseparable from such implications" (Colapietro, 2005; Peirce, 1931, p. 467). Thus, while pragmatism can assume the attitude of scientific realism[1] in the sense that it recognizes a reality outside our consciousness, it does not recognize our ability to study reality for what it really is, just how we can relate to it through our purposes and interests.

To go further from the basic pragmatist attitude toward knowledge and get a grasp of what pragmatic peace research should do with its concepts, theories explanations and understandings, we will have to go a little further into the interface between reality and practical knowledge. Due to the fact that classical pragmatists did not consider meaning-giving as the interpretationists did it is difficult to find classical formulations about the pragmatist relationship between reality, theory, concepts, and claims that would satisfy today's peace researchers. However, George Herbert Mead (Mead, 1934; Scheffler, 1974) has presented a formulation that this book can use as the starting point. According to Mead:

1. What is real for us depends on our own active intervention. Things do not tell us what they are, knowledge about the world

---

[1] Scientific realism is a position according to which reality exists outside our consciousness and can be studied for what it is (Russell, 1984).

does not impose itself on us. Knowledge requires an interpretative process. We never see reality in the raw.

2. Knowledge is constantly being tried out in situations and is judged by its usefulness. Perspectives are judged by the individual (or humanity, as in this book) in terms of applicability.

3. Objects we encounter in situations are defined according to their use for us. So, not only the knowledge judged by use, but we also see things in our environment according to their use. *What things mean to us depend on how we intend to use them.*

If the criterion of knowledge and theory is their practical value, two questions arise. Whose purposes and what kinds of objectives should peace research serve? The first question leads us to the question of egoist relativism versus universalism/cosmopolitanism. Should we all just care about our own purposes and objectives, or should science and knowledge in peace research serve some more universal subjects. Dewey opted for the Universalist option. Dewey saw pragmatic truth as a result of some kind of discursive democracy where "free social inquiry is insolubly wedded to the art of full and moving communication" as much as to the facts discovered (Dewey, 1993, p. xiv).[2]

Cosmopolitanism is an ethical theory, first introduced to peace research by Immanuel Kant (1999), according to which political organization should be based on a recognition of the universal, equal value of all people regardless of nationality. Political organization should be constructed in a way that would maximize the voice, values, and interests of global citizens.

For security studies this question relates to our thinking of the referent object of security. Is it me, my race, my nation or is it humankind? To some extent the question is easier for peace research, which is more universalist in nature. Peace cannot be on one side of the conflict only (while security could be). It is possible to "secure the village by

---

[2] From the point of view of peace research, there are some interesting further developments from Deweyan universalism to cosmopolitan ethics (Bray, 2009).

killing all the people in it", while it would be madness to call that destruction of the village a peace strategy: destruction is not peace, although it can be security for some. Thus, it would be natural to say, pragmatic peace research is based on a cosmopolitan conception of purpose: The peace that peace research has to produce has to be for all, not just for some. However, instead of accepting this as something "natural", we could start from the observation that the vast majority of humanity wants peace, and that peace is the purpose of humanity. Thus peace research, as an instrument of humanity, has to subscribe to inter-subjective (rather than objectivist) universalism and cosmopolitan ethics (Kant, 1999), where the lives of all human beings are equally important. The founder of peace research, Johan Galtung, felt like this, declaring that the purpose of peace research is to reduce violence — violence against anyone (Galtung, 1964). Pragmatist peace researchers want to serve humanity rather than any partisan national or racial purpose, and thus they subscribe to cosmopolitan ethics. I hope this is a normative starting point that my reader can tolerate.

However, when constructing peaceful structures it is clear that the terms of peace are always part of the peace, and thus what is pragmatic and whose pragmatic interpretation matters is always related to popular preferences. There are no rational meaning-giving or correct, neutral pragmatic interpretations, but instead, when defining knowledge and interpretations that are pragmatic from the point of view of the security of humankind, humankind should itself somehow be involved in this definition. While a scholar is destined to make his own interpretations of knowledge pragmatic for humankind, pragmatic science should be sympathetic towards the efforts of Habermas and others to develop procedural criteria of discursive rationality that could help define pragmatic consciousness in a manner that would allow participation in a rational manner (Habermas, 1984). I will return to this question once I have introduced the conclusions for pragmatism of the realization that social realities are constructed in social interaction as this realization changes and emphasizes the importance of the definition of criteria of knowledge in a participatory process.

For some pragmatists, serving a purpose means the same as maximizing someone's utility. It would be possible to define utility in a broad way as simply anything people want, but in some pragmatist writing, purpose is defined as hedonistic pleasure. Many critical readings of utilitarianist ethics take this line and claim that for example Benthamian utilitarianism is hedonism and this is probably to some extent justified as Bentham is occasionally open to this interpretation (Bentham, 1890). If we assume that people can give different kinds of meanings to realities around them, hedonism would lead to problems when connected with pragmatism. If my purpose is simply pleasure and happiness then why not give positive meanings to everything around me? When people are killed in genocide we will just assume a sadistic line and enjoy the pleasure. And if we turn out to be the next ones to be tortured, we can take a masochistic approach to life. In this way we could be happy and make the most of our realities. However, since we have genuine purposes, we cannot be happy about killings and genocide. This is why we act against it. Our attitude toward violence should be disapproving, so that we can motivate our sometimes hard and demanding action against violence. Thus, purposes cannot be simply pleasure-seeking, yet it would be against the pragmatist starting point of seeing scholarship as instrumental to life to define what kinds of purposes we should have. Despite the fact that the question of what we should purposefully do is a normative one, we would not be able to define "purposes" from outside life: purposes are what humanity desires as willing subjects. Defining purposes from static dogma of science would again objectify life and subjects, and this would be against the basic ideas of subjugating science to life rather than the other way around. The only thing we can say about purpose is that it should not be conceived as something given to subjects, it is what defines the subject, as it derives from the subject. When pragmatist peace research defines purpose as the reduction of violence, both structural and direct, this is not something that defines what people should do. Quite the contrary: since people want to avoid violence, we have invented pragmatist peace research as a tool for our living objective.

Since there is movement and a purpose for the reduction of violence, we can study conflicts and social interaction from the point of view of this interest. We can follow Johan Galtung's definition of violence and define it either as direct action that in its most extreme form kills people (direct violence) or deprives people of years of their lives by means of a structure that causes untimely deaths (structural violence). While it is easy to understand what Galtung means by direct violence (killing in war, for example), the concept of structural violence is trickier. If an apartheid system taxes black people but denies them their access to national health care, and if as a result, say 500,000 black people have their life expectancies reduced by two years, we can measure the severity of structural violence in the apartheid system as 1 million years of life in one generation (Galtung & Höivik, 1971). This we could compare to violence in a war, where 25,000 young men with life expectancies at 60 years are killed on average at the age of 20 years. As a result, we can see that the latter category of violence deprives combatants of 1 million years. It is difficult to find a fair way of comparing structural and direct violence,

---

Violence is a direct or indirect intentional action by one person or a group of people that results in a death of another person or a group of people (direct violence that deprives one of years of life) or a quality of a structure that systematically deprives years of life from a group of people by reducing their life expectancy (structural violence that deprives one of years of life).

On a less serious level, violence could also be action or a quality of a structure that brings the quality of life further from the level the target of the action of the subject's structure has wanted it to be.

Conflict is often defined as "a contested incompatibility that concerns government and/or territory, where the use of armed force between two parties, of which at least one is the government of a state, results in at least 25 battle-related deaths". War again is a conflict that causes at least 1,000 conflict fatalities per year (Lacina & Gleditsch, 2005; Singer, 1980). If we accept the idea of severe (fatal) and less severe (life-quality-lowering) violence, we could say that severe violence is a quality that does not belong to a peaceful society, while in the absence of severe violence, we could see different levels of less severe violence in various terms of peace. A capitulationist state would have to settle for a peace that has a lot of life-quality-lowering violence, while a better peace would have less.

and it is not easy to compare actual life expectancy in an imaginary fair structure. Does life expectancy in the latter case depend on reckoning that everyone has an equal income, or is life expectancy related to everyone getting what they deserve according to her/his contribution, or is it something else? In any case the virtue of Galtung's concept of structural violence is that it points to the fact that a stable structure can be violent and that it, indeed, can contribute to the deprivation of years of life, just as the direct violence of wars can. Without the concept, violence would be very much a *status quo*-biased concept that associated stability with peace, even the stability of apartheid South Africa, cruel, deadly versions of unregulated market economy, Pol Pot's Cambodia or Stalin's rule by means of gulags.

Finally, introduction to the classical form of pragmatism should define its relationship to the idea of eclecticism in peace research. According to two eclecticist pragmatists, Sil and Katzenstein, pragmatist instrumentalism has to rule out the demand of coherence in the explanation and investigation of peace and conflicts (Sil & Katzenstein, 2010). Eclecticism rejects the need to have only one coherent theory of the world, and the need for explanations of particular things to fit coherently to that total view of the world. If it is more practical, according to Sil and Katzenstein, one should not hesitate to create models that are internally incoherent with any world view, just as long as the model manages to offer explanations that help actors stay on "top of things" in their role as peacemakers. At the same time, according to James, new opinions can be judged useful also to the extent they "melt" into the previous experience and previous beliefs (James, 1913, p. 44). It seems that there is a conflict between Katzenstein's and Sil's view on the one hand and the position of James on the other. Furthermore, Dewey and James seem to insist not only on coherence between different dimensions of our world view, but they also insist that truth is somehow a product of consensus and a coherence of views. According to Dewey, "to represent things as they are is to represent them in ways that tend to maintain the common understanding" (Dewey, 1993, p. 13). While these positions are not very clearly argued for either by Dewey or by James, it is easy to understand that a conception of a conflict situation cannot be very productive if it is internally contradictory. To explain causes of a conflict by assuming that conflicting parties are rational and at the same time expecting them to be irrational is certainly not what Sil and Katzenstein mean by eclecticism. However, if James and Dewey assume that consensus defines something true — say, consensus about Jews as the ultimate problem of Germany — it would be difficult to insist on consistency with such a consensus. If we are left with a dissident view, we might think twice whether we really have good grounds for our deviation. At the same time, a consensus cannot define Jews as the problem, since even people who participate in that consensus consider Jews a problem because of other things, not because of the consensus. They arrive at the consensual view due to considerations that cannot be the consensus as once they arrive at that view, the consensus does not yet exist. Thinking otherwise would also lead us into a circular argument. We believe in a view that is consensual because it is consensual, and it is consensual by definition because we all believe in it. Thus, we cannot accept this part of James's and Dewey's theory of knowledge.

On the issue of coherence between elements of the world view we will also need to disagree with James and accept the eclecticist view of Sil and Katzenstein. If we consider praxis to be the starting point of pragmatist peace research, we cannot also accept the need for totalizing, coherent world views that define our lives and praxis inside absolute scientific truth. We started our development of pragmatic peace research by defining it as an instrument for the global movement of humankind against violence, and thus it would not be our goal to insist on total consistency for our findings with a totalizing world view. Thus, in this sense, we also abandon part of classical pragmatism and opt for a more post-modern, eclectic version already at this stage.

2.2. Pragmatism with a Constructivist Twist

The philosopher that first used the word pragmatism in reference to his own position, Charles S. Peirce, was a natural scientist by training, and some of the useful ideas that were less useful for peace research can be traced to the orientations of natural sciences in Peirce's times.

In this section, pragmatism will be adjusted to the realities of social sciences before it can be used to assess the value of various paradigms to peace research. Since much of this adjustment will lead us closer to the Constructivist paradigm, we will call this adjustment the "Constructivist twist" to the meta-theory of pragmatism.

For both Peirce and James anything real could be experienced and empirically observed. This position can be separated from instrumentalist ideas of knowledge that are important in James' and Peirce's work. We will reject the anti-rationalist position of Peirce, Dewey and James that considers real to be only those things that we can have empirical evidence of (James, 1977). Partly this is due to the problem of empirically observing potentialities. As will be discussed in Chapter 4 on free will, we must assume that social settings have potentials that will never be actualized, and yet they are real as potentials. These potentials can naturally not be empirically observed, as they do not materialize, and yet, we cannot imagine free will or purposive action that could resolve conflicts unless we assume that social situations permit potentials that could be actualized or that will not be actualized (Kurki, 2008; Lebow, 2009b; Patomäki & Wight, 2000).

It is also practical for peace research to consider ideative realities that are important to consider real for a practical understanding of peace and conflicts. However, also they are often not possible to observe empirically. State borders cannot be empirically observed, and yet the study of international conflicts is well advised to take them very seriously and consider them to be real. Social structures of peace and war are conditioned by material realities, but they are first and foremost constituted by our thinking, language, practices, and ideas. The issue of the reality of socially constructed facts will be returned to in the chapter on social construction, but in order to construct our meta-theoretical criterion that we will then use to assess the value of different paradigms for peace, we will have to think what social constructs and the ideative constitution of social realities mean for our pragmatist assessment of paradigms. If there are material conditions, such as insufficient nutrition for a group of people, that prevents peaceful interaction, the problem is outside our knowledge and we can use classical pragmatist criteria for the assessment of the usefulness for peace of a way of thinking. When the focus is on materially constituted realities our assessment of practicality of knowledge can be instrumental. Whichever intellectual paradigm can help us deal with the lack of food is pragmatic in an instrumental sense. However, if the reality is constituted by our thoughts we cannot just consider instrumental pragmatism. We cannot just consider what tools a paradigm offers for the fixing of a material condition, but instead, we will have to think what kind of realities our paradigm constitutes. A paradigm of race purity in a racist state can have instrumental value for the management of something we understand as races, but the very "knowledge" of races and the purity of races already creates social agency of these races. Instead of just thinking whether theories of race purity can be used for something practical, we will also have to consider whether the existence of races as political actors that the theory and its concepts construct, is a positive, pragmatic reality. When classical pragmatism only considers instrumentally what can we do with certain knowledge or certain paradigm, constructivist pragmatism also considers what that knowledge does to us and our social realities. A classical pragmatist ponders whether knowledge about the hardness of a stone is useful for us if we want to avoid being injured by hard objects. Knowledge for a classical pragmatist is thus an instrument for acting in a pragmatic manner. However, a constructivist pragmatist would also have to consider theories and concepts for the usefulness of the entity they constitute, as without our knowledge, theories and understanding (and convention) of many ideative entities, such as states as actors of international relations or money as an instrument of economic exchange, such realities would not exist. Thus, due to the constructivist twist we will have to extend our use of the pragmatist criteria in our assessment of the practical value of paradigms from considerations of their instrumental value to the practicality of realities they constitute.

We will return to the definition of constructivist pragmatism once we have discussed the paradigm of constructivism. Before that we simply refer to post-classical versions of pragmatism as neo-pragmatism.

2.3. Pragmatism and the "False Gods" of Peace Research

We have now defined some basic tenets of all pragmatist thinking. After this, it will make sense to define what pragmatism cannot be: i.e. what implicit criteria for scholarship pragmatist peace research has to try to stay clear of. One such "value" for peace research, and criteria of the quality of analysis of conflicts and peace is the innovativeness and creativity of theoretical constructs (Jutila *et al.*, 2008). It is understandable that the relevance of a study is partly dependent on how many new innovations it offers. Yet, innovativeness is a value only if it offers new, usable ideas for peace. A huge amount of peace research is done about the most exotic topics that demonstrate originality and innovation, but which are entirely useless in helping people avoid violence. There is, of course, no point in inventing the law on liberal democratic peace again, but if we can modify the existing understanding of the relationship between peace and democracy in a way that helps us save lives and reduce violence, then we should do that despite the fact that such a modification might not be original and innovative after decades and centuries of theories on the relationship between peace and democracy.

Academic merit is often better served with theoretical constructs that have a high level of abstraction (Patomäki, 1996). If a theory has generic features it could serve peace in many situations and in this way it could be of greater pragmatic value. But at the same time, peace research theories that cannot be applied all the way to the level that gives concrete advice to concrete people in concrete situations does not have pragmatic value. In this sense, pragmatic peace research is like building a house. The architect might get a higher salary than the mason and the electrician, but without them the designs of the architect would be useless. Similarly, basic research has a place just as applied research that uses discoveries of basic research does. One should not think that only applied research has practical utility or that generic explanations are of higher value, they both contribute to the same purpose.

In positivistic peace research scholars often seek laws that could cover a greater number of cases and thus be more generalizable

(Hempel, 1965). This, too, could serve pragmatic interests of peace as the same laws would be able to be used in the explanation of more cases. However, on one hand laws that bind people's behavior more do not give us more freedom to work for peace (see Chapter 4), while at the same time the nature of the laws could be much more important for their practicality than the number of cases they apply to. The ideal of broader coverage often also appears in scholarship that in no way subscribes to positivistic ideals and is combined with the ideal of higher levels of abstraction. For example, Milja Kurki, a critical realist, suggests that her model of causality is better than the so-called Humean model of causality as it is "wider" and "deeper" and integrates several approaches to the study of international relations (Kurki, 2008). If such a model really enables us to talk to a wider scholarly community and learn more ideas which are practical for peacemaking, that could be useful. But if a wider concept of causality simply helps us to speak about entirely different things (such as mutual constitution and material causality) with similar concepts it does not really offer anything new to scholarship, perhaps it just contributes to confusion.

Much of social science aims at parsimonious models (King *et al.*, 1994). According to Stein, human action cannot be explained with complicated models as their logic escapes the people whose actions we want to explain (Stein, 1990). Furthermore, overcomplicated models fail to produce heuristic value. Yet, outcomes of actors in conflict situations can be traced from complicated structures of interaction (without assuming that actors fully understand them), and for this, one might have to reconstruct these complex structures and develop complicated models. Failing to do this and modeling complicated structures as simple ones could distort the diagnosis of the situation and it could lead the analysis to wrong prescriptions. While taking complex structures under control might require analysis that separates each of the simple elements of the complicated structure, a model that aims at useful diagnoses has to be careful not to simplify complicated realities so much that elements that need to be taken into account for the sake of pragmatic prescriptions are left out of the analysis. In Chapter 4, we will be discussing the parsimonious model of "prisoner's dilemma", in which structures of interaction are assumed to have only one cooperative alternative. In such a model conflicting parties can either choose to cooperate or not to cooperate (deceive) and thus failure of cooperation is always caused by deception: a conscious choice not to cooperate, but to seek partisan benefits by deceiving the other conflicting parties. Here for the sake of simplicity and parsimony one then models cooperation in a way that rules out the problem of whose terms of cooperation actors will adopt when choosing to cooperate. Yet, analysis of real-life conflicts seems to suggest that this is the main difficulty in peacemaking. Almost all conflicting parties want peace; they just want their own peace, not the peace their enemy is offering. Thus, modeling conflict with the parsimonious model of the prisoner's dilemma almost always fails to factor in the most difficult problem of peacemaking — the bargaining between various terms of peace — and thus this model advises peacemakers wrongly and in a destructive manner that will be discussed in detail in Chapter 4.

While parsimonious modeling is often a virtue, in some subfields of peace studies complexity also shows methodological rigor and is seen as a virtue. In some game theoretical journals (*International Journal of Mathematics, Game Theory and Algebra* or *International Journal of Game Theory* for instance)[3] the complexity of models has become a virtue in its own right, even if such complex models were then never really even tried to be used for the strategic planning of anything. Description of a structure or a process needs to consider the strategic value of each detail and leave out details that do not affect the accuracy of the diagnosis and the prescription. Methodological sophistication should not become a virtue in itself, but instead, it should be considered useful only to the degree it offers better prescriptions and puts the peacemakers "on top of things" in a conflict situation.

While positivistic scholarship has many criteria with which research can be judged for its "scientific quality", such criteria are

---

[3] Undoubtedly these journals are not meant to be practical support for the creation of practical prescriptions for peace, and thus these journals are here taken as less confrontational examples.

normally judged on the basis of their ability to create correspondence between claims and reality. However, since the theory of truth in positivistic scholarship does not problematize the type of correspondence there could be between sentences of a study and the reality these sentences describe, scholarship is often affected by the simplistic metaphor in which a sentence is like a picture of reality, which can then be compared to reality by means of empirical observation. Yet reality is not just something one can observe, something that reveals all its meanings to the pure observation, certainly not when we are thinking of elements of conflict realities. The meaning of an assault rifle does not reveal itself to the observer, but instead its meanings are given by its use and our purposes for this tool. Thus criteria of "scientific analysis" do not necessarily produce interpretations that are useful. On the contrary, the ideal that arises from the metaphor of a photograph, that science has to stay aloof from interests in order to be objective, confuses the whole idea of truth and gives an illusion that there is a correspondence between scholarly discoveries and the reality that would be objective, directly driven from the object itself. The ideal of objective truths that true science has to discover often then means that the very virtues of the "scientific method" are developed in absence of considerations of how these methods serve life and peace, and thus these virtues live their own life and obscure rather than serve the pragmatic purpose of analysis. Chapter 3 will show, though, that, in reality, many of the "scientific" virtues of the method, in fact, have a pragmatic grounding and that despite the explicit commitment to objective truths positivistic causal analysis explicitly considers the relevance of the study in question in a way that is in line with the ideals of the classical version of pragmatism.

While rejecting positivist scientific ideas, post-positivist analyses have often also developed their own criteria of "scientificness", much as a counterargument to the argument of "positivist real scientists" that post-positivist scholarship is just opinion writing or journalism. G. B. Madison has created strict criteria for postmodern hermeneutics that guide scholarly investigation and distinguishes it from opinion writing. According to Madison, interpretations of reality have to be thorough (all questions must be answered, as if that was possible without defining a set of criteria based on the purposes and interests we have *vis-à-vis* the object of our study), it has to be comprehensive and contextual regardless of the strategic value of the context for our interests in knowing the object of our study, and it has to be appropriate in the meaning that the interpretation has to rise from the text rather than from the interpreter, as if there could be ways of interpreting anything without implicit ideas arising from the interpreter of the interests in knowing. Finally, interpretations have to be fertile and stimulate the imagination (Gadamer, 1989; Madison, 1988, pp. 29–30). The need to show methodological discipline and to distance oneself from non-scientific writing has created a lot of false gods in scholarly investigation, false gods that distance investigation from the relevance and practical value of scholarship.

Relevance is often a value in the social sciences, but it is a value among other values. This presentation of the "false gods" of peace research has listed just a few of the values that often compete with the values of pragmatism. This list is in fact much longer, but the one presented above is given to exemplify how competing scientific ideals often compromise the ways in which social scientific research and paradigms can be in the service of peace.

Chapter 3
Positivism: Social Engineering of Peace

Social Engineering is a concept that Popper (2012) coined in his theory of the use of social sciences. According to him, social research, just like engineering, should be focused on social problems. Once the scholar understands the conditions that are associated with the problems and once she knows the mechanisms by which conditions cause the problems, the social scientist should be able to tell how to fix these problems (that is, if they can be fixed with the available resources), just as an engineer knows how to fix an engine. In peace research, the problem would then be violence. Social engineering would then be scholarship that seeks correlative relationships between different conditions and peace or war, and the possible mechanisms that lead from conditions to wars or peace. In this way she produces knowledge for the engineering of peace. In this book we will simplify things slightly and use the common expression of *positivist peace research* as something which refers to all peace research that could be fitted into the frame of the social engineering of peace.

3.1. Classical Pragmatist Science and Engineering

Classical pragmatism was "scientific" in the sense that it was committed to empiricism and strong ideals of natural sciences even in the study of societies. In this way the ideas of classical pragmatism go together with the positivist mainstream of peace research, which still dominates such central outlets of peace research as the *Journal of Peace Research*, the *Journal of Conflict Resolution*, and *International Security*. Since judging the pragmatism of peace research that sees social science as different from the natural sciences requires a slightly different meta-theoretical approach, let us call it neo-pragmatism. We could call the pragmatic applications of the mainstream peace research classical pragmatist peace research and the pragmatic post-positivist approaches (approaches that reject the engineering view of the social sciences) to peace research neo-pragmatic peace research.

Since neither classical pragmatism nor mainstream positivist peace research distinguishes between natural and social sciences, but instead derives the maxims of social science from the natural sciences, classical pragmatist peace research looks a lot like engineering. When there is a problem with a physical machine, technologists are needed to create prescriptions for the mechanics on how to fix the engine. Similarly, classical pragmatist peace research engineers problems of conflict and peacemakers follow the prescriptions of peace researchers. Thus, according to Dewey, social engineering is the purpose of pragmatist social sciences (Dewey, 1993, p. xiv). But pragmatist reflection is also needed for the diagnosis of the problem and it's just settlement: Efficiency is just a mechanistic interpretation of pragmatism while Dewey also wants pragmatism to be used for the definition of the direction of the solution (Dewey, 1993, p. xv).

For Dewey, "Knowing is a way of employing empirical occurrences with respect to increasing power to direct the consequences which flow from things, the application of the conclusions must be made to philosophy itself" (Dewey, 1917, p. 1). Some of the intelligence-thinking in strategic studies comes close to such a concept of knowledge about peace and war. According to Breakspear, "Intelligence is a corporate capability to forecast change in time to do something about it. The capability involves foresight and insight, and is intended to identify impending change which may be positive, representing opportunity or negative, representing threat" (Breakspear, 2013, p. 678).

The way in which social engineering in peace research has traditionally studied occurrences to increase the power of the ones who know about these occurrences, is related to causality. If we know what conditions or events cause conflict, we can engineer peace by systematically avoiding those conditions and events. If democracy is a condition of peaceful inter-state interaction, then peace practitioners could promote democracy in order to promote peace (Gleditsch & Hegre, 1997; Russett, 1993, 1996). Despite the problems later discovered in this kind of thinking, peace research that has followed the maxims of social engineering, has managed to create a lot of knowledge which is useful for peacemakers. Discussion with practical peacemakers about the use of social sciences reveals that most mediators as well as planners of national security think about knowledge on peace and war within an intellectual framing of social engineering. They think of conditions that could help create peace and conditions and situations that could be prevented in order to prevent war or the escalation of violence. They think about the causes of war and think of ways to prevent these causes. This is why it is useful to take the use of peace research as social engineering very seriously. For example, the theory of relative deprivation (Gurr, 1970; Runciman, 1966), according to which changes for the worse in the relative wellbeing of groups of people often trigger war, has affected the way in which development planners promote conflict sensitive development (Kamatsiko, 2014). The social engineering of peace can save, and indeed, has saved many lives, and thus regardless of problems related to it, it can be used in a useful manner. Furthermore, the social engineering frame of peace research also needs to be taken seriously because of the problems involved in it. If most practitioners of peace and security think of knowledge in their practice of the social engineering of peace, pragmatist peace research must also take this framing seriously as something that needs to be criticized and developed further, as the flaws of the social engineering frame also kill people in wars. While this book will deal with the critique later in the transformation of classical pragmatist, positivist peace research into a neo-pragmatist post-positivist program in peace research, the treatment of social engineering of peace will follow in this chapter by developing the practical side of the program further.

3.2. Mainstream Peace Research as Social Engineering

Social engineering of peace in the main peace research journals (*Journal of Peace Research, Journal of Conflict Resolution and International Security*) tends to recognize the complexity of causal relations in peace and conflict situations. Instead of looking at single deterministic independent variables that could explain peace and war in their entirety, most scholars follow long and complex causal chains and acknowledge the probabilistic nature of causality. Instead of claiming that poverty causes war, scholars of *relative deprivation*, for example, claim that economic decline and ethnic diversity together with the ethnic functionalization of the economy causes relative deprivation which, again, increases the risk of conflict (Gurr, 1993; Runciman, 1966; Singer, 1980).

The frame of social engineering of peace by using causal models has resulted in several useful theories. While causal modeling simulates causal mechanisms in the natural sciences, in the social engineering of peace, they have often sought explanations for causal relationships from a frame that seems to assume purposive action and a certain voluntarism. War causes have been explained by conditions that:

1. Make existing peace frustrating or intolerable (Gurr, 1970; Runciman, 1966; Singer, 1980).
2. Make violence attractive (Collier *et al.*, 2003; Collier & Hoeffler, 2004).
3. Create opportunities for gainful violence (Tilly, 1978), or
4. Block alternative ways of political influence and thereby force people into violence (Brown *et al.*, 1996; Lichbach & Gurr, 1981; Rummel, 1995).

Theories do not tend to explain the contradiction between voluntarism and causation, as the former suggests that people can decide what they want while the latter suggests that at least in a probabilistic manner human action is determined by certain conditions. Wendt suggests that these theories assume an objective set of preferences with a given logic of rationality that determine human action. If then conditions are changed in a way that increases the utility of violence, the likelihood of violence increases. In such a framing humans might be purposive but not free, as their purpose is to maximize utility in a set of preferences that are given to them (Wendt, 1998). Fukuyama, despite his historical interpretation of the development of cooperation and warfare with clear purposive elements, explicates such an ontology by seeking the origin of preferences all the way from human physiology. According to Fukuyama: "What economists call preferences and what others refer to as desires, wishes, impulses, and the like, originate in the limbic system, and the ancient part of the brain that includes the hippocampus and the amygdala. The limbic system is the seat of the emotions, and the hypothalamus interacts directly with the endocrine system, which in turn secretes hormones regulating body temperature, heartbeat, and the like" (Fukuyama, 2000, p. 182).

The example above of relative deprivation is probably the best example of the first type of causal social engineering. In this model the *status quo* becomes intolerable for a group of people when the level of their wellbeing declines in relation to other groups or in relation to the past. This theory treats the independent variable as an objective condition, while in reality it could also be treated as something people just perceive (Winarso, 2014): the fact that people can compare their current wellbeing to something else creates the gap between expected and real wellbeing, and this creates the frustration that fuels aggression. It is not the level of wellbeing in itself, but the perception that it could be better that gives rise to the frustration. However, in the theory itself, this nuance is not considered important: instead, the objective condition of reduced economic welfare or the growth of disparity between two groups are treated as objective conditions that trigger a chain or causal events that lead to frustration-aggression (Gurr, 1970).

Thus, for example, because of the ethnic diversity of Indonesia, and the fact that food stores and shops in several areas of the country were largely owned by ethnic Chinese, the collapse of the national currency, the rupiah, in 1997–1998, created a situation where people felt that rich Chinese shop owners increased their prices in an unreasonable manner at the same time as people were laid off from work.

As a result there was a perception that the Chinese (who, in reality, had to increase their rupiah prices of those products that had foreign components) were getting rich while the majority population, in many places the Javanese, were getting poorer. This created relative deprivation (i.e. impoverishment of a group in comparison to previous and/or to other groups) and frustration, which in parts of Indonesia led to violent anti-Chinese rioting (Kivimäki, 2001c).

Furthermore, most food riots in the world are related to the frustration caused by economic trouble or economic fluctuations. Indonesian conflict peaks took place in the mid-1960s and after the 1997 economic crises, while the demand for independence in East Timor was emphasized by the frustration caused by the Asian financial crisis. East Timor was the most import-reliant and poor province of Indonesia, and thus not coincidentally also the most violent one after the collapse of the value of the rupiah. Rioting and occasional near chaos in Greece and Spain during the economic troubles in 2010–2011 did not at that time just take place coincidentally.

This knowledge of the complex probabilistic causal chains that led to frustration and aggression could teach planners of Indonesian peace and stability elsewhere many lessons. It is not good to encourage or allow strong ethnic functionalization of the economy: the Javanese should also be encouraged to get involved in small-scale trade. Furthermore, Indonesia, like Greece and Spain, or indeed any economy, should be designed in a way that avoids drastic fluctuations so that destabilizing and extreme relative deprivation could be avoided (Kivimäki & Pasch, 2009). Development cooperation in most countries has already for some time been wary of following the cold logic of markets in transforming too much agricultural land into cash crops, as such a development often exposes the society to drought — or flood-induced drastic economic fluctuations. Measures to tackle relative deprivation have largely been useful for peace, and thus, the theory of relative deprivation, with all its theoretical flaws (which we will come back to later) has been a good theory from the pragmatist point of view.

In addition to relative deprivation, absolute, stable levels of misery lower the threshold of violence, and as a result there are conflict motives for improving the intolerable situation. According to a calculation by the World Bank, the level of per capita GNP is among the best predictors of conflict. An increase in per capita income by a percent reduces the likelihood of conflict during the next five years by 1%. From the level of 1,800 USD/year, the likelihood doubles with the halving of the per capita GNP and declines by half with the doubling of the per capita GNP (Collier *et al.*, 2003). This is why relative deprivation in Spain caused rioting and chaos but no fatalities, while any frustration aggression in Sierra Leone is likely to result in massive loss of life. Poverty alleviation, therefore, is peace work and should not be compromised in development cooperation for the sake of more indirect ways of addressing conflict motives (Ruohomäki & Kivimäki, 2001). This has been noted by several donor agencies as the seminal World Bank study, breaking the conflict trap, exemplifies (Collier *et al.*, 2003).

Theories emphasizing violence as gainfully motivated activity have emerged as a challenge to theories of frustration violence. For theorists it is important to investigate whether gains or grievances explain conflict better. However, for a pragmatist the relative merits of the two theories make no difference: absolute merits are more important, as precautions concerning frustration-aggression do not rule out opportunities for the prevention of gainful aggression as well.

Theories of gainful violence often take their start from the observation that the discovery of natural resources in countries where political competition is not institutionally regulated often sparks conflict. Separatist conflicts often flair up in areas where people from a separatist territory have an incentive to fight because of the locally found natural resources. Natural resources in areas where economic competition is not institutionally regulated cause conflict partly because they offer a pool of wealth to fight for (Collier *et al.*, 2003; Collier & Hoeffler, 2004). Another possibility is that natural resources in the hands of the government enable it to ignore its people as the state does not need people as tax payers. As a result, state repression is harsher, while popular participation in politics is restricted and limited (De Sousa, 2000; Sovacool, 2010). Thus, violence is driven by incentives offered either for the rebels or for the state to use violence gainfully.

Theories about the causal chain from gains to violence have also been useful for the planning of peaceful societies. Aid can offer riches to fight for (Auvinen & Kivimäki, 2000) and therefore the donor community has been warned in most policy papers on conflict-sensitive aid programming about being careless with aid distribution (Collier *et al.*, 2003). Developing societies are well advised to focus seriously on the creation of an institutional framework for economic competition in order to avoid wasting energy in fighting over natural resources. Despite theoretical and philosophical problems, the theory of gainful violence has also been very useful for practical conflict prevention.

Close to the theory of gainful violence is the idea of conflict opportunities being the cause of conflicts. If states are too weak to regulate their societies, groups with grievances or gains to achieve will resort to violence. With regard to international conflicts the opportunity-driven theory of conflict is one of the mainstream approaches to international relations theory. According to this international application, conflicts in world politics can be attributed to the anarchic structure of world politics, where order can only be guaranteed within states due to the monopoly of legitimate violence and law enforcement, while in the international system wars are endemic due to the lack of an authority that could enforce order in the global system (Waltz, 1968, 1979). Charles Tilly in his analysis of civil wars focused on the difference between states in preventing the mobilization of rebellious groups and claimed that this variation in state capacity to regulate predicts conflict: the weaker the state, the weaker the motives — grievant or gainful — needed for the initiation of violence (Tilly, 1978). This theory of resource mobilization prescribes the strengthening of police forces and the justice system as the main recipe for peace (Collier *et al.*, 2003). Also these prescriptions have saved lives, if the regulating system of the state has had the legitimacy and prudence to enforce an order that is not intolerably unfair or violent in itself. Thus, this approach has also had its merits in the development of pragmatist peace research.

If we minimize the incentives to fight and the deprivations that push people to rebellion, as well as opportunities to fight then we only have one motive-related option unexplored for the social engineering of peace. This option is to create non-violent options for changes that people would otherwise pursue violently. The lack of such options can be a cause of conflict, since only in the absence of non-violent channels of change will people, groups and states resort to violence. Democracy has been suggested most often as the most appropriate non-violent channel of political change. While democracy offers opportunities for mobilization, it also reduces grievances and the motivations for fighting as it offers more appealing ways of achieving goals that would otherwise be attempted through violence. According to Rummel, Boulding, Gurr, and Lichbach this is the reason why democracies are more peaceful than autocracies (Boulding, 1978; Gurr, 1993; Lichbach & Gurr, 1981; Rummel, 1995). As a result, the likelihood of a citizen dying in a conflict is merely 0.24% if one lives in a democracy while it is 0.56%, more than twice as high, if one lives in an autocracy (Rummel, 1995).

The ability to influence without using violence is seen to be associated with international violence through a process of diversion. When the government is unresponsive to the needs of people and thus internal stability is difficult to sustain, autocratic regimes are often tempted to divert the frustration of people by offering them an external enemy (Levy, 1989; Rivlin, 2008; Wright, 1965). Yet similar diversionary temptations have sometimes also been found in democracies (Gelpi, 1997; Russett, 1990; Smith, 1996).

Democratic, non-violent opportunities are also seen as a source of trust among democracies: opinion polls among democracies suggest that part of the explanation for the fact that democracies rarely (or never) fight each other is because people from democracies tend to trust other democracies not to attack as they share a non-violent way of settling disputes (Tomz & Weeks, 2013).[1]

---

[1] Otherwise explanations to the theory of democratic peace tend to relate to common identities among democracies, or liberal interdependence, common capitalist norms or problems of legitimacy of aggression against a "free" democracy (Gleditsch, 1995; McDonald, 2009). These explanations, despite their self-identification in the tradition of positivism, require taking the socially constructed realities of identities and the logics of appropriateness very seriously.

Support for democracy has also been a major undertaking in peace promotion. Consciousness about the causal relationship between democracy and peace has also underplayed the autocratic tendency to legitimize limitations of democracy by references to security: If democracy is causally connected to peace, autocrats should not use security needs as a justification for the maintenance of their political privileges.

3.3. Optimizing Pragmatism in Traditional Causal Analysis

While positivist peace research, or social engineering of peace has its problems that need fixing, it is clear from the above that this research program has managed to serve as an adequate tool for the praxis of peace making. To develop this program further, it is possible to create maxims for causal analysis by using the logic of maximization of expected utilities, where utility is defined as the ability of knowledge to help reduce violence by revealing conditions that cause violence. Following the principle of maximization of expected utilities leads us to surprisingly similar maxims of peace research as those followed in positivistic causal analysis. From the point of view of maximization of expected utilities:

1. It is important to prioritize links in the causal chain to war that have a strong relationship with war, in other words those which

    a. Increase the *probability* of war most and which;
    b. Are related to the greatest severity of violence (the biggest losses of lives).

        If we can see that in all inter-state wars at least one of the states is autocratic, then we can make very practical conclusions with this association. If we can expand the community of democracies we can create zones of peace. We will later, in our critique of social engineering of peace, see why this prescription has gone so horribly wrong. In current warfare, up to 70% of conflict fatalities are a result of wars that have been at least partly justified by the interest of advancing democracy (see Chapter 4). However, if we can find genuine correlations and if we can interpret them correctly, it should be possible for us to prevent more violence the stronger the correlative relationship that we can explain causally. In other words we are looking at high correlations and steep regression curves, which are something causal analysis always aims at. The higher the correlations and the steeper the regression curves the more certain we can be that the association between war and the condition is not coincidental, assuming that we can see that the correlative relationship is not due to a third factor that causes both war and the associated condition, that war does not cause the condition and that the relationship is not purely interactive (in which case it might be that we can prevent the condition only if we can simultaneously prevent wars as such). The probability of a causal effect under certain conditions is dependent on two things that have different practical effects. The probability is dependent on:

c. How necessary the condition is for the conflict to be ignited or for the peace to emerge (necessary conditions). If we can manipulate such conditions that are almost necessary or extremely probable in the chain of events leading to war, we can focus on removing them and thereby reduce the likelihood of war drastically. In cases of interstate wars the controlling of offensive weaponry that can hit strategic targets of the potential enemies can be a good strategy because without the potential to wage wars efficiently, there will not be wars between these nations. At the same time ethnic conflicts cannot be prevented by removing weapons due to the physical proximity of potential enemies. If weapons can be replaced by agricultural or hunting tools, controlling weapons will not work, because weapons are not necessary for warfare (Kivimäki, 2012a). It is often the case that the selection of traditional primitive weapons in conflict is very systematic. Madurese warriors in West Kalimantan, for example, always choose sickles (traditional Madurese knifes). Yet despite this strong correlation between the production of sickles and serious violence, Madurese conflict behavior suggests that this is not an important link in the causal chain: in the absence of sickles it would still be easy for the Madurese to use something else in violent actions.

d. How sufficient the condition is for the ignition of warfare or the emergence of peace? If we know statistically highly probabilistic sufficient conditions for peace, it would be practical to focus on the production of such conditions. Anything else would not be useful since this condition alone could bring peace. The example of common democracy between states as a sufficient condition for bringing peace between these states is a good example of the usefulness of working with sufficient conditions for peace (Gleditsch & Hegre, 1997; Russett, 1996; Tomz & Weeks, 2013). There are not as good sufficient causal conditions for warfare as there are for peace. However, there is scholarship suggesting such a sufficient condition of war with a relatively high probability. This scholarship suggests that while wars could occur without arms races, with an arms race the probability of wars would be greatly increased (Diehl, 1983; Wallace, 1979).

In addition to the degree of probability, the severity of conflict development is crucial to pragmatic prioritization. It is important to prioritize causal links, where a condition is associated with the most severe conflict developments (and not some benign developments). Partly this is a simple question of a steep regression curve in the association between this condition and battle deaths. However, the question can also be qualitative or part of a more complex causal path. For example, the emergence of public debate about a corruption case might, with very high probability, create frustration, and non-violent disputes. However, the step from non-existence to the existence of a heated debate is not a very serious one and thus it would not warrant an analysis of how to prevent publicity on divisive issues. Taken that publicity tends to give verbal, non-violent channels of protest and change, and that it tends to reduce the likelihood of public corruption, military abuse, administrative discrimination, and many other problems, which are all activities that increase the likelihood of violent war, it is often suggested by conflict scholars that openness and transparency, even concerning divisive, emotional and frustrating topics is useful for the prevention of violent conflicts (Lindley, 2007; Rummel, 1983). This is even though openness reduces the probability of violent conflicts much less than it increases the probability of lower levels of non-violent expressions of conflict. Thus the issue of severity of conflict development that a cause is associated with is important in our analysis of the causal chains in conflicts.

2. It is important to prioritize the study and explanation of causal conditions that only/mainly link to negative (or positive) developments instead of focusing on links that contribute to both conflict and its resolution (strong probabilistic sufficient causes). In some cases something might increase the probability of a conflict of some seriousness, and yet it would be too costly to remove this link from the causal chain in war because of the positive contributions it has. The emergence of ethnic or religious identities increases the probability of horizontal conflict since it is clear that in intra-state conflicts there is a need for collective identities that could then be mobilized for conflict. However, since both ethnicity and religion also have positive functions, it would not be so interesting from our point of view to study the emergence of ethnic or religious group identities. Religion and religious leaders have served an important role in peace education in many parts of the world and they have had a very positive role in conflict resolution (Svensson & Lingren, 2013). Thus, instead of focusing on links that create (the identities of the) potential conflicting parties (such as ethnic groups) it would be better to focus on the emergence of the antagonism between collective entities or antagonistic identities because antagonism between collective entities does not serve any positive purpose in conflicts, but it is linked to violent mobilization, the emergence of militant true believer cultures, and the emergence of violent collective motivations and thus conflict violence.

3. It would be important if causal peace research could focus on explanations that could be generalized to as many cases as possible. This is why social engineering of peace aims at generalizations and covering laws with a maximal scope. While this is not a consideration of the causal relationship itself, it is a consideration related to the economy of research. If we know that Kim Jong-il used violence against his citizens to preempt rebellions, we will only know that we should have tried to find ways to change this pattern or that we should have tried a regime change before or during his power in order to prevent autocratic violence. However, if we knew the conditions under which all autocratic rulers use violence against their people, this knowledge would kill many birds with a single stone (if such a violent expression is allowed in this context). Thus the scientific objective of positivistic peace research to find greater and greater generalizations is perfectly within the logic of maximization of expected utility, and thus generalizability yields pragmatic value.

4. Finally, also the feasibility of intervention in a specific link of causal chain is important. The fact that it was not entirely easy for the Madurese in West Kalimantan to identify the Dayaks, or in Bosnia and Herzegovina to identify Bosniaks, Serbs, or Croats must have inhibited the intensity of violence (this is why in these conflicts targets of aggression were often people attending religious rites, as religion was one of the things that identified the Dayaks, Bosniaks, Serbs, and Croats). Clearly this was an issue in the explanation of the intensity of violence, but one that could not be manipulated, and thus, not an interesting issue from the point of view of pragmatic conflict studies. More specifically, three issues related to the feasibility of an intervention give weight to the relevance of the study of a specific link in the causal chain to violence. These three issues are the following:

   a. What kind of probabilities are there for an intervention to cut a link to violence?

   b. What kind of costs would an intervention have? Supplying a protective vest to all people would reduce the number of casualties of stray bullets in conflicts, but it would be too costly an option for peace-building.

   c. What kind of other consequences would it have? One cannot kill the villagers in order to end a village conflict, even though the existence of the villagers is a necessary condition for conflict in that village. This would be throwing out the baby with the bathwater.

Before moving on to the critique of classical pragmatism and its peace research (the social engineering of peace), it is useful first to say a few words about how we should not criticize the positivist program.

3.4. Critique of the Social Engineering of Peace

There are good grounds for opposing a program that studies human behavior by seeking covering laws that could explain it. This book will proceed to these reasons in a little while. However, there are also poor reasons for criticizing such a program. The first is the idea of treating all behavior as voluntary and thus beyond regularities and covering laws. Whenever we find strong correlations between conditions and violence we might be observing the kind of behavior that is not quite free. We should not think that only such behavior exists (the deterministic position) or that only such behavior should be studied (the position of most positivist social sciences), but nor should we think that such behavior does not exist, especially when we can observe it. Thus, while we should not build our understanding of the world on regularities (especially since they are not many and in most cases they are not very regular anyway), we should utilize the study of such regularities whenever we find them. Regularities are practical as they help us predict things and change things by manipulating conditions if we know regularities that they are related to. Therefore, generalizations of regularities are pragmatic and thus justified in peace research.

Sometimes regularities are criticized on formal grounds. Hidemi Suganami, who has probably contributed more than anyone else to the pragmatic peace research program, criticized research emanating from the so-called Correlates of War (COW) project and the studies by Rudolph Rummel on the basis of the data produced by the project (Rummel, 1995) for meaningless correlative regularities, which, for relationships between regime qualities and wars, at best could not reach higher than a correlation coefficient of 0.35. This critique could be serious if we were interested in measuring research projects for their formal merits. Perhaps some other projects have managed to identify higher correlations. However, when judging the COW project from the pragmatic point of view, we must recognize that global correlations between conditions and wars at levels of 0.35 explain more than 12% of variation in all wars, meaning that if one can prevent a COW-identified condition that has a 0.35 correlation with wars, this could save 4.5 million people in a century like the 20th century, where there were about 36 million battle deaths in the world according to the project. For the 4.5 million people who would be rescued because of the project's ability to identify this regularity, the virtues of the project would not be meaningless.

Many opponents of covering laws and correlative causal analysis of war and peace point to problems in data or quantitative methods that render conclusions on associations between potential causes and war formally insignificant. Suganami, for example, identifies reliability problems in Wallace's calculations about the correlation between arms races and warfare. On the basis of these problems Suganami then rejects the claim by Wallace that arms races are a probabilistic sufficient condition of war. Suganami's proof refers to the differences of Diehl's and Wallace's definitions, methods and findings on the relationship between war and arms race (Suganami, 1996, p. 96). His conclusion is that the different results at different times by using slightly different definitions renders both studies useless. Yet, both Diehl and Wallace clearly show a strong correlation between the arms race and conflict, even though they do end up in different correlation coefficients. While in the sciences one wants to be certain that one's observations are sufficient to rule out the possibility of a conclusion on an association being coincidental, from the pragmatic point of view when studying risks, a conclusion on an association between a causal condition, say the arms race, and an outbreak of a war, is useful even with higher likelihoods of conclusions being wrong. An association between potential causes and effects is significant as soon as the likelihood of the observation of their association being coincidental is lower than 5%. It is highly significant if that likelihood is lower than 2%. However, if the arms race predicts or causes war, as it is associated with a greater risk (Wallace says this risk is greater, whereas Diehl, who looks at a different period, also finds a correlation albeit a smaller one), knowing about that is pragmatically useful, even if there are risks of inaccuracies and reliability problems. If the likelihood that the arms race and war are associated is 97% or 99%, it has very little difference for the planner of evacuations or for decision makers who think how seriously one should take the arms race and the risk of war. This is despite the fact that a scientist would conclude that there is not sufficient evidence to suggest that there is an association between the arms race and war if the likelihood of this association is systematic.

In the case of the association between peace and democratic dyads, the likelihood of this association being coincidental is almost nil. The random probability of the absence of wars between democracies between 1816 and 1980 is 0.0000000000000000002% (Russett, 1996, p. 345) and yet democratic war, during that period, has been virtually non-existent (Rummel, 1983). There might be disagreements on how this association between democracy and war should be interpreted, but one should not consider the finding about the association unreliable or coincidental. Yet, this is exactly what Suganami does. According to him, this association "could be a coincidence" (Suganami, 1996, p. 107). Undoubtedly, it could, but the likelihood of it being a coincidence is so low that one should not even consider it, let alone ignore the correlative relationship.

In addition to inaccuracies, causal analysis has been accused of inconclusiveness. According to Dessler, for example, studies on correlative relations have added knowledge about regularities, but they have not managed to offer integrative explanations that could integrate the different regularities in a more holistic understanding of how peace and war work. "Integrative progress suggests a qualitative rather than a quantitative improvement of knowledge; it requires not more findings, or better findings, but better connected findings" (Dessler, 1991, p. 340; Harré, & Madden, 1975). Yet, instead of complementing correlative causal analysis with qualitative investigation Dessler, Lebow, Patomäki, and many other critics of positivistic peace research simply reject correlative analysis as if it was not useful for the integrative understanding to know the correlative associations and add knowledge about them (Dessler, 1991; Lebow, 2009a; Patomäki, 1996).

One of the arguments to reject considering correlations is that world politics, conflicts and peace are not regulated by covering laws. Politics in general is not regular, and in the next chapters I will show why to some extent I agree with this statement. But even if politics was regular, observation and systematic study of any regularities is very practical as they help us know, understand and predict things that repeat themselves. The fact that one cannot claim that there would not be such things as correlative regularities already proves that such things do exist. Furthermore, to say that all things in wars and peace are so unique and irregular that peace research should be totally idiographic and not nomothetic, is problematic. This would mean that we cannot even use language in our study of conflicts as language is already generalizing in a way that assumes some regularities. To say "conflict" assumes that there are some similarities in all or most conflicts that then could be generalized as abstract concepts, as the abstract word "conflict" does not refer to just one specific conflict. Thus we cannot avoid generalizations, no matter how much we emphasize historical path dependence or structural (cultural, political, etc.) context specificity in the causation of war, and therefore we should not try to avoid regularities especially since they are practical from the point of view of planning action that maximizes expected utility (i.e. the minimization of the likelihood of fatalities of violence).

The other reason why correlative regularities are criticized by many post-positivist scholars is the fact that they are not believed to be a condition for causality. Causality that generates something is not a correlative phenomenon, or something that is related to regularities or covering laws (Harré & Madden, 1975). While this may be so, there could be unique mechanisms related to causal powers to produce peace or war, correlations might still be useful for the discovery of causal powers. If democracy and conditions defined in the theory of democratic peace only once caused peace, and if in other exactly similar conditions democracy fails to produce peace, it would be difficult to claim that democracy has causal power over peace in general. Rather the co-occurrence of democracy and peace could in the first case be assumed to be coincidental.

Furthermore, the idea of totally unique causal mechanisms is a suspect. Even in the most specific cases of the historical generation of effects, it would not be possible to claim that a cause generated an effect unless it would generate the same effect in exactly similar conditions. The introduction of actions of free will does not change the correlative nature of causality. If Napoleon was under conditions C the cause of a rebellion being crushed, the fact that in another otherwise similar set of conditions C he would not want to crush the rebellion does not mean that he did not have causal powers to do so, since conditions were not the same unless in both situations he wanted to do that. This cannot be changed by the fact that in politics it would be methodologically impossible to observe identical conditions, as we do have permission to speak contra-factually and imagine what would happen in exactly the same conditions. In this sense causality is regularity, even in the most specific historical situations, where the regularity would not be possible to observe by means of correlations (in fact, it is common that correlative analysis fails to prove associations due to the small number of cases when the causal conditions exist). This is not in conflict with the fact that causes are generative: Cause means the power to make something happen, while the correlative relationship proves this power. Thus a correlative relationship is, as positivist social sciences admit, only part of the story. There has to be a mechanism through which forces with causal powers produce causal effects (Rios, 2004). For pragmatic causal analysis this means that in addition to correlation one needs to establish the mechanism of causality in order to prove the correlative relationship and make it intelligible (Coleman, 1990; Rios, 2004; von Wright, 1971) and useful. Only if we understand the causal mechanism can we fully manipulate it for the social engineering of peace. If, for example, we realize that there is a correlative relationship between the condition of social diversity and intra-state conflict (Rummel, 1997) or between social bipolarity (the division of society into two groups) and civil wars

(Collier & Hoeffler, 2004), and we know that somehow bipolarity or plurality causes conflict, we cannot still know what to do to prevent conflict. Let us assume, for example, that bipolarity/plurality causes conflict by raising demands for special treatment for the local population. Perhaps this then leads to disputes between locals and "migrants" and demands by the locals that migrants must leave the areas. This could lead to the increased probability of conflict. In this case we cannot draw conclusions from the causal relationship between plurality and conflict that plurality should be avoided in order to avoid conflict, since demands to avoid plurality is one of the steps in the causal chain from plurality to conflict.

In addition to regularities, traditional causal analysis of peace has been criticized for some of the conditions it sets for the study of causal relations. In order to avoid tautological reasoning — i.e. peace is caused by a condition in which nobody fights anybody in a violent manner — traditional, Humean, causality requires analytical independence between cause and effect. Causal analysis can only focus on synthetic relationships, rather than analytic, as otherwise statements on causality can be purely conceptual as is the relationship between people not fighting and peace: one cannot say that if people do not fight this causes peace because, people not fighting *is* peace conceptually and analytically.

For some opponents of social engineering of peace the distinction between analytical truths — i.e. truths that are not empirically but conceptually true — and synthetic truths — i.e. truths that observation of reality could falsify — is a positivistic anachronism that research could do without (Harré & Madden, 1975; Kurki, 2008; Lebow, 2009a; Patomäki, 1996; Wight, 2006). According to Herré and Madden, the identification of independent and dependent variables as independent of each other is a positivist illusion because "considered as cause and effects they are not independent for they are related through the generating mechanisms upon which they operate and through with they are produced" (Harré & Madden, 1975, p. 130). Yet, it is useful to make a difference between the association between war and fighting (conceptual/analytical) and democracy and peace (synthetic). Only the latter types of associations are useful for the pragmatic analysis of causality, as one cannot manipulate an analytic condition of war in order to prevent wars simply because an analytic condition is already conceptually part of war. The distinction between analytical and synchronic associations/correlations is useful when talking about natural science types of causality (the condition of a democratic dyad is associated with peace between the two democracies). To deny that there is a difference between analytical and real associations would allow us to discover tautological causations.

However, once we talk about socially constructed realities the situation becomes more complex: there is a grey zone between simple conceptual associations (tautologies) and analytically independent variables and this something seems very useful to analyze for the praxis of conflict prevention. Identities and norms are "variables" in the grey zone. For example, one cannot claim that there is a norm — say according to which states do not interfere in each other's domestic disputes — unless there is at least some kind of compliance of that norm in the behavior of states. Thus, compliance is partly assumed analytically in the concept of a norm. If we then say that in East Asia the norm of non-interference has contributed to peace after 1979, our dependent and independent variables are not analytically entirely independent. If there is a norm against certain conflict behavior (military interference in each other's internal disputes), this cannot be the case without the actual existence of such behavior. Thus, our independent and dependent variables are analytically connected and thus our claim is partly tautological. With identities the relationship is the same. If East Asian states are now seen as instruments of wellbeing and economic development, that rules out behavior that would focus all the attention on war fighting, expansion and revolution. Thus, also the relationship between a developmentalist identity and peaceful behavior is partly analytical and conceptual rather than synchronic. Yet, a pragmatist would say that working with state identities or negotiating about norms pays in peacemaking, and thus there is no reason to shy away totally from the study of relationships that are partly tautological.

However, also here the strict distinction between analytical and synchronic associations, and total focus on the latter in the social engineering of peace is just a limitation, not something that could make the limited area studied somehow valueless. There is no need to reject a positivist causal analysis of war, instead, one just needs to reinterpret and supplement it.

In short, social engineering of peace works. It has its side effects that we will tackle in this book as we proceed toward neo-pragmatism, but this will not mean that we should bury social engineering of peace: it has saved a lot of lives and it will continue to do so and thus it is valuable.

3.5. Moving from Classical Pragmatist Peace Research to Neo-Pragmatist Peace Research

Classical pragmatism may have implicitly dealt with some or even most of the ideas I present as ones that transform classical pragmatism into neo-pragmatism. Emphasizing the difference of the two in this book is therefore a simplification. However, as empiricists, classical pragmatists did not systematically study the implications of purposiveness for the social sciences. In the social sciences the concern is with subjects rather than objects, and with the fact that such subjects give meanings to the realities around them, and thus create social realities in people's minds. Since classical pragmatists did not do that, they were unable to interrogate naturalized concepts that structure social practices and realities as being externally given, or that serve partisan interests, or interests of the past. On the level of theory this means that classical pragmatist peace research cannot systematically explore the ways in which new interpretations in peace research as such can change the world by deconstructing and constructing social realities. This means that part of the tool box for activist peace research remains unused.

On the level of meta-theory (and the instruments of evaluation of theories of peace research) it also means that classical pragmatists see the relationship between knowledge and reality in a way that is useful for our relationship with material realities, but not with social realities. Knowledge is not just a practical way of relating to the realities that surround us, but also a practical way of creating social reality.

For classical pragmatists it is useful to consider a brick wall as real, otherwise, we get hurt ignoring it and bumping into it. Similarly, neo-pragmatists would claim we should consider social realities. It is useful for us to consider money as real or race as real in politics, if and only if a common regime or truth, culture, approach or a discourse that considers money as real or race as a political reality creates useful social conventions and realities. If, for example, we do not see the utility of economic exchange that money makes possible or if we do not like racial segregation in politics, we should criticize money or race as a construction. This means for a meta-theory that in addition to the instrumental value of peace research — the value of a theory as an instrument for a practitioner — theories and knowledge should be considered for the practicality of the social structures they constitute. Theory is no longer like a hammer that could be used for the building of a bridge, but instead theory is the bridge and should therefore be judged for its usefulness as a bridge.

Also positivist modeling of peace and war fails if it does not take into account the social creation of social realities, and thus it is useful to reform the core epistemological ideas implicit in positivist peace research. This is why it is useful and pedagogical to make a distinction between classical pragmatism and neo-pragmatism in this book. For purely pedagogical reasons the book has first imagined pragmatist peace research without any of the four more developed later innovations in social sciences (anti-determinism, interpretationism, constructivism and critical/poststructuralist theory). I started with the notion of "the social engineering of peace" and then add later innovations one by one to complement the picture of peace research so that it is up-to-date with current useful innovations in the social sciences, and yet committed to the philosophical program of pragmatism. This has been done in a way that draws from the metaphor of progress, and uses ideas that assume that before an innovation, people's understanding was more incomplete than after. My approach is not intended to be completely true to the historical development of ideas: many post-positivist ideas predate positivism, while many of the "pre-constructivist" positivist ideas represent the state of the art in current peace research.

Chapter 4
Toward a Social Science of Peace

Determinism is a belief according to which whatever happens in the world happens out of necessity because of conditions that determined it to happen. Deterministic explanations of peace and war seek the determinants that cause them. What kind of external conditions make a fighter kill, or what kind of internal characteristics of a society of an individual determines their violent behavior are then questions deterministic scholarship seeks answers to. Most peace research is deterministic only in a probabilistic sense. This means that conditions determine peaceful or belligerent actions only with a certain probability, or that conditions increase such actions with a certain probability. Rejection of determinism then means an approach in which a scholar does not seek determinants of belligerence or peacefulness but for example, tries to understand action from inside the logic of the ones committing them. The assumption there is not that something determines action and thus action can be explained only by finding the determinants of it, but instead, conflict developments are not fully determined but, instead, genuine decisions are made at will. This way violent or peaceful actions are better understood by looking at what actors of violence wanted to achieve than by looking at what kind of conditions determined these actions. Hollis and Smith call deterministic and anti-deterministic objectives in social sciences simply the objective of *explaining* and the objective of *understanding* social realities (Hollis & Smith, 1990).

4.1. Problems of Deterministic Knowledge of Peace and War

If we acknowledge that some conflict behavior is intentional/purposive, that does not mean that all conflict behavior is such. The conflicting parties might be unable to see that there are opportunities in terms of making a choice and thus they might act in accordance with some apparent external cause. Such behavior could coexist with genuine, intentional/purposive action that cannot be understood without reference to the individual's or her/his group's/state's free will. Many scholars who approach peace research from the perspective of social engineering have struggled with the realization that social engineering can only tackle the unintentional, non-genuine[1] conflict action. Singer, for example, who led the project on the Correlates of War, had serious reservations with this problem. His project sought to find causal conditions that could explain wars, and thus predict them. Armed with this knowledge, he intended to help practitioners remove these causal conditions in order to prevent wars. However, Singer eventually became frustrated with the entire venture of finding causal conditions and settled for correlative associations between various condition and conflict or peace. Part of his frustration was due to the fact that he recognized the existence of a DOF (of will), but could not model it into his causal model. Yet he was convinced that his project on the correlative relations of war was very valuable for the progress of peace research and that peace research needed evidence, not just interpretation and theorizing (Singer, 1969, 1976). He was undoubtedly right. Yet, we must go beyond correlations and deterministic causalities in order to know how to use Singer's correlations and other evidence that could help peace practitioners.

Correlative associations of the type that Singer was talking about can at least explain behavioral patterns that are somehow unintentional or unreflexive. Such behavior can be explained by external

---

[1] Coleman considers action genuine only if it is intentional. Accidental causing of something is not really an action for Coleman, as it is not intended (Coleman, 1966, 1990).

conditions, while genuine action always assumes intentionality that is internal to the true subject.[2] Freedom of will, again, means unpredictability, and the refutation of correlative regularities. While Singer's regularities could be very useful, the idea that conflict phenomenon can only be explained if one can find the external conditions that explain the phenomenon effectively rules out the study of genuine action and genuine politics from the study of war, politics, and human action. The fact that all positivistic modeling in peace research presents probabilistic conclusions — we no longer claim to know the absolute necessary or sufficient conditions for peace or war — does not change the situation. If a model explains 20% of the variation in conflict behavior, it is focused on the 20% that is determined and not on the 80% that is somehow genuine human action. It is important to explain the part of behavior that is not genuine action, as it is externally determined. To say, however, that peace science should only be focused on that automatic, externally determined part of human activity really means that genuine action is not the object of peace sciences. Only if we can define a model that explains 100% of the variation in conflict behavior can we consider the model perfect and stop studying that type of behavior. If we can only consider the part of the action that is not genuinely free as something we have "explained" then we do not really understand genuine conflict actions at all.

However, if conflicting parties interpret their social realities deterministically this has an impact on the reality of the conflict situation and some of these impacts are not positive. At least the following negative consequences can be identified:

1. Deterministic thinking implies human behavior that fails to recognize the human opportunities for choice.
2. Deterministic thinking makes pragmatic peace work impossible, or limits it to the elites.

---

[2] True subject here, means someone who is responsible for her/his actions, as she/he has done them intentionally.

3. Deterministic thinking of one's own behavior or the behavioral environment opens the door to unaccountable immoral conflict action.
4. Deterministic thinking about one's enemy rules out opportunities for conflict resolution.
5. Determinist actors in conflict-related interaction risk being exploited by self-consciously free actors.

I will briefly describe these problems before moving on to the kind of explanation to which peace research has to resort once the determinism of the social engineering of peace is rejected.

The determinism involved in the type of understandings that the social engineering of peace exemplifies has ruled out opportunities for the use of the political imagination of peace-actors. Fromm, Heidegger, and Gadamer, each from their own very different theoretical perspectives, criticize the positivistic world view of the social engineering of peace for losing sight of genuine action and the options and choices people have in their lives. This shrinks the "human" out of people (Fromm, 1973; Gadamer, 1989; Heidegger, 1962). In the same vein, Lebow claims that the main problem in covering laws and social engineering of peace is the problem that our consciousness (or false consciousness) of the laws and regularities covering human behavior affects our behavior. A "False consciousness" or an "unpractical knowledge" of the "laws" that regulate our free choices could make us behave in what we believe is the only/natural way of behaving. Thus, deterministic knowledge about covering laws could be a self-fulfilling prophesy. Lebow, for example, says that these kinds of unpractical epistemic orientations are very prominent in the explanation of conflict behavior. Cognitive frames that prevent us from seeing some options (such as those that go against the covering laws in which we believe) and emphasize others (those that are consistent with covering laws) are treated in Lebow's causal analysis as forming the deepest level of causality that influences people, societies, and states. This is why Lebow claims that causal analysis in the social engineering of peace narrows our map of causality rather than widening it (Lebow, 2009a, p. 215).

For pragmatic peace research strict determinism (even if based on probabilistic determination) of positivist scholarship is a problem as it leaves no room for acts designed to create peace that are based on the use of free will and intentional actions. Thus, for pragmatic purposes, it seems useful to be able to consider alternative futures that our reflections could affect. Otherwise, it would appear to be useless to produce knowledge that would enable us to come to better decisions regarding the issue of peace and war. Committing to ontologies copied from natural sciences is thus very difficult, as is using the methods of causal analysis from the natural sciences. As Berger says, we do not doubt freedom, and yet, since it is its own cause and a special kind of cause it is excluded from this system of positivistic research (Berger, 1963).

While classical pragmatists felt that science is a process of exploration that starts from someone's interest in the realities around her/him, the assumption in social engineering and in the search for determinants assumes that outside this process of exploration purposive action does not exist. This, of course, is either contradictory or it puts purposive human action beyond the scope of social sciences such as peace research. If peace research assumes that only the explorer/peace researcher is purposive, while the actions of others are determined, then the foundation of the explanation of deterministic peace research is that human beings are purposive and that they are not purposive (A and −A). With such ontological premises, it is not possible to design models that can make social phenomena intelligible. Yet, making something intelligible is part of the ambition of social engineering: In order to define the content and limits of our covering laws, we will need to have a basic understanding of the objects of our study. A system that is based on assumptions A and −A cannot produce that basic understanding.

Thus, in a deterministic setting we will have to assume both free and intentional actions, and determined actions, and then simply limit ourselves to the analysis of the latter or to the analysis of the "surroundings" of purposive action. Game theory and the rationalist paradigm in social sciences that are based on the modeling of purposive (but not necessarily free) strategic action have done this by distinguishing between flexible and rigid actors (Coleman, 1990; Harsanyi, 1956) or the form of action that chooses the best course of action as the typical, pure form of action and degenerate forms of action that are not purposive but determined (Van Parijs, 1981). Whenever there are covering laws that can predict human behavior, we must be talking about degenerate, rigid behavior, as a law related to the actor's objective character (instincts) or to the environment of the actor (response models) causes behavior, not the free will of the actor. This reveals the limits of research for social engineering: it necessarily leaves out real human behavior and only focuses on degenerate forms of behavior. If the main action in conflicts and peace remains unexplored we will necessarily lose many options for prescriptions on how to make peace.

If we study this limitation further, we will discover another problem. If the assumption is that there are regulated actions and free actions, and that social engineering is aimed at manipulating regulated action, this divides people into two categories: engineers and the engineered. The main category of peace-seeking actions that are being ruled beyond the focus of classical pragmatic peace research are strategies where we all mobilize for peace and where the crucial peace-seeking actors jointly search for peace. Instead, social engineering focuses on finding ways for elites to engineer peace in societies. It is easy to see how peace research as social engineering commits to rather elitist and autocratic strategies, and that taken the inherently political nature of peace, this involves unfortunate political consequences. The fact that there is no peace without the terms of peace means that elitist engineering of societal peace gives elites the ability to define the terms of peace. Thus there are negative political implications, not just theoretical ones, with the selective assumption of freedom.

Another negative political implication that stems from determinism is related to morality. The kind of scholarly understanding and truth regime that sees that human action is determined by external conditions leads to the idea that an action that we can explain cannot be morally accountable. Responsibility for the actions that we take as a result of our free will has been the foundation of our understanding of morality. At least Immanuel Kant, John Rawls, Jeremy Bentham, Rousseau, Mills, John Locke, and Hayek have made this very explicit in their analysis of ethics. Even if there are compatibilist views that see that determinism is compatible with moral accountability (For a philosophical review both on compatibilist and incompatibilist views, see Fischer *et al.*, 2007), it seems that in conflict situations determinist truth regimes are used to avoid moral accountability. Thus if we do not incorporate some degree of freedom (DOF) into our study of peace and war, we cannot incorporate norms and morality in our analysis either.

If, for example, we believe that there is no room for morality in world politics as realists and neo-realists have suggested (Morgenthau, 2006; Waltz, 1979), states will act in the expectation of not finding any room for morality and norms, and, thus, they, too, will act egoistically without applying normal normative codes to their foreign policy. In doing this, they will also verify the "covering law" on the dissociation between world politics and political morals, and thus further strengthen the idea that world politics is an immoral zone. During the cold war, the US Secretary of State, Henry Kissinger (Kissinger, 1973), and, for example, Finland's President Urho Kekkonen (Kekkonen, 1967), explicitly declared that in their view morality was not relevant to world politics. Then they both committed acts that clearly emanated from this belief by sidelining morality and norms as things for which world politics had no place (rather than making conscious decisions to choose immoral strategies). Clearly their way of avoiding moral blame was simply to consider the moral as something that is not relevant in world politics, just as Morgenthau and many other realists have theorized. The political consequences of covering laws can be traced everywhere in world politics.

The positivistic conclusion that war and peace are the results of deterministically caused conditions can be abused in politics in a way that demonstrates the pragmatic problems in such deterministic cognitive frames and epistemic orientations. On the one hand it is possible to get away with immoral choices in politics if one considers that the outcomes are caused deterministically. In addition to the above example about "the reality of world politics as a moral free zone", we can draw examples from the so-called root cause discussion. In this discussion, the conflicting parties treat their own aggression as something that has been caused by some root causes of the conflict. The logic of this rhetorical strategy is strange as it expects that the adversary can make choices and thus can be criticized for his actions, while one's own side simply reacts to the actions of the opponent (as a causal effect of the opponent's action).

According to Netanyahu, during his seven-day military campaign in Gaza in November 2012 "terrorists" had the initiative while Israel was ready to "take whatever action" was "necessary". (Israel launches retaliation strikes against Hamas rocket attacks, 2012). In the Israeli rhetoric, the notion of national security and national interest made such action a necessity, as if Israel was the only country in the world and thus the only actor that can prioritize its interests as non-negotiable, natural, and objective necessities. Israel's aggression is not a moral or immoral choice, but simply a mechanistic causal effect of the threat that plagues Israel's security.

The view that one's own use of violence is a causal reaction to someone else's is even more common among rebels or even terrorists than among states. The Palestinian side of the seven-day conflict in November 2012 also often used the root cause metaphor based on causal models of grievance-based rebellion and violence. According to Diana Buttu, a Palestinian lawyer close to the Hamas government, "if we're going to move forward in reaching a ceasefire agreement we have to look beyond just the question of rockets and bombs but actually begin to address the root causes. And in this case the root cause is Israel's 45-year military control over the Gaza Strip and most particularly a very brutal six-year blockade that has been imposed on the Gaza Strip, which has effectively ensured that the Gaza Strip, in the words of the United Nations, in a few short years will become unlivable. So if anything we have to begin to address these root causes and that is the 45-year denial of freedom to the Palestinians" (Sales, 2012).

In West Kalimantan, Malay cannibalistic aggression against the Madurese migrant population was seen as a mechanical reaction to the abuse and denial of indigenous rights in their own lands. According to a Malay leader of the district, where a Malay rampage and cannibalistic rioting against the Madurese population took place, the Malay soul was like a spring: Once it had been pushed back far enough it had to bounce back (Rasyid, 2008). Interestingly in the preceding conflict between ethnic Dayak and ethnic Manurese between December 1997 and February 1998, the grievances of the indigenous Dayak population were seen as the reason for the Dayak population showing a similar level of brutality toward the Madurese "migrants" (Bamba, 2003). The metaphor of this physical deterministic process was rather widespread and was revealed in quite a lot of the interviews with some of the key mobilizers of the Malay and Dayak aggression, and it clearly helped both populations to avoid any moral condemnation of their violence: Killing perhaps a 1,000 Madurese migrants, and terrorizing them by publicly eating organs of their bodies and parading in public with Madurese sculls hanging from their belts was a deterministic reaction rather than an immoral choice (Kivimäki, 2012a).

When determinism affects one's own identity it takes away morality, but when "knowledge" of determinism affects one's perception of the enemy it removes the resolution of conflicts from our menu of options. If a party to a conflict has a deterministic view of its enemy — it is the characteristics of the enemy that cause their violence (instinctivism) or it is the conditions to which the given preferences of the enemy mechanistically reacts (environmentalism) — conflict could not be reconciled. Very often this thinking leads to the perception that the enemy has to be stopped or liquidated before he/she does any more damage. The most common narrative used in support of realism against idealism was the story of the British Prime Minister, Neville Chamberlain, who trusted agreements and failed to stop the evil Nazis in time. It is very rare to find an account of the Second World War which argues that the interested of the main powers could have been reconciled in a manner that could have satisfied everyone. The causes of the war is diagnosed as stemming from the vicious character of Hitler or Germany at the time and the prescription offered is the destruction of Nazis. The need to stop crazy dictators is in a more general way part of a narrative that starts with the need to stop Hitler and continues with the need to stop Stalin, Khruschev, Breshnev, the Ayatollah Khomeini, Saddam Hussein, Osama bin Laden, etc.

George W. Bush revealed that this narrative was behind his decision to invade Iraq when he explained his decision to go to war and repeated the idea of Saddam Hussein as a madman: "So I had a choice to make: either to forget the lessons of September 11 and trust a madman who is a sworn enemy of the United States of America, or take action necessary to defend this country. (Remarks in St. Paul, Minnesota, August 18, 2004 in Bush & Register, 2004, p. 1724)" This narrative has justified a lot of violence. Ken Booth and Nicholas J. Wheeler talk about this type of determinism as lack of "security dilemma sensitivity", in which the origin of the threat is seen in the deterministic characteristics of the enemy, not in an antagonistic interaction or a security dilemma let alone an interactively constructed social structure (Booth & Wheeler, 2008, pp. 65–70). Booth and Wheeler see such a narrative concerning the US attitude towards the Soviet Union since the National Security Council characterization of the Soviet Threat in the NSC-68 document from the 1950s. This document defined the Soviet threat as being "animated by a new fanatic faith, anti-thetical to our own and (seeking) to impose its absolute authority over the rest of the world" (cited in Booth & Wheeler, 2008, p. 65). Booth and Wheeler mentioned Reagan's rhetoric about evil states (p. 67), Bush's "axis-of-evil" rhetoric and the rhetoric of rogue states of the US National Security Strategy in 2002 as examples of this dangerous rhetoric of determinism. Robert Jervis calls spirals of hostilities, "deep security dilemmas". In such dilemmas, the dangerous social structure of a security dilemma is present and the sensitivity of the danger of such a structure is made more poignant by the determinism involved in the perception of the conflicting parties of each other (Jervis, 2001, p. 41).

The view that a particular threat emanates from the objective characteristics of the enemy has been resorted to even when it has been founded on a less than credible argument. For example, in 2002, the United States argued that the anti-democratic character of several states was a deterministic characteristic that made those states dangerous for the United States. However, many of the US allies were much more autocratic than the enemies identified, which were regarded as a threat precisely because of their supposedly autocratic character. When George W. Bush launched his campaign against the axis of evil, he based his rationale for opposing Iran on his general program against the tyrants of the world. Yet Iran had been a tyranny all through the decades during which it was a US ally (1953–1979), while in 2002, when it was against US oil interests and against the US's ally Israel, it was, according to Polity IV data, the most democratic Muslim country in the Middle East (If Turkey is considered a Middle Eastern power, Iran was the second most democratic) (Kivimäki, 2012b). It is very clear that this idea of "knowing" the enemy through its deterministic characteristics has not served peace. Instead it has constituted the basis for legitimate military "reactions" against vicious leaders.

As in many conflicts between migrants and "locals", in West Kalimantan, the activities of the migrant population during the conflict were seen as being caused by the vicious character of the Madurese. During and soon after the conflict between the Madurese on the one hand and the Dayaks and the Malays on the other, the dominant explanation of the conflict used two deterministic processes in the analysis. The above explained "reaction" to Madurese violence was the one of them, while the original Madurese violence was explained by referring to the primordial characteristics of the Madurese (Bamba, 2003; Hermanus, 2005; Kivimäki, 2003b). Later the explanation changed and the same people interviewed earlier said that Madurese culture was incompatible with the local Dayak and Malay cultures (Marsellino, 2005; Rasyid, 2008). The conclusion was the same regardless of whether the regime of truth emphasized determinism in terms of race or culture: "The Madurese had to be expelled from the district and those who refused to leave had to be killed" (YD, 2001). Only much later, did the diagnosis of the "local"[3] conflicting parties start to change and more structural explanations for the disputes (the idea that

---

[3] I use words local and migrant in the context of West Kalimantan inside quotation marks to denote that according to the Dayak and Malay conflicting parties, the Madurese are migrants, while the Dayak and Malay are indigenous to the area. However, most Madurese people considered themselves indigenous Indonesians and thus as having equal rights to those of the other parties to the conflict in Indonesia (Thoha, 2005).

it was the lack of police that had escalated the Madurese criminal violence before the cannibalistic riots, the idea that there were disagreements with the rights and duties of "local" and "migrant" populations) started to emerge in 2006–2008, which allowed a more constructive approach to the task of reaching a settlement of the conflict.

In the Gaza conflict in November 2012, and earlier in 2008, the identification of Hamas as a terrorist organization by Israel and the US determines causally, for these conflicting parties, the behavioral pattern of aggression against citizens. Both security-oriented and religiously-oriented Israeli circles tended to support this causal interpretation, while Sherifa Zuhur's analysis of the Israeli discourse on Hamas and the Palestinians reveals that there are also compromise-oriented forces in Israel who focus on interests rather than the characteristics of their enemies and who want a resolution of the dispute and reject the idea that Hamas and the Palestinians will not be moved by compromise (Zuhur, 2009).

At the same time, Hamas (and Iran, for example), understand Israeli behavior in terms of their perception of Israel as a Zionist, occupying state. As a result, there is little room for conflict resolution and reconciling the interests of these enemies. Instead, the party with vicious characteristics has to be eliminated, expelled, deterred, or fought against in self-defense. According to Mohammed Deif, Hamas' elusive military commander, Hamas "must invest all resources to uproot this aggressor from our land" (Deif, 2012). This is according to this deterministic thinker because Israeli aggression takes place because of Israel's nature as an occupying Zionist state. Egyptian Foreign Minister Mohammed Kamel Amr, in talks with the US Secretary of State, demanded an immediate US intervention to stop Israeli aggression (Fox News November 15, 2012 (http://www.foxnews.com/world/2012/11/15/3-dead-after-gaza-rocket-strikes-southern-israel.html).), referring to the aggressive nature of Israel.

However, in addition to determinism creating problems for norms and conflict resolution, deterministic thinking of one's adversaries can also be manipulated and exploited by agents that understand their freedom of action. According to Ted Robert Gurr, conflict is probabilistically caused by relative deprivation. If we assume this, we will have to appease violent offenders and this exposes our thinking to manipulation. Our opponents can exploit our belief in the model of relative deprivation by manufacturing empirical evidence of a similar reaction in them with regards to all those grievances they want to address. A rational reaction from us as peacemakers would be to give in to their demands quickly. Yet, to prescribe capitulation as a formula for peace would be too easy. Only if we realize that some things can be explained by referring to the purposes and the free will of actors can we make a distinction between justified claims and unjustified ones, and thus only by incorporating free will into our thinking about peace and war can we identify unfair manipulation and exploitation of grievance-based theories of war.

Clearly in order for the conflicting parties to see the potential of managing conflict behavior, the resolution of disputes or the transformation of the structures of interaction we have to recognize the potential of voluntary actions for peace, within the limits of the social and material structures set for peacemaking.

4.2. Modeling Purposive Conflict Behavior

By now it seems clear that a true pragmatist cannot limit research to the type of action in conflicts that can be explained by looking at its external determination. However, moving from deterministic to non-deterministic peace research is not easy. I will discuss this leap in this section by starting with some methodological questions on what non-deterministic research cannot be, what kind of interaction can it have with deterministic processes and finally how the non-deterministic dynamics of peace and war can be understood and how they could be modeled.

Our intuition suggests that in most social situations we have opportunities alternative to the ones we choose. Thus alternative futures, in addition to the course we end up choosing are part of the reality in which we live (Kurki, 2008; Patomäki, 2013). However, even if this is common sense, this has implications on our way of understanding the substantiation of our claims concerning peace and war. Empirical evidence no longer tells us anything about causal patterns, as social situations are open to alternative paths, and thus empirical evidence about pathways to peace or war only prove that a particular path to peace or war was possible, not that it was causally determined. Thus, we cannot expect to find regularities that explain why purposive behavior necessarily has to take certain forms in conflicts. Rigid covering laws in conflict dynamics can therefore only be found in the realm where human behavior is not genuine action, but a simple, unreflexive reaction to external conditions. We will have to approach real action from a different angle. However, before moving on to the unpredictable realm of real conflict behavior and peace action, I will demonstrate some alternative ways of modeling some rather durable deep structures[4] that can be imagined even if we assume that human and group action has an element of freedom.

Even if we assume that humans, groups, states, and other actors in peace and conflict have a certain freedom of choice, this does not mean that there might not be limits to alternative futures. Even genuinely free action has many types of limits. Some are analytical (and yet tell us something about reality). We might imagine a situation in which an actor is able to choose between more or less economic resources. Since the outcomes she/he can materialize (things she can buy) with a smaller amount of money are a subset of the outcomes she can materialize with a lot of money, it is logical, regardless of her/his preferences to assume that she/he will prefer more rather than less economic resources. It is logically not possible to find better outcomes from a subset of a set of outcomes than from the full set of outcomes.

If we think of power resources in world politics as similar additive resources to money, we could similarly say that it is logical to assume that people will prefer more power resources to less power resources, if the outcomes one can materialize with smaller power resources is a subset of the outcomes one can materialize with bigger power resources.[5] These considerations rule out rational preferences for

---

[4] By "deep structures" I mean structures that are rather fundamental and durable and that condition other social formations that could then be called surface structures. For Marx power structures of production were such deep structures that then formed a foundation for cultural formations.

[5] Of course power resources are not necessarily additive. Great military resources could for example provoke one's neighboring country to rule out the option of living

smaller power resources and less money (under conditions where less power or smaller amounts of money do not offer anything that more power or more money would not offer) and give rise to an economic (Smith, 2001) or political realist (Morgenthau, 2006) modeling of action that is not dependent on preferences.

Yet, focusing only on these "logical preferences", puts many realities of peace and war outside our focus. Even if we believe that logical preferences are somehow fundamental as they are so common to all, we cannot reduce conflict developments to these preferences only. How do people use their money or power, how much are they willing to sacrifice other values to get more money or more power, how much more, if any, would more money or more power offer to the actors of conflict situations are all issues that cannot be studied without assuming and studying the purposes and preferences that derive from a will that is at least somewhat free.

Similarly, in collective action, we can find logical ways to predict outcomes irrespective of free will and the preferences that free will wishes. If the outcome can be materialized by a group that is a subgroup of another group, the outcome will be materialized with a smaller probability than in the case where its materialization was available for any of the members of the whole group. Thus, for example, it could be useful for global security to limit the number of states that have the capacity to cause an accidental nuclear holocaust, since the more powers that could make such a mistake the greater probability of it happening. Furthermore, if a political system is without a coordinating and regulating authority that can prevent an individual sabotaging order, such a system is more vulnerable than a system where plurality has been limited by means of unifying norms. Thus, the lack of centrally imposed rules for the global exercise of power, in other words, a condition of international anarchy, by definition creates risks to peace as it allows many actors instead of just a few to use violence in the international

---

peacefully with its neighbors without an arms race. This would mean that greater power resources would not offer a set of outcomes that has to include all the outcomes one could get with less power resources.

system (Waltz, 1979). Yet, again, logic can lead to some rather trivial results, while the reality of an open system of world politics often interferes with the premises of such logical deductions. For example, could this increased danger make states more careful or could one country's nuclear potential deter another country's carelessness with nuclear issues? To solve this problem requires answers to many other questions that cannot be given without understanding the purposes and preferences of potential actors of conflicts.

Materiality can also create deep structures that can be taken as a starting point of analysis disregarding preferences. If something material (such as survival) is instrumental to an actor's influence in a conflict situation or in society in general, then we could take the preference for survival as our starting point of analysis.[6] It would be possible to imagine alternative preferences, too, but actors with such alternative preferences would not be influential for long, due to the material unsustainability of self-destructive preferences. This allows us to conclude that some deep structures of societies do not change when people change their preferences and purposes. Survivalist conflict analysis could develop rational models that start from the common preference for survival and then develop prescriptions as to how such survival-oriented actors should act to guarantee their survival in a given structure (Snauwaert, 2015). However, given the commonness of pro-survival preferences, it is possible to base peace research on an ontological deep structure that helps one understand the foundations of societies that are in conflict. One such attempt is based on the material necessity of the production of livelihoods in the Marxist theory of politics, societies, and conflicts. If production is somehow primary and instrumental for all societal life, common to all societies and members of all societies, then it is useful to look at the main forms of production and the power relationships involved in these forms in order to understand societies, politics, and peace and war. The theory of imperialist wars looks at conflicts by starting from the commonness of the preference for survival, the instrumentality of production for survival, and finally the power relationship, once the

---

[6] Obviously this would not be a good starting point in an analysis that focused on suicide terrorism or kamikaze operations.

money economy had taken over from the feudal mode of production, between the two groups of people involved in production: the capitalist and the worker (Lenin, 1980; Marx, 1990).

An alternative route from the same generalization of the preference for survival is taken by Fukuyama, Elias, and Pinker, who look at the avoidance of violent death as the fundamental basis for the preference for survival, and explain how violence has declined in the world. The organization of security benefitted from the presence and action of larger groups, and thus facilitated, when material foundations afforded greater and greater organization, the move from families, clans to city states, nation states, military alliances and perhaps one day global government. Once security communities, within which there were rules for human interaction and some sense of a common identity, were enlarged each step of enlargement implied a progressive step toward diminishing violence and increasing peace (Elias, 1939, 1982; Fukuyama, 2011; Pinker, 2011).

Thus, it is possible to utilize models of economic rationality, classical realism and survivalism's models of power behavior, models of neo-realism on anarchy, Marxist models of economic power structures, and modernist models on the development of governance as deep structures, simply by assuming a preference for survival over death. However, while material or logical limitations to possible futures can offer some deep structures to the political context of peace and war, in the end we will have to be able to model intentional, purposive free behavior, no matter how unpredictable and how impossible it is to explain it by means of exogenous covering laws. I will start with some philosophical considerations and proceed towards the realities of peace and conflict and the new kind of pragmatic approach to them.

The thing that distinguishes a fighter from water is the former's underdetermined[7] ability to consider his actions. Thus there is an element, will, that we cannot, by definition, determine, and yet we

---

[7] Underdetermination refers to the fact that action and consideration cannot be fully explained from the characteristics of the actor or the environment the actor is in. Thus, even if there are factors that influence human consideration, those factors do not fully determine what the actor is going to choose (Sartre, 1984).

should not assume it away. Assuming it away would rule out the "subject" and politics from our analysis (Gadamer, 1989). This "will" does have causal powers, but, at the same time, even though it is not fully determined it is affected by many things outside itself.

On the one hand, the element of under-determination in a person's will makes it unpredictable and different from essential beings that are defined by their characteristics. Sartre puts this in puzzling terms by saying that subjects with a will are not what they are (in essential sense, i.e. as they are determined by their characteristics, instincts, and the environment), but that instead, they are what they are not, and thus they demonstrate their subjectivity by doing something that is not in their character or role (Sartre, 1984). Instead of being what they are, humans are "in the state of becoming", unfolding, acting, not something essential with fixed characteristics (Mead, 1934). Doty, in her analysis of the dialogue between actors and material and social structure suggest that this gives the study of social practices a radical element of under-determination (Doty, 1997). Only by understanding the potential for something and the freedom from total determination of themselves can people be authentic selves, according to Heidegger (Heidegger, 1962).

On the other hand, the free will interacts with material realities that set limits to purposive action. A soldier cannot survive bullets by sheer will power, and outcomes do not entirely depend on his preferences. Furthermore, the limits of his brain limit his ability to consider exactly what he wants or what consequences will follow from different actions. Social structures also limit (even if they also facilitate) purposive action. This will be discussed further once the social engineering approach to peace is widened in a constructivist and symbolic interactionist direction, but one cannot avoid some elements of social structures when defining the limits of individual will. Elements in subjective agency that are their own causes are partly created in a social process. People are born in a system of meanings, facilitating and limiting institutional facts, and collective ideas of appropriateness. These social realities not only limit what people can do, but also affect what they want. In the past, soldiers were allowed to kill enemy civilians, while today, they would not want to identify themselves as terrorists and thus they try to avoid such fatalities. However, if soldiers can live with the idea that they are terrorists, they are now able to do acts of terrorism as this category of acts has been created. Finally, due to the fact that soldiers are born in a system of meanings where they themselves are defined as an Indonesian or as an American, they are able to have social preferences: they can "want as part of a nation", and their wanting together with the wanting of other Indonesians or Americans create a "we-intention" (Tuomela, 2005; Tuomela & Miller, 1985), a collective purpose, and a collective subjectivity/agency. Thus,

1. Free individual's will is limited from doing things that cannot be done in a material and social structure;
2. His/her will is regulated by existing social norms and identities, while;
3. It's (will's) objects are sometimes created in social conventions. Finally;
4. Individual will can also be an element or a part of the will, purpose, and intention of a collectivity.

While it is clear that the subject creates and transforms the structures he/she is surrounded by, it is also clear that in at least the above four ways the free will of an individual is linked and created by the surrounding structures. Thus, everything related to peace and war does not happen as we want (despite the freedom of our will) it to happen: If it did there would be no need for research as peace could be brought about simply in accordance to our will and if people wanted war, it would not be practical or democratic to go against the popular will by being a peace practitioner. At the same time, if everything was externally determined, cognitive orientations, knowledge and theories, let alone social engineering, would not be possible either as everything was already externally determined. Pragmatist peace research has its place at the crossroads of external determination and underdetermined will. It is where the two meet, where knowledge is needed, as the basic axioms of classical pragmatism have already made clear: knowledge gives us, that is, underdetermined subjects, the opportunity to choose a pragmatic approach to the realities that surround us. However, in matters of peace and war external realities are not just material limitations or opportunities, but are themselves also underdetermined subjects, with whom our interaction creates social realities. Since this crossroads of structures and agencies not only implies the free will of an individual but also the creation of social meanings and social realities in the action of social beings, we will have to transform the classical pragmatist paradigm. Since the objects of the natural sciences do not give meanings to their actions — water, for example just boils and lets others interpret it — and since the natural sciences cannot offer ways to understand social structures that are created according to different conventions and interpretation (Water does not create conventions either), neo-pragmatism has to distance itself from the natural sciences. Not only do we have to see how peace can be engineered in a reality where purposive actors interact with material realities, but we also have to see how peace can be engineered in a structural environment of many purposive actors. We can begin such an investigation by looking at one pre-constructivist, pre-interpretivist way of studying the meeting of the will and the realities of peace and conflict. This mobilizes a mathematical modeling of the structures of interaction between purposive subjects. In its difficult formalism this approach has often caused rashes and allergies among post-positivists. As a result, much of post-positivist thinking has targeted sometimes very unfair critical characterizations of game theory that could very well be a useful tool in the hands (and minds) of peace researchers and peace practitioners.

What freedom of will requires to explain peace and war are descriptions of the reasons that make conflict behavior understandable. These descriptions are based on understanding the motives and intentions of conflict actors for what they do (Hollis & Smith, 1990). This is clearly something that goes beyond the kind of explanation to be found in the natural sciences: the reasons that water has for its boiling cannot be understood as it has no purposes, preferences, or interests. It is important for a peace practitioner to understand the reasons behind conflict behavior. This, rather than the explanations of the determination of such actions, is the beginning of the ability of peace actors to start resolving conflicts.

However, to know the reasons for the behavior of parties to a conflict is not enough. If conflict behavior was simply a voluntary act, there would be no need to interfere: people do what they want and, thus, if they fight, that is what they want. There must be structural realities that affect conflict as presumably the people involved in conflicts do not want violence and destruction as such. Interviews in most conflicts with the parties to a conflict tend to prove that most people in conflict zones want peace, but peace on their terms. Somehow, thus, structures of interaction twist the outcome of action of actors with peaceful preferences into acts that result in war and destruction. Such structural realities seem to be especially important for peace research. However, in more general terms, non-deterministic pragmatist peace research needs to aim at understanding the reasons for behavior as well as the structures that create social results and the purposive behavior of many actors. Pragmatic peace research needs to study the interplay, or dialectics, between free action and the facilitating and limiting structures, in order to understand outcomes like war, which is partly the product of free will and yet is still the unwanted outcome of the self-same agents who helped to produce it. To put it simply, pragmatic peace research has to study approaches to the external reality of free subjects to see what works for conflict prevention and what does not.

Game theory can do all of this, even if it lacks tools for the reconstruction of constructs and meanings that constitute the games. The constitution of games will be introduced after the introduction of the most relevant game theory models for pragmatic peace research. Yet, before presenting these two most relevant models — models that explain the structures that make peaceful individuals act in a belligerent manner — I will defend game theory against the most usual arguments given for rejecting this methodological tool. Since game theory is formal, mathematical, and difficult, it would be nice if we could say that it does not provide us with anything useful and therefore that we don't need to study it. This must be one of the main reasons why the critique of game theory has gained so much popularity. However, since game theory can reveal the structures that make peaceful actors act in a belligerent manner, we will have to take the trouble of learning about this methodology.

4.3. The Relevance of Game Theory for Modeling the Reasons for Action

Game theory is a formal method that addresses the interaction between the purposive action of actors and the structure formed partly by material realities and partly by realities that the existence of several causally potent purposive actors constitute. While most of the game theory work conducted by theorists of security has assumed that the agency of states is something given, and that the political interests of powerful states is natural (Schelling, 1980; Ellsberg, 1968), game theory is not limited to this practice (Wendt, 2001, p. 1021). Game theory can model all kinds of preferences, a willingness to avoid power, a preference for death over life, and losing money for no reason, by any kind of purposive actor: namely, a human being, a social class (with common purposes) a terrorist group, a multinational corporation, an activist group, an epistemic community, or a football club. This is why it is true when Wendt says that much of game theory's modeling of security, deterrence, conflicts, and strategies is based on ontology where the people and nations involved are given, but it is not true that game theory is destined to model only such ontologies.

Whatever the preference of an actor is, and whoever the actor may be, game theory describes preferences — even the free will of subjects — numerically by allocating a greater number to the outcomes the actor prefers most, and a smaller number to those the actor prefers less. Game theory often talks about utilities, which are the descriptions of the degree to which actors prefer something. Outcomes that we prefer most give us the highest utility, while the ones we prefer less give a lower utility. If we then follow our free will in our behavior, game theorists will say that we maximize our utility, while if we consider the outcomes of our actions probabilistically game theorists will say that we maximize our expected utility.

Thus, besides the methodology, game theory is simply committed to an ontology where actors are purposive (try to achieve some consequentialist goals) within their own system of beliefs. Owing to simplicity, most game theory applications assume that preferences are related to material outcomes, rather than the preferences of others, or processes of interaction, or probabilities (risk avoidance or risk-seeking behavior). When actors have relational preferences — when A wants B to be satisfied or B wants misery for A — or when agents try to avoid having to bargain, or when they seek risks in their lives, or when different limits to purposive rationality exist due to psychological or neurological characteristics of the actors (Lebow, 2009) simple game theory models are clumsier.[8] Yet, even consequentialism (in the sense of preferences being related to outcomes, rather than processes, relations, or risks) cannot be considered as something given in game theory. It is possible for a game theorist to build models that take all these different types of preferences into account. Changing preferences as well as learning can also be modeled in game theory, just as it is possible to model games where the game structure is being negotiated on a meta-game level (Kivimäki, 2002, 2003a).

Wendt has suggested that there is a sharp distinction between game theory's logic of consequences and the normative logic of appropriateness (Wendt, 2001). Action justified by the utility of its consequences can be game theorized, while action that follows normative rules cannot. Yet, when we discuss with the fighters or decision makers that decide on matters of peace and war we are almost always confronted with the confusion of the two logics. On the one hand, action can produce good outcomes, say money or security, but, on the other hand, it could be wrong. In a situation where conflicting

---

[8]While game theory can model structures that are constituted by different material, psychological, or purposive forces, this does not mean that game theory can explain the constitution of such structures. Game theory can explain purposive structures and how they affect outcomes and choices within such structure, but not necessarily how structures are constituted. The fact that agent A prefers outcome Y, the fact that she/he cannot identify strategy s2, and that outcome X is not possible are all questions, in addition to the purposive structure, that game theory can explain, which affect the outcomes and choices and that might sometimes need to be studied to produce a pragmatic knowledge useful for peace making. While finding answers to some of these questions cannot be helped by employing game theory's methods, some can. Conflicting parties often negotiate their negotiation setting — they meta-bargain their interpretations of the elements on the table — and obviously this could be studied as bargaining.

parties have to make decisions they will have to consider both normative and utility motives, and each of these motives will have its own weight in the calculations of the conflicting parties. Thus, practice forces them into a single logic where normative institutions are given a utility value, as is the case with money and security. An action or a decision will have to consider different kinds of payoffs and to say that normative payoffs are fundamentally different from immoral payoffs does not seem convincing given the practice of conflict decisions. Rather than different logics, the selfish, immoral consequences of one's actions can reflect a construct with a different agency (individual) than moral, normative consequences, which as a rule perhaps serve a more collective agent (collective) by maximizing the utility of a group instead of an individual. In any case, methodologically, one could just as well describe normative consequences as utilities as one can such consequences as money and security, and attach a utility value to the consequences of following a norm. It may be difficult to compare the utility of honoring sovereignty to the utility of gaining a piece of land, but in practice decision makers will have to make the comparison to reach a decision, and thus pragmatist peace research has to be able to follow that one logic of practice rather than theorizing some fundamental differences between the logic of consequences and the logic of appropriateness.

Behind game theory modeling there can also be an ontology that assumes that utilities can be taken as given — everybody wants money and power — but there is no reason why this should be the case. It is easier to create game theory models if we assume preferences instead of going to the trouble of actually investigating what different actors want. Furthermore, this investigation is something game theory cannot help the investigator with. But any game theorist understands that given preferences are just simplifications that any modeling sometimes needs to make, and that such simplifications can thus be suspect if realism is expected from a model.

Without given preferences or game structures, though, game theory is much less of a theory claiming anything about the reality. It is mostly a methodology for the study of the interaction between an agent and the structure of purposive agents. Yet, there are structural regularities that relate to simple, but common situations of interaction between purposive agents, and the understanding of some of them is very useful for peace research. These realities are somehow material as they force themselves on us and exist even when we do not recognize them (unlike social realities), and affect our lives even when we do not have any idea of them (unlike categories that exist only in a heuristic sense). Yet, they are based on preferences that actors are free to change, and a setting that actors can negotiate and bargain about on a meta-game level: actors can reconsider their agency, create new strategies, construct new outcomes, etc. Yet, once there is a setting of agency, preferences, and strategies that agents construct in their interaction, there is also a structure that actors do not control, that has causal effects on how actors behave and what outcomes they produce with their actions. This structure is the focus of attention of game theorists.

4.4. Social Structures that Make Peaceful Actors Choose Belligerence

I will present two game theory models that help us understand how free actors that do not want war still end up engaging in or going to war. The models are the two most common structures that involve a strong contradiction between individual and social rationality, that is, they are structures in which acting rationally (in the sense of maximizing one's utility = doing what needs to be done to bring about the outcomes one prefers) leads individuals to outcomes that are worse than would have been the case if everyone had opted for a suboptimal strategy. The anatomy of such structures is crucial for the study of conflicts as the main puzzle about conflicts is the fact that somehow people who generally do not want war tend to end up in one despite their anti-war preferences.

The first of the models is the prisoner's dilemma, which is the model most used in peace research, and the other is the bargaining game model, which counters some of the recommendations of the first. I will argue that the latter is a more realistic model of most conflict situations, although I admit that the former also has value in the analysis of conflict structures.

4.4.1. Structures that make peaceful actors choose belligerence: The anatomy of the prisoner's dilemma model

The durability of a peaceful state of affairs often requires that former conflicting parties mutually adhere to the norms that they have agreed upon. Agents might have agreed to limit their offensive weapons in order to bring about a degree of stability to a crisis concerning their border. Yet, both agents might be tempted to choose a deceptive strategy in order to avoid being fooled if the opponent decides to have a secret weapons program, or in order to gain the upper hand if the opponent sticks to its promise not to arm itself with offensive weapons. Such a situation where both parties are better off if they both stick to a cooperative strategy (not arming themselves with offensive weapons), but where both are presented with a temptation to deceive the other party (that is to build offensive weapons) regardless of what their opponent does, is called the prisoner's dilemma. The structure of such a dilemma can be summarized in the following matrix (See Matrix 4.1), which presents the utility values of each outcome for each agent as numbers in the respective halves of the boxes of the matrix. Each of the boxes represent one of the outcomes that can be reached in an interactive situation between two agents (A and B) where each party can choose one of two strategies, namely, cooperation or deception.

The usefulness of this model for peace research is that it presents one structural constraint to peace making, namely, the structure where social rationality contradicts individual rationality. Individually purposive agents will maximize their utility by choosing a deceptive strategy regardless of how they assume their opponent will act. Yet, if

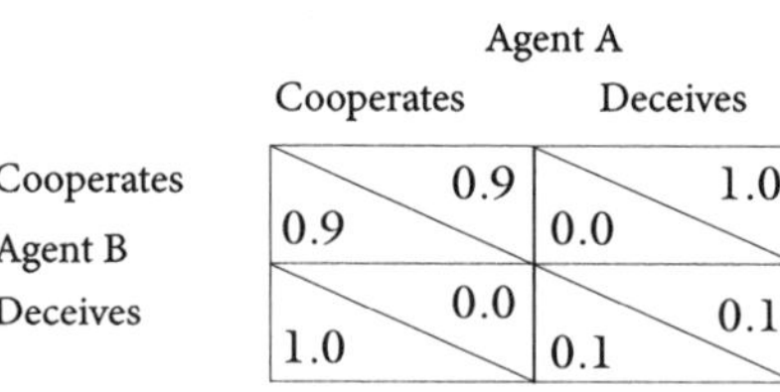

Matrix 4.1.   Simple prisoner's dilemma

both are individually rational and choose a deceptive strategy, they will both end up with only one ninth of what they could achieve by choosing to cooperate.

This model has been used to analyze security issues and the need for international cooperation and coordination. If all nations pursue their own security in a situation where there is no clear difference between offensive and defensive weapons, this leads to a special prisoner's dilemma, which is usually called the security dilemma, in which one agent's efforts to gain security lead to the insecurity of other agents. In this structure, dominant, individually rational strategies to secure oneself become socially irrational (Hertz, 1950). In different versions of the model, the security dilemma and the logic of anarchy (where deception cannot be controlled by supra-national regulation) have been at the core of many structural explanations of international warfare. It can be found in the classic work by John Hertz, who coined the concept of the security dilemma, and in the work of Kenneth Waltz, who established neo-realism (or structural realism, see Hertz, 1950, 1959; Waltz, 1968, 1979). But the same logic of explanation for warfare can also be found in the classic works of many earlier writers such as Harold Butterfield, and even Thucydides, well before this logic was called the "security dilemma" (Butterfield, 1949, 1951; Thucydides, 1972). For all these theorists, world politics was about the purposive behavior of nations, and yet, due to the structure of the prisoner's dilemma, no malign motives or preferences were needed (just the interests of self-preservation) but states will still behave in a violent manner: "Even if one wants no harm to the other and wants nothing from the other save guarantees of non-aggression, there is no guarantee about the intentions of the other. Thus both have to prepare for the others hostility and thus the power of one is the insecurity of the other." (Butterfield, 1951, p. 21).

The same structure found in the prisoner's dilemma and the security dilemma has been found at the heart of intra-state conflicts where ethnic groups arm themselves for their own security in the absence of legitimate law enforcement. The result is often an unstable balance between various groups, similar to the balance that existed before the groups started arming themselves, but now with a greatly increased capacity to kill and thus a greatly increased risk of conflict escalation (Fearon, 1995; Kaufmann, 1997; Kaufmann, 2001, 2006; Lake & Rothchild, 1997; Poulton & Youssouf, 1998). In some of these explanations, based on the security dilemma, the conflicting parties are treated as unitary and rational (Fearon, 1995), whilst in others the role of various intra-party actors, such as gainful[9] ethnic leaders are analyzed in detail, and the construction of the symbolic targets of preferences are treated, which complicates the basic logic of the security dilemma and the prisoner's dilemma (Kaufmann, 2001, 2006).

The prisoner's dilemma model has also been used as a model to analyze the problem of burden sharing in the production of indivisible common values (public goods) like security (Olson, 2009; Starr, 2000). Policing the world demands resources, energy, money, and sacrifices, which all nations would like to avoid. The United States cannot produce security only for itself — for example, by enforcing a nuclear non-proliferation regime in Iran or in North Korea — and thus, in terms of the prisoner's dilemma, it might be tempted to take a free ride and let others deal with rogue nations like Iran. The structure of the prisoner's dilemma has been used to analyze various "global problems" such as the insistence by Iran of its right to develop nuclear capabilities (Sisodia & Behuria, 2007).

The pragmatic value of game theory can be demonstrated by the fact that the prisoner's dilemma model not only offers a diagnosis of a problem, but also a prescription of how one can get out of situations where there is a contradiction between individual and social rationality. This prescription is the foundation of the neo-liberal institutionalist theory of international cooperation (Axelrod, 1985). It is based on

---

[9] "Gainful" is a term that characterizes the motive of a party to a conflict. Instead of being frustrated, a gainful actor is motivated by the possible gains the use of violence might offer her/him (Tanter, 1999).

a super-strategy,[10] which identifies how agents can choose their strategy in any prisoner's dilemma situation by referring to the strategy their opponent had chosen in a previous case where the prisoner's dilemma had occurred. As its starting point, the neo-liberal institutionalist prescription is to choose a cooperative strategy. However, if an opponent had deceived the other party in the previous game the prescription would be to do the same to it in the next game. This super-strategy of reciprocity gives an opponent an incentive to cooperate because each game provides a clue as to what will happen in the next game. What the opponent does this time determines what the reciprocal actor will do the next time. The way in which the strategy of reciprocity reconciles the contradiction between social and individual rationality can be seen in Matrix 4.2. Since Agent B knows that Agent A will meet cooperation with cooperation and deception with deception, and since Agent A's deception always reduces the expected utility for B in the next game by 0.9 utility points, this amount can be added to the payoff matrix as the effect of the clue to the future.

It is easy to see that a reciprocal super-strategy employed by Agent A will make cooperation the dominant strategy for Agent B. Since this is the case, it is also rational for player A to stick to the reciprocal super-strategy, and not start deceiving the other party, as deception would destroy the super-game strategy that has made cooperation a

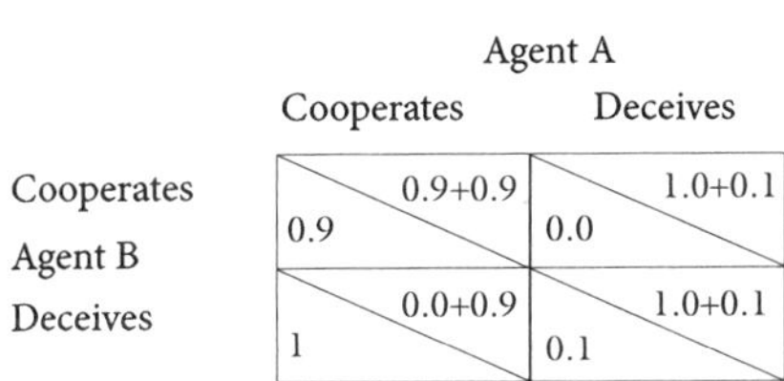

Matrix 4.2. The prisoner's dilemma and the impact of the super-strategy of reciprocity

---

[10] A super-strategy is a strategy that guides not only a game (interactive situation), but a row of games (Axelrod, 1985). One's game strategy could be to cooperate, while one's super-strategy could be to cooperate always after the opponent has cooperated in the previous game.

dominant option for B. Deceiving now would deprive Agent A of the benefit (0.9 utility points) of B's cooperation next time.

When there are commonly accepted cooperative solutions, say an existing agreement on arms control or a reciprocal agreement on confidence building, the logic of the prisoner's dilemma is very useful for the parties involved. If there is a reciprocal, verified procedure for disarming the parties to an ethnic conflict and an agreement to allow and facilitate the police in having a monopoly in terms of law enforcement (as was the case in West Kalimantan since 2009, Kivimäki, 2012a) all the ethnic groups will be better off as none of them would have to fear that one of them might mobilize or arm itself. Knowledge of the problematic structure where individual and social rationality are in conflict with each other, together with the neo-liberal institutionalist super-game solution are very clear examples of the type of practical knowledge that empowers peacemakers and enables them to settle a conflict. Furthermore, this knowledge, which does not expect and is not based on the determinism of the behavior of the conflicting parties, empowers not just third parties to the conflict but also the conflicting parties themselves to find solutions to their problems.

4.4.2. *Problems in seeing conflict settings as prisoner's dilemma structures*

The virtue of the prisoner's dilemma in explaining conflict situations is that it emphasizes the interactive nature of conflicts. Conflicts usually arise as the result of a process of escalation rather than as a consequence of the characteristics of one of the parties to the conflict (even though one cannot totally rule out the possibility of such situations). When conflicting parties understand the impact of their actions on their opponent and realize how their use of violence or resort to arms provokes violence and a resort to arms by others, one can begin to address the social irrationality of the situation. Robert Jervis calls security dilemma situations where the conflicting parties do not realize the interactive nature of the process of conflict escalation "deep security dilemma" situations, while Booth and Wheeler argue that "security dilemma sensitive behavior" is not possible in such situations (Booth & Wheeler, 2008, pp. 7, 28, 167–168; Jervis, 2001, p. 41).

With their ability to explain the collapse of peaceful cooperation among perfectly peaceful actors and even to solve such problems in real-life, it is no wonder that the prisoner's dilemma and the security dilemma have become such powerful models in the study of security and cooperation. The original models of the security dilemma utilized this model to show how international relations were inherently plagued by insecurity (Hertz, 1950). It was argued that it was utopian and idealistic to deny the inevitability of the logic of the prisoner's dilemma or of the security dilemma in international relations. Equally sensational for our understanding of security and cooperation was the discovery of the super-strategy of reciprocity, which fixed the problem of security dilemma (Axelrod, 1985).

However the prisoner's dilemma model is an incorrect description of most conflict and cooperation structures. On the one hand, the model fails to identify more than one cooperative outcome making it impossible to understand the way in which conflicting parties choose between several ways of cooperating. On the other hand, as a consequence of the first problem, the application of the prisoner's dilemma to security studies cannot locate the use of violence correctly. Owing to the lack of perspective to bargaining between several terms of peace prisoner's dilemma insists on treating violence and threats as part of outcomes that some of the parties to conflict prefer. In reality, however, violence is almost always just a vehicle in the process of bargaining about the terms for cooperating and peace. Violence in conflicts is almost always instrumental rather than an end in itself (Fromm, 1973).

Some theorists of the security dilemma have revealed problems with the prisoner's dilemma. However, to date, critics have not found an alternative to the prisoner's dilemma model. Stuart Kaufmann, for example, has noted the problem, yet failed to solve it. Kaufmann emphasizes the role played by fear and the problem of the intentions of other people, their mentalities, or ways of thinking, which one cannot know for sure, but he also says that conflicts are often the results of aggression where the conflicting parties aim at securing a political basis for their security. For Armenians, for example, the fear of another Armenian genocide made them claim Nagorno-Karabah from the Azerbaijanis. This could have been a defensive move in the sense that its intention was to prevent Muslims ruling over Christian areas, but, at the same time, the move was very offensive toward the Azerbaijanis. Thus the situation was not about cooperation and deception: The Azerbaijanis were not responsible for the Turkish genocide of Armenians almost a century earlier, and thus Azerbaijan's decision not to yield to these peace terms cannot be regarded as deception. Clearly there is an element of bargaining about peace terms in Kaufmann's model even if he characterizes the conflict as a security dilemma with a spiral of increasing violence (Kaufmann, 2001, pp. 82–83).

Another theorist that moves the security dilemma model toward bargaining models is Thomas J. Christensen. According to him, security dilemma theorists have misunderstood the security dynamics of the China–Taiwan–US relationship. They have assumed that ensuring or trying to ensure security equals ensuring or trying to ensure one's safety. However in Taiwan, according to Christensen, and in my opinion everywhere else, trying to ensure or ensuring one's security entails trying to ensure that particular peace terms are recognized. Even technically defensive weapons in the hands of Taiwan may seem provocative in the eyes of China if those weapons encourage Taiwan to declare independence (in Taiwanese eyes, one method of ensuring Taiwan's security, peace, and political existence) (Christensen, 2002, pp. 11–13). This would be an existential threat to China (since in the Chinese interpretation, of course, Taiwan is part of China) and would go against the Chinese definition of its security. Thus physical safety is not at the core of the security debate, and safety for both/all cannot be the only cooperative option. Violence is not an objective of a non-cooperative strategy for players of the security dilemma game, violence is a means to a definite type of peace. Violence is a tool in bargaining, it is not a deceptive strategy. Thus, continuing Christensen's analysis, defense is not a means to secure physical safety, but a tool for bargaining over a specific political formula for peace. Hence, someone else's security is a threat to my concept of security, not because it might threaten my physical safety, but because it threatens the political interests that I want to protect. US Nuclear Missile Defense, for instance, threatens China, according to Christensen, because of the fact that if the US had a first strike capability and the ability to defend itself against Chinese retaliation, the US would be able to do what it wants concerning Taiwan, which China considers to be part of its territory and thus an element of its existence (Christensen, 2002, p. 13).

However, while Christensen simply criticizes the use of security dilemma modeling, he does not challenge the entire model. This is a mistake since the lack of alternative cooperative strategies — peace with Taiwan legally independent, peace with Taiwan as part of China and peace with Taiwan *de facto* independent — should all be included in the modeling of the dispute. None of them are necessarily the product of deception. Thus the problem with theorizing about the Taiwan conflict using the security dilemma does not lie in the way in which the model has been used. It lies in the model itself, because the prisoner's dilemma model as applied in the form of the security dilemma, does not allow for competition or bargaining between alternative cooperative outcomes. The model of the prisoner's dilemma only allows one cooperative outcome, as if security problems are simply a matter of apolitical physical safety, and as if violence that threatens that safety was an objective itself rather than a means of coercive bargaining that seeks alternative cooperative outcomes.

One of the key theorists of the security dilemma, Robert Jervis joins the critique of the simplified view of cooperative outcomes. According to Jervis, "there are ambiguities in the basic concept of security, including what the object of security is (e.g. individuals, the regime, the state, or the values that any of these hold dear) and what is needed to make states or individuals feel secure. Even more troubling, the terms we commonly use to characterize states and the sources of their conduct — "aggressive", "expansionistic", "opportunity driven", risk-acceptant", "*status quo*", "security-seeking", "risk-averse" — are problematic, just as the definition of self-defense as a justification for murder is contentious"(Jervis, 2001, p. 39). What Jervis is driving at here is that the protection of "values that (security actors)… hold dear" by means of "self-defense" and "murder" means that it is not possible to classify strategies, as the prisoner's dilemma suggests, neatly into cooperative and non-cooperative ones. The protection of a set of values that one holds dear means protecting one type of peace. Thus the promotion of other types of peace in a way that is not compatible with the type of peace that one wishes to materialize seems like uncooperative behavior. It is uncooperative in relation to one's own vision of peace. But this does not mean that promotion of a particular terms of peace means violence or denial of physical safety, because violence in both one's own self-defense and in the opponent's behavior are just means to the protection of one type of peace (say peace with Taiwan being legally independent or peace with Taiwan as part of the PRC).

Yet, even after the realization that the world (and the cold war) is more complex than the model of the security dilemma seems to allow, Jervis fails to point to the main problem in the model — the lack of alternative cooperative outcomes — and fails to develop an alternative model that allows for the analysis of the bargaining between alternative forms of security.

Kaufmann, Jervis, and Christensen are not alone in their inconsistent use of the model of the security dilemma and the prisoner's dilemma. In fact the definition of a conflict in most conflict datasets stipulates that one can only consider a situation a conflict if there is a presence of an incompatibility of political (or ethno-political, religious, etc.) positions about the terms of peace (Lacina & Gleditsch, 2005; Singer, 1979). In absence of such incompatibility, we cannot consider the situation as conflict. Thus, both the security dilemma model and the use of the prisoner's dilemma fail to reveal the conflict-aspect of conflicts. The problem with the prisoner's dilemma in the analysis of conflicts and cooperation is that it only has one, given, cooperative solution and thus it cannot model the incompatibility of or the competition (conflict) between several alternative peaceful solutions. Yet as we know the cold war was about a communist and a capitalist model of peace, not between peaceful nations and imperialists (as Soviet propaganda asserted) nor between free nations and crazy, deceptive dictators (as Western propaganda asserted). The conflict in Palestine is not about terrorists willing to destroy peace, nor about a Zionist mission to destroy Muslims/Palestinians, but between Israeli and Palestinian conceptions of what constitutes a fair or just peace. For the Acehnese rebels, peace for an independent Aceh was a dream, while the Indonesian government was dreaming of peace for Aceh as an integral part of Indonesia. Neither party's objectives could be described as the product of deception or inherently belligerent, and yet their conflict behavior was violence. Whilst the prisoner's dilemma is useful in situations where the parties have already agreed upon the terms of peace, and have thus found one cooperative option any breach of which would be the product of deception, it is not as useful for most conflict situations where the main challenge is not whether to make peace and cooperate, but whether to make peace on my terms or on yours.

In addition to theoretical deficiencies, the prisoner's dilemma-type of framing conflict also has negative practical consequences. Before presenting an alternative model that tackles the problem of the terms of cooperation/peace, I will briefly discuss the practical pitfalls of rigidly applying the model of the prisoner's dilemma to situations where there is no one agreed view of what might constitute the terms for cooperation. This is due to the fact that there are some very pressing pragmatic political reasons to address this unhelpful "knowledge" about the nature of international problems of peace.

The interpretation of problems of international cooperation as prisoner's dilemmas has been adopted by much of American political rhetoric. The idea of offsetting the temptation to free ride in global governance by means of a super-strategy of reciprocity has been explicitly used in US policies toward US allies and even in relations with powers not allied with the western world, powers that utterly disagree with most of the US's conceptions of the terms of peace in the world (Dumbrell, 2009, p. 116).[11] The case of US-Chinese relations is in that sense very important for world peace as peace and fair terms of cooperation are an important precondition for the preven-

---

[11] It has been claimed, though, that the super-strategy of reciprocity cannot be applied in the war on terror, and, as a result, George W. Bush has introduced an exception to the US foreign policy tradition of reciprocity (Osiel, 2009).

tion of the next "battle of the titans", between the hegemon and the hegemonic challenger. Furthermore, since the idea of free riding in US-Chinese relations is often related to the question of how to deal with rogue nations, which in itself is one of the key questions of peace and war in world politics, the question of over using the prisoner's dilemma model is crucial for a better understanding of the challenges faced in the relationship between knowledge and war/peace.

Prisoner's dilemma exists on two levels in US-Chinese relations. On the one hand, there is the prisoner's dilemma, which US foreign-policy rhetoric identifies in the relationship between responsible nations and the deceptive, so-called rogue states (North Korea, Syria, and Iran. Formerly also Burma and Iraq and many others also belonged to this category). On the other level of prisoner's dilemmas exist also between the responsible powers who feel responsible for the regulation of rogue states. Between these powers, the prisoner's dilemma is related to burden sharing. When regulating rogue states, responsible powers need to use super-strategies of reciprocity by puni-shing nations that fail to respect international norms with sanctions. This regulating of world politics is costly, as imposing sanctions requires the use of economic might, and sometimes even military power. Order in the world, again, benefits all, and countries that do not impose sanctions cannot be denied the benefits in terms of peace that come from imposing sanctions. Thus contributing to the regula-tion of order in the world is modeled as a prisoner's dilemma. Nations that benefit from such order may be tempted to take a free ride by letting others do the regulating, but if everybody did this everybody would suffer the consequences in the form of lapses in the regulation of the world.

The first level of the prisoner's dilemma thus applies to the US relationship with rogue states, while the second applies, among oth-ers, to US-Chinese relations, as the US accuses China of not taking its share of responsibility in regulating the world. David Shambaugh, one of the leading authorities on US-Chinese relations, for example, uses the logic of the prisoner's dilemma in his analysis of US-Chinese relations. He talks about reciprocation and free riding. When talking about China's lack of contribution to global governance, Shambaugh talks about calls to contribute more to global "public goods" and about the accusation that China is "a free rider" in the global system (Shambaugh, 2013, p. 130). He concludes that instead of supporting "coalitions of the willing", China opts for passivity or resistance to solutions in order to avoid the burden of responsibility for global policing and governance (Shambaugh, 2013, pp. 8–9, 306). China's "full moral integration into the international system remains a work-in-progress" (Shambaugh, 2013, p. 153). If all did this, and opted for responsibility aversion, the world would be left without governance and policing, and it would remain in a natural state of anarchy. However, both the interpretation that US or Chinese policies toward global problems can be analyzed as reciprocal super-strategies and the applicability of the prisoner's dilemma in analyzing global coopera-tion can be questioned.

In order for the problem to be analyzed in terms of the prisoner's dilemma, the starting point for the uncooperative reciprocation by the "coalition of the willing" (which China decided not to join) had to be one in which a rogue state failed to cooperate. However, this assumption has not always been beyond doubt in the US regulation of the world. As we now know, Iraq did not have weapons of mass destruction, and thus it was actually cooperating with the Non-Proliferation Treaty (NPT) regime when the US decided to "recipro-cate" with an uncooperative strategy. In Iran the question of whether the country is developing nuclear weapons may also be subject to doubt. According to the assessment of US security agencies, there have been no programs to advance Iran's nuclear weapons capability since 2003 (Risen & Mazzetti, 2012). Joining sanctions or military action as a way of "reciprocating" Iran's lack of cooperation would not necessarily be within the neo-liberal institutionalist formula for promoting global cooperation.

Furthermore, if we criticize Chinese policies towards the main global security problems for sabotaging the strategy of reciprocity found in the coalitions of the willing, then we will have to be able to establish that in these issues the US has been cooperative to start with. Reciprocating uncooperative strategies with uncooperative responses would not work if the United States and coalitions of the willing were uncooperative to start with. If we look at disputes between the United States and Iran related to Iran's failure to comply with the norm of non-proliferation, this too can be called into question. To start with the treaty on non-proliferation is asymmetric and thus difficult to model as a norm whose compliance and non-compliance could be reciprocated. After all, the treaty does not allow Iran to manufacture nuclear weapons, while allowing the US, the world's only user of nuclear weapons, to do so.

However, if we simply look at the dispute as it has been framed by the United States we can introduce some balance to the views by using the concepts compliance and non-compliance with the NPT and its additional protocols in defining cooperative and deceptive strategies. When the United States started to push Iran to change its nuclear policies the bone of content was the so-called Additional Protocol of the NPT. The United States did not accuse Iran of being in non-compliance with the treaty itself, but, instead, the United States wanted Iran to ratify the part of the treaty that related to more intrusive verification procedures, the so-called Additional Protocol agreed by the IAEA's Board of Governors in 1997. This protocol was voluntary, only about two thirds of the signatories of the NPT have ratified this protocol, and it is in force in about half of the NPT countries. Thus failure to ratify was not really a failure to comply with a mutually accepted norm. Instead, the need for Iran to ratify was more of an *ad hoc* necessity for regional security. The *ad hoc* nature of the demands presented to Iran makes the idea of applying a super-strategy of reciprocation a bit shaky. However, the issue of the US's compliance with the Additional Protocol, a subject rarely mentioned let alone discussed in public, makes the idea of reciprocity even more difficult to apply. At the time when the US started to claim that Iran was in non-compliance with the protocol, the United States had ratified the protocol, but not changed her legislation to comply with it. It took the United States a decade to change her legislation to comply with the stipulations of the protocol. In this sense the United States was in violation of its own voluntary commitments, while Iran had simply failed to make that commitment in the first place. Later, the question of Iran's enrichment of uranium raised similar problems: Iran had undertaken no legal or other obligations not to enrich uranium, whereas the United States did enrich its own uranium.

In Syria the September 2013 agreement between Russia and the United States on the dismantling of Syria's chemical weapons was also framed as a matter of compliance and non-compliance (Diplomatic Push for Assad to Give up Chemical Weapons Could Prevent Military Strike, 2013; United States, Russia Begin Discussing Syrian Chemical Weapons Disarmament in Geneva, 2013). The United States felt that it had a right and a responsibility to monitor Syria's compliance, and reciprocate with punishments in case of non-compliance (House Republican Leaders Endorse Military Action in Syria, 2013; Kane, 2014). However, the US and Russian "reciprocity" was found under a formula that committed Syria itself to a regime that prohibited chemical weapons, a regime to which neither the United States nor Russia complied. Thus it is difficult to see how the logic of the prisoner's dilemma, which has implicitly been used in Shambaugh's analysis, applies to the argument according to which China should support the global order by reciprocating Syria's, Iraq's, or Iran's failure to cooperate by joining the coalition of the willing to punish rogue states for their "non-cooperation". In fact by not selling strategic assets to Israel or India, China is more in line with the regime of non-proliferation than the United States. Inaction can sometimes be more constructive than action.

Furthermore, sanctions or military action would not be symmetrical with non-cooperation in the non-proliferation regime. Reciprocity in the form of military action should in the logic of neo-liberal institutionalism be required as a reaction to a violation of the norm against military violence. In problems related to indivisible collective goods, such as non-proliferation, reciprocity would be difficult to implement due to the fact that the US cannot end its commitments under the NPT only in its relationship with North Korea, Iran or Saddam Hussein's Iraq. Thus the whole idea of talking about reciprocity in relation to norms that are indivisible is problematic. And so is the claim that China fails to join in reciprocity-related fixing of global problems.

China's failure to "reciprocate" against Syria, Iran, Iraq, and North Korea might actually be better for global governance due to the dubious consequences of interpreting problems of cooperation as prisoner's dilemmas. While there are three uncooperative outcomes that players might end up in the prisoner's dilemma, there is just one cooperative outcome in the setting. Thus this model rules issues of distribution out of its analysis of cooperation. With only one cooperative outcome it is not possible to imagine alternative terms of cooperation with differing ways of distributing the benefits of cooperation. This could be a serious problem for the analysis of cooperation and global governance — a problem with analytical as well as political consequences. What if Iran wanted to cooperate, but not on the basis of peace terms unilaterally defined by the United States? What if China was not free riding in a US-led system of global governance but promoting its own approach towards global governance? What if global governance was not about intruding into everything that one could not accept, but instead about silently working for greater respect for the equal sovereignty of nations, international legality, the centrality of the UN, and international democracy? All of these various cooperative moves would be considered free riding and to be "reciprocated" with uncooperative moves if one modeled international interactions in terms of the prisoner's dilemma.

It is easy to imagine the political consequences of the interpretation of global governance as politics challenged by prisoner's dilemma type of problems. Such an interpretation of global governance gives all the power to the actor that sets the agenda and defines what is cooperative and what constitutes a failure to cooperate in world politics. What is even more alarming is that fact that the framing of global affairs in terms of prisoner's dilemmas requires the global hegemon constantly to react to uncooperative behavior with uncooperative moves. In cases where the hegemonic response cannot be of the same nature as the original "offense" (due to the indivisibility problem), reciprocity and the maintenance of global order will have to mean various types of punishments for countries and actors that do not comply with the hegemonic interpretation of the rules and strategic necessities.

One way of looking at the successfulness of global governance from the point of view of security, is to look at how many people die in conflicts and wars. I have done this in my analysis of the China's refusal of its US-designated role as a responsible stakeholder in the world (Kivimäki, 2014c). The fact that China has not joined the US-led global governance seems also from that point of view as a good choice. It seems that conflicts that are initiated by a US intervention with various coalitions of the willing or interventions with drones that constitute part of the global war on terror by the same coalitions now cost between 40% and 74% of all fatalities of wars and conflicts in the world.

The "global governance" which the US suggests as the only option for China should to join in could be considered the main global problem. According to Shambaugh, "When one examines a number of other (than North Korea) recent international challenges or crises — Sudan, Iran, Iraq, Syria, Libya, Afghanistan, Somalia — an aloof and unhelpful China is also evident" (Shambaugh, 2013, p. 46). But the conflict fatalities involved in US-led global governance suggests that China is merely refusing to contribute to what might be considered the main international problem. Thus leading "coalitions of the unwilling" might actually not be such a poor a strategy for China.

Instead of focusing on the imposition of a set of norms that only one side has drafted, the focus in the settlement of global problems should be on the negotiation between several different sets of peace terms. However, this cannot be done if we stick to the model of the prisoner's dilemma. Instead of continuing to use the prisoner's dilemma model in an inconsistent manner, there is a need for a model that describes the dynamics of violence bargaining between alternative peace terms. Such a model should include various competing, alternative peace terms, and the risk of parties failing to agree. Such a model has been developed in microeconomics by John Nash, Frederik Zeuthen, and John Harsanyi (Harsanyi, 1956; Nash, 1950, 1953; Zeuthen, 1930). It is called the bargaining game model, and it needs to be brought from economics into the modeling of peace and war. In classic security studies by Thomas Schelling, Daniel Ellsberg, and

William Zartman some elements of bargaining have already been introduced to the study of peace (Ellsberg, 1968; Schelling, 1980; Zartman, 1977). However, in none of their theories has the dominance of the security dilemma models been challenged, nor has bargaining been presented as an alternative to the dominant prisoner's dilemma modeling of conflict and cooperation. This is what will be attempted below. In the following section I will first reveal the structure of all such interaction, where actors have different ideas of the terms of cooperation and use the threat of failure of cooperation (and the beginning of a war) as a way to persuade their opponents into accepting their terms of peace. I will call such a structure the structure of bargaining, even if parties did not explicitly bargaining anything as in negotiations. I will use the word bargaining in a loose sense because of the fact that in world politics and in conflicts bargaining and negotiation often takes very different forms as conflicting parties might argue with their demonstrative action. After revealing the structure I will show how such a structure easily leads to conflicts and orientations that make conflicts more likely by looking at politics that aim at improving country's or other entity's bargaining power.

4.4.3. *Structures that make peaceful actors choose belligerence: The bargaining game model*

Bargaining structures are situations where two or more agents aim at cooperative solutions, but have different terms for cooperating (each suggesting terms that are more advantageous to themselves). If no agreement can be reached as to whose terms for cooperation/peace to follow, no cooperation will be reached (the worst outcome for both = conflict). Bargaining proceeds in two directions at the same time. In one direction the parties seek ways to find peaceful cooperative solutions, or the Pareto optimal frontier (Illustration 4.1). Pareto optimality refers to a possible solution, agreement, or suggested settlement, where there are no changes that would leave all the players with at least an equal payoff and at least one player better off (Pareto, 1897, 1971, pp. 108–109). In conflict analysis the Pareto optimal solution often refers to a set of peaceful alternative solutions to a conflict.

The move towards a solution commences with a starting point — a situation with no agreement — and proceeds toward the Pareto optimal frontier. In conflicts, the starting point often involves violent conflict behavior (in the so-called extended bargaining game). This zero point for both parties is the best alternative to a negotiated solution (BATNA), which, in conflicts, is naturally a worse outcome than Pareto optimal negotiated solutions (see Illustration 4.1 below).

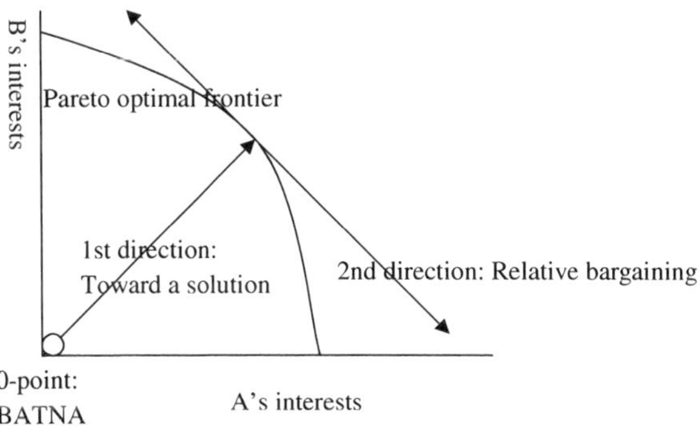

Illustration 4.1. Two directions of bargaining

While the rationality of bargainers presumes that the conflicting parties will eventually reach the Pareto optimal frontier, relative bargaining logic defines where on the Pareto optimal frontier the conflicting parties will find their agreement, that is, how much each of the parties has to compromise in terms of their original demands in order to find a peaceful Pareto optimal solution. Defining the solution point in the Pareto optimal frontier (relative bargaining) is the other component in bargaining. This process is necessary in all bargaining situations where more than one alternative Pareto optimal solution point can be identified. In reality, any conflict involves both conflict resolution (first direction), to reach the Pareto optimal frontier (getting to "yes", finding a peaceful solution), and haggling, related to how much each conflict party has to yield (2nd direction, relative bargaining, defining whose terms peace must be followed).

The bargaining leverage in the process of defining the solution point within the Pareto optimal area depends on two relative things:

the bargainers' determination in relation to the terms of agreement, and their dependence on a negotiated solution.

The simplest model of bargaining can be presented by assuming that there are two actors A and B. In the simplest bargaining game, both A and B take an initial position by demanding a distribution of benefits that we name c' and c'' (c' is A's position and c'' is B's position). The utility payoff that c' gives to player A is $u(A, c')$ and $u(B, c')$ is the utility payoff for player B if a bargaining solution is found in c'. The zero utility point of the bargaining game is at the point, where instead of cooperative solutions (c', c'', c''', c'''', etc.), cooperation fails and the uncooperative state n prevails. This point is the point that was called BATNA (best alternative to a negotiated agreement) above, the cutoff point or the security point (Ellsberg, 1968; Young, 1991b; Zartman, 1977). The utility player A gets in the BATNA situation with threats carried out is $u(A, n)$. In order to avoid being committed to absolute measuring scales, we do not present utility values such as $u(A, c')$ without reference to the arbitrated zero point n. Therefore, when we present the value of a cooperative solution c' to A, we compare it to the BATNA, $u(A, c')-u(A, n)$, and simply measure how much better player A considers his own terms of peace than the outcome where bargainers do not reach a solution and end up at war.

If the two claims c' and c'' are not identical, one of the players has to yield in the direction of the other's demand. If a solution is not reached, there will be no deal and neither will get anything from their bargaining. Intuition leads us to think that in this situation the player whose relative loss, or critical risk, to use Ellsberg's terminology, is smaller will stand firm while the other will concede (Ellsberg, 1968). The one who thinks that the difference between the two demands is smaller compared to the loss that might occur if no solution is reached is more anxious to salvage the negotiations. If, for example, we assume that player A feels that $u(A, c'')$ is close to $u(A, n)$ and that player B feels that $u(B, c')$ is closer to $u(B, c'')$ than to $u(B, n)$, then it is obvious that player B has more to lose if the negotiations cannot result in a solution. Mathematically, we shall end up with the following equation, which will give us the bargaining leverage of player A.

If the relative bargaining leverage of A is larger than 1, player B has to yield; if it is less than 1, player A has to yield (see Equation 4.1):

Equation 4.1.   Determinants of bargaining leverage

$$\frac{\dfrac{u(A,\, c') - u(A,\, c'')}{u(A,\, c') - u(A,\, n)}}{\dfrac{u(B,\, c'') - u(B,\, c')}{u(B,\, c'') - u(B,\, n)}} = \text{A's bargaining leverage in relation to the leverage of player B}$$

$u(A,\, c') - u(A,\, c'')$ represents the difference that player A perceives in the desirability between his original claim and the opponent's original claim. Similarly, $u(B,\, c'') - u(B,\, c')$ represents how much more player B prefers a solution on the basis of his claim to a solution than on the basis of the opponent's demand. Let us call this difference bargainers' *determination* in questions over the distribution of benefits in bargaining (*sensitivity toward terms of a settlement*). The equation reveals that the bigger a player perceives the question of distribution in bargaining to be, the stronger his bargaining leverage is. This is only natural: a bargainer is more determined to get his way if he believes that the issues of distribution make a big difference.

$u(A,\, c') - u(A,\, n)$ represents the utility value for player A of a solution on the basis of A's original demand compared to the situation in which a cooperative solution cannot be found. Similarly, $u(B,\, c'') - u(B,\, n)$ is the utility value of a solution on the basis of c'' for B. The bigger $u(A,\, c') - u(A,\, n)$ is, the weaker A's leverage is; and the bigger $u(B,\, c'') - u(B,\, n)$ is, the weaker B's leverage is. $u(A,\, c') - u(A,\, n)$ consists of $u(A,\, c') - u(A,\, c'')$ and $u(A,\, c'') - u(A,\, n)$, and $u(A,\, c') - u(A,\, c'')$ implies leverage. But what is critical for player A's leverage is how much it values a solution on the basis of the opponent's demand. The more the player values this solution with its disadvantageous distribution of benefits, the weaker his bargaining position is at this stage; the more vulnerable in relation to a cooperative solution and the more dependent the agent is on the opponent, the weaker his leverage is. Let us call this element of the bargaining leverage *dependence on a settlement.* The more dependent a bargainer is the more he/she has to compromise.[12]

After one of the players has moved toward the other's demands by giving up his original demand and presenting a compromise demand, we shall again see which of the bargainers is relatively more sensitive about reaching a negotiated solution; and that decides who is going to yield in this round. If for example B has compromised his claim c'', and moved it closer to claim c' (let us call the new claim c''', the difference between $u(B, c''')$ and $u(B, n)$ – B's critical risk – is reduced: B is no longer as scared of war, because even in peace he would now be worse off than he would have been if his terms of peace c'' had been accepted. At the same time, since A has not changed his claim, his critical risk (loss if war continues/starts) has not diminished. Thus, in the new setting, B's bargaining leverage has improved, and it might be that A will have to make the next compromising move to balance the situation. This procedure is repeated until the demands of the players meet.

The equation of rational bargaining can also be presented without formal logical equations, and can be reduced to a conclusion that

---

[12] Of course, in simple exchange negotiations where, for example, an agreement gives money to the player and a good distribution means a bit more money, it is often the case that if the player appreciates the additional money from the good distribution (that is, the player is sensitive about the distribution issue = determined) he also tends to appreciate the money that results from the agreement. In other words, she/he is equally sensitive about cooperation (dependence) if the utility function toward money is linear. If this is the case for both players in relation to their opponent's contributions, it is easy to see how the Nash–Harsanyi solution automatically leads to a 50–50 share of the benefits. These conditions are sometimes erroneously seen as universal in negotiations. However, as often happens in international negotiations, the value that cooperation produces can be something completely different from the value that is distributed: all the elements in the bargaining equation become equally important in the definition of the negotiation solution. For example, security cooperation can be perceived to produce security, and the distribution issue is about how to distribute the costs of producing this security in cooperation, as in the case of negotiations on the rent payment for military bases. Thus, the one who is sensitive to security loses in the distribution while the one who is sensitive to money wins. This is the structure in which many developing countries have been very successful in bargaining with their superpower allies (Kivimäki, 1995, 2003).

explains a party's bargaining leverage on the basis of two sources: determination and independence. In an extended form, we can spell out the factors that determine the bargaining power for player A:

1. The less dependent player A is on a solution, the stronger A is as a bargainer.
2. The more dependent player B is on a solution, the stronger A is as a bargainer.
3. The more determined player A is to get her/his way in bargaining, the stronger bargainer A is.
4. The less determined player B is, the stronger bargainer player A is.

The four elements that determine one's bargaining leverage carry the essential ideas of the structure of bargaining in any conflict, assuming that the conflicting parties aim at something in their dispute, and assuming that their action reflects this aim. Quite like the situation in the prisoner's dilemma, the structure of bargaining also involves a major dilemma for peace, even if this dilemma is not as well known as the conflict between individual and social rationality in the prisoner' dilemma. The contradiction between the social and individual rationality of the bargaining structure is not as immediate as it is in the prisoner's dilemma. Rational players in an optimal situation will end up in a socially rational outcome: the one who is more dependent on peace and who is less determined about his/her own terms of peace will be wise enough to yield. However, the elements of bargaining leverage encourage manipulation and bargaining tricks that are socially irrational simply because of the imperfections of real-life bargaining situations. This is mainly because of the fact that conflict realities do not express themselves as material realities do: there will always be different interpretations about the elements that define an agent's bargaining leverage. In many cases these elements are largely defined by interpretations and social constructs. Thus in wars or in coercive bargaining that uses the threat of war as leverage, perceptions of realities and social constructs and interpretations are always influenced to the partisan advantage by war mythologies and propaganda. Bargainers have a partisan incentive to manipulate their preferences, the preferences of their opponents, the identities of the agents, outcomes, and strategies in a way that is individually rational, but socially irrational. To see this we will look at elements of bargaining leverage to see their impact on partisan bargaining power in conflicts (individual rationality), and for their impact on the prospects for peace (social rationality). Since war propaganda is the most concrete expression of partisan manipulation of bargaining leverage in conflict situations, such propaganda, and war mythology, will be the main focus in our investigation and exemplification of the conflict between social and individual rationality in conflict bargaining.

To become more independent of a solution than one's opponent means two things: that one's opponent becomes anxious to reach a solution and that oneself becomes less anxious for peace. These two elements of the structure of bargaining already explain how agents that do not want war *per se* get into one when trying to gain bargaining leverage.

4.4.3.1. *Making the opponent more dependent on a solution*

The way to get one's opponent more dependent on a reaching a solution (and thus more willing to make favorable compromises) in a conflict is to make the absence of a solution, that is, the conflict, as painful for the opponent as possible. The ability and willingness of conflicting parties to kill in a war and damage their enemies is generally not because the conflicting parties originally hated each other (hatred often comes as part of the conflict process, though), or that they are violent by nature, but because making the opponent feel dependent on the return of peace is good for the agent's partisan bargaining power. This seems to correspond to the empirical studies of human destructiveness. So, for example, Erich Fromm concludes that violence is used by the vast majority of people in a purely instrumental way, and is not motivated by violent instincts or experiences that induce violent behavior. Violence is most often (but not in the rare cases of mentally ill people) instrumental and can only be explained by models that investigate the dialectics of structures and purposive behavior (Fromm, 1973, p. 210). Conflicting parties hurt their opponent so that their opponent will compromise: give them independence, accept staying as part of a country, accept giving up territory, decide not to claim territory, accept selling oil, or not to demand oil etc.

Making one's opponent more dependent on a peaceful solution in the pursuit of bargaining leverage explains why actors that do not want war end up at war, in order to promote their own cause in interaction with others. This explanation can be applied under the most trivial ontological assumptions: (A) the assumption that conflicting parties act in order to get outcomes they want to achieve and (B) the assumption that agents define their preferences and their agency in a way that puts them in a structural position that game theorists define as a bargaining game (i.e. their preferences are such that the agents prefer different terms of interaction, and that there will be a loss for both if none of the solutions can be reached). Agents create the structure (a game setting) with their preferences and with their understanding of agency, but once they have done so, structural logic takes over. In this structure, just like in the prisoner's dilemma, partisan rationality, acts that are functional from the point of view of one agent's purposes, lead the agents to outcomes that are dysfunctional for all.

The ability and willingness to hurt one's enemy is needed for victory on one's own terms. Thus hatred brings hope. A credible threat, again, is necessary for partisan bargaining purposes, as it makes one's enemy/opponent more dependent on peace. The logic behind the justification of patriotic hatred is very similar in wartime propaganda, regardless of culture, political system, or historical time. This is simply because of the stability of the structure of bargaining over time and across cultures. Naturally, in different cultures hatred has been cultivated by focusing on the enemy's destruction of one's values, although different political systems may have different methods of promoting hatred of the enemy. Yet, notwithstanding differences in nuances, the logic of seeing hatred as a patriotic function for the nation, and the idea of associating the enemy with the destruction brought about by war seems to be universal.

The need to get one's opponents more committed to a solution (and thus more willing to compromise) in order to get what one wants, pushes the conflicting parties not only to violence against others, but to many other kinds of practices and orientations that increase the opponent's eagerness to find a solution to the dispute about the terms of interaction. If hurting the enemy is important, then arming oneself in order to facilitate violence becomes useful for bargaining, too. This applies especially to offensive weaponry as that is the most useful material capacity to increase one's opponent's need for peace. In coercive bargaining, powerful nations tend to win (unless there are normative or institutional constructs that prevent this). This is simply because of the fact that they can make their opponents more dependent on peace, because if weak powers do not yield they might be crushed by powerful nations.

Furthermore, the need to be able to hurt enemies for bargaining leverage, demands normative orientations that are good for the nation, but not so useful for international peace. Warriors need to be able to kill, and softness cannot enter their mindset. This logic is exemplified by Marine Colonel Lewis Puller who told his soldiers: "Our Country won't go on forever, if we stay as soft as we are now. There won't be an America — because some foreign soldiers will invade us and take our women and breed a hardier race" (Goulden, 1982, p. 336). But although softness is arguably a global virtue, all security apparatuses are treating it as a problem. Any stable society needs norms against violence, and these norms become detrimental in coercive bargaining. In most societies, soldiers are somehow exempted from the peaceful norms of ordinary people and yet killing is still difficult even in wartime. According to Randolph Collins, 75% of front line soldiers never try to hit their enemy, because killing is not something people normally tolerate morally or mentally (Collins, 2008). War propaganda often deals with this issue, by inciting hatred toward the enemy or by reifying the enemy action as a mechanistic cause of the enemy's characteristics (see above) (Brewer, 2009, pp. 141–170). Brewer explains campaigns by the US government and the entertainment industry to mobilize Americans for war and has examples that directly deal with the difficulty of killing an enemy, which, of course, is necessary unless a nation wants to surrender on the enemy's terms. He analyzes the narratives that, for example, the Warner Brothers' film Sergeant York (1941) presents for a Tennessee farmer (Alvin York, a real character from WWI, played in the film by Gary Cooper), who wrestles with his conscience about the commandment "thou shalt not kill". Killing was necessary for "liberty", national and global, which was the marketing slogan for the US peace terms (Brewer, 2009, p. 91).

To mobilize a nation's power to make the opponent dependent on peace starts with the control of information, which relates to making moral decisions between peace and violence. Even in democracies misinformation and the controlling of information (journalists and peace researchers) is common and sometimes takes place even during peace time (Mariager, 2013). During wars, outright lies are a rule rather than an exception when it comes to moral issues the country's war effort. During the Second World War and in Vietnam the US government, for example, claimed that US bombing were well targeted and did not involve civilian fatalities (Brewer, 2009, p. 125). Speaking about the dropping of the first atomic bomb, President Truman called Hiroshima a military base, rather than a city, since Americans did not like civilian casualties, and revealing that it was a civilian target would have made the population less willing to accept it (*ibid.*, p. 136). Yet, during the two last years of the war the US killed between 240,000 and 300,000 Japanese, mostly civilians. Yet, even in peace time, moral condemnation of violent special operations and espionage is avoided through secrecy. According to a former CIA operative, Victor Marchetti, the United States, from the field operative to the president habitually lies to the public, and to other members of the decision-making apparatus about intrusive operations in potentially hostile and even friendly countries (Marchetti & Marks, 1974, p. 34).

In addition to the control of information and the ideological justification of war, hate of the enemy is useful for the bargainer's ability to make the opponent dependent on peace. According to Lasswell, it is a necessary element in coercive bargaining (Lasswell, 1995, p. 15). In order to incite hatred of an enemy, parties to a conflict commonly try to associate the enemy with the sorrow and destruction caused by the war. Patriotic Soviet newspapers during the Second World War described the relationship between hatred caused by the destruction inflicted by the enemy, hatred and the power and strength of one's own side very well. After describing the destruction caused by the Nazis in the Ukraine, Ilia Ehrenburg, a well-known ideologist, explains more optimistically that "sorrow feeds hatred. Hatred strengthens hope" (*Krasnaia Zvezda* September 27, 1941, translated and cited by Berkhoff, 2012, p. 41). Ehrensburg's text also shows another rhetorical technique in its associations between the enemy and one's own sorrow, and the war effort on one's own side and hope. Whilst one's own side is always associated with virtuous goals and good peace terms, one's enemies' identity is always tied to the destruction of war in hate speech. "While we are the ones that aim at liberty, anti-imperialism, socialism etc, the enemy is the one that causes destruction, threatens our families and way of life."

In most conflicts linguistic strategies are used to demonize or dehumanize the enemy (Kriesberg, 1998). In Papua, the Indonesian police often referred to the rebel Papuans (Kivimäki, 2006) as "smelly bugs", while in the ethnic war in West Kalimantan, enemies were called black dogs (Kivimäki, 2012a). A Pravda editorial on July 11, 1942 used the same rhetorical strategy of dehumanization by talking about Germans as "fascist dogs". In some cases the media portrayed Germans poisonous, or associated the occupiers with "beasts" and "cannibals" (Berkhoff, 2012, p. 174). More subtle rhetorical means of dehumanizing the enemy were used in the USA during the First World War. When President William McKinley of the United States tried to mobilize his people for war against the Philippines he used the racist colonial mentality of hierarchy between civilizations to lower the threshold of violence thus enabling the killing of the Philippine enemy. In his rhetoric the Philippine were "little brown brothers", who needed American help to maintain law and order (Brewer, 2009, p. 8). When President Woodrow Wilson's Commission for Public Information (CPI) tried to mobilize the American people to participate in the First World War, their campaigns used racial language to subhumanize the Germans. Germans were portrayed as barbaric Huns, dangerous and less than human. One CPI poster said "Hun or Home, buy more liberty bonds" and the picture showed an American woman with a child on her lap and an approaching, faceless, animal-like man ("the Hun") with a spike helmet (Brewer, 2009, p. 61). While this poster used many rhetorical strategies, one of them was the portrayal of the enemy as animal-like. In previous wars, especially the war with the Philippines in 1898, the enemy had been from a different, previously colonized civilization, and the US war was treated as one being fought against a barbaric people (in accordance to colonial rhetoric) (Brewer, 2009, p. 4). This same strategy was now adopted to mobilize Americans against the Germans, who were similarly portrayed as animal-like "Huns." In reality, of course, far from being barbaric and colonial, this enemy was the land of Luther, Goethe, Eucken, Beethoven, Bach, Schumann, Schubert, Brahms, and Mendelsohn-Bartholdy. And of course Germany was not only a culturally developed country but was also one of the new giants of the industrial age represented by firms like Mercedes, Siemens, etc.

In most countries the language of killing has become somewhat clinical by substituting words such as "elimination", "collateral damage", or "destruction", instead of the words kill or killing while the act of going after enemies with the intent of killing them has been described with words that in normal usage do not have anything to do with killing or fighting. This way the context of conflict was made exceptional, one in which normal norms did not apply. In the conflict in West Kalimantan, the combatants often talked about "hunting" (Kivimäki, 2012a; Rasyid, 2008), a word that has also been used in the war on terror in phrases like hunting down terrorists (Bush: We will hunt down terrorists | Mail Online, n.d.). Since the word "hunting" is normally used when speaking about animals, the use of it in this context implicitly associates the enemy with animals thus making it easier to use violence against them.

The technology of modern warfare has also enabled states and other combatants to wage war from a distance, thus separating the soldier or airman even more than was the case in the past from the actual battlefield. The use of unmanned weaponry, such as drones and missiles represent a technology that makes it easier for their operators to kill. This makes countries using such technology better coercive bargainers by making the threat of retaliation more credible for their opponents. Der Spiegel's seminal interview with Brandon Bryant reveals that drone warfare is not quite as clean as expected, and killing causes mental distress even when it is done thousands of kilometers from the target by using predator drones (Former Drone Operator 'Haunted' By His '1600 Hits' Scorecard, n.d., 2013). Yet, if distress starts haunting a soldier only after more than 1,600 reported kills, violence during the time of drones is certainly more effective and painless than during the time of traditional warfare.

In many conflict situations killing is also made possible by mobilizing old stereotypical masculine identities. According to Brewer, some US propaganda posters showed US soldiers attacking "hulking, ape-like attackers of women and children" (Brewer, 2009, p. 60). While such images made Americans more demanding with regards to the peace terms that they would be prepared to accept — soldiers would not want to settle for a peace that enabled "the Huns" to harass American women — they also hinted at the opportunity to use violence against Germany that was now open to young men. War and killing offered young men, who were maturing to manhood, a way to enact their masculinity, and thus interpretations of the war as one between the strong heroic defenders of American women and "the Huns." A Salvation Army poster showed a "virtuous American woman" whom the boys were fighting to protect. Their reward for a job well done would be to return home and marry someone just as nice. At the movies, which were also used by the American propaganda apparatus, "Americans saw their soldiers portrayed as rescuers of threatened women" (Brewer, 2009, pp. 65–66). While this facilitated violent masculine agency, it also denied feminine agency by constructing women as victims, i.e. objects of violence (Åhäll, 2012; Parashar, 2009). This way the rhetoric of violence was only partially rational in a partisan manner, as the exclusion of the violent potential of women was ruled out due to the masculine origin of the rhetoric (Tickner, 2004, pp. 43–44).

In societies where there is a strong belief in the power of magic, magic may be used to enable combatants to fight and hurt their enemies. It has been found that in surprisingly many conflicts combatants have been fighting under the influence of a trance or a spell of a witch doctor. This raises the question of whether they can be regarded as wholly responsible for their violent actions. Acting under such influences allows combatants to circumvent the moral norms of everyday life. This way also magic can serve conflicting party's bargaining power. In Fiji, fighters blame the drinking of kava for their violent acts (AA, 2006) and among the Malay fighters of West Kalimantan, Indonesia, a charmed water called *air tolak balak* is cited as the reason for the violence of the otherwise benevolent Malays (Darwis, 2009; YD, 2001). In some Dayak communities in West Kalimantan, the spells of witch doctors (*dukuns*) result in a trance where people are no longer in control of their bodies. Instead, it is claimed, ancestors of their ethnic community take over and use the bodies to wage holy war against the enemies of their ethnic community (Bernardinus, 2006; Hermanus, 2005; YD, 2001). This mystical knowledge that takes over individual fighters helps to create a fearsome reputation for these communities, which their enemies need to take into account. Possessing such a reputation clearly improves the bargaining power of these communities: one should not offend them or else. Yet, knowledge of the spells, charmed water, traditions, and trances that make tame people wild is not useful when it comes to making peace or in terms of social rationality.

4.4.3.2. *Making oneself less dependent on a solution*

The need to be less dependent on a peaceful solution than one's opponent also requires conflicting parties to try to reduce their own dependence on peace. The most obvious material means of doing this is to develop country's/conflicting party's defensive capabilities. Defensive weaponry reduces a country's need to find peaceful solutions as its enemies cannot hurt it as it has the the ability to defend itself. However, material means can be complemented by ideational means. How touched one is on the objective destruction of war is a matter of interpretation

Terrorists who do not care about their own death or the destruction of a plane full of hostages that they have hijacked are in a good bargaining position simply because they do not care about the possibility of any negotiations failing and the airplane exploding with them and the hostages. This strategy of a madman's bargaining was theorized by Daniel Ellsberg (Ellsberg, 1968), who to his great dismay found Nixon using it in his seemingly insensitive and mad escalation of the Vietnam War (Young, 2000). According to the documentary material Young refers to in his study, Nixon and Kissinger wanted to demonstrate their insensitivity *vis-à-vis* the destruction of war in order to show that the United States was not about to budge and that destructive war was about to continue unless the Communists yielded towards the demands of the United States. While Nixon's escalation of the Vietnam War did not improve the US's bargaining position in the peace talks regarding Vietnam, the logic of the bargaining situation was what motivated escalation. For terrorists the use of blackmail does not always succeed, but it certainly has a better chance if the terrorists manage to convince their opponents that they are willing to sacrifice their own lives if their demands are not met. Thus, socially disastrous strategies in a bargaining setting may be individually rational.

Here, instead of making peaceful people violent, the bargaining logic pushes parties to conflicts toward tolerating the sufferings of war and gives them direct motives against wanting to make peace. This way the structure of bargaining seems to make it more understandable that peaceful people are willing to kill instead of seeking peace.

A situation in which a combatant (a country or other entity) is less concerned about reaching a peaceful outcome may actually push the conflicting parties to adopt a tough attitude, which then in itself becomes something of a virtue, and makes the ability to take a hit a virtue too. The idea that there are rewards for religious warriors, a feature that can be found in almost all religions, could also be a reflection of this element in the logic of bargaining. Rewards are needed for partisan bargaining benefits. The beauty of dying in a war for one's motherland makes sense in peaceful societies only within a structure where less eagerness to seek settlements offers partisan benefits. The need to be tough also explains some of the organizational peculiarities in the management of security. People who are normally inclined and encouraged by the domestic order not to be violent have to be kept in the dark or isolated from decision making about war, because popular anti-war pressures against the government, caused by the suffering of war, make nations weak bargainers. This is why even democratic countries try to avoid showing their own people the fatalities on their own side (whilst still making claims, for the sake of the international community, about the brutality of their enemies). In the first Gulf War, journalists with privileged access to combat operations were asked not to report on American fatalities and banned from filming body bags. The same policy was followed during the second Gulf War, and, according to a Defense Department directive in March 2003, "There will be no arrival ceremonies for, or media coverage of, deceased military personnel returning to or departing from Ramstein (Germany) airbase or Dover (Del.) base, (and) to include interim stops" (Pentagon Manages War Coverage By Limiting Coffin Pictures, 2003). According to Brewer, the casualties at Pearl Harbor were concealed and then underreported all through the war (Brewer, 2009, p. 96), and for the first 21 months of the US's participation in the Second World War no pictures of American dead were allowed to be published (*ibid.*, 122). Furthermore, American deaths have often not been portrayed because it was felt that this might create panic and undermine the country's resolve to continue tough bargaining with its opponents. According to Moeller, in official announcements, war journalism and pictures that pass official wartime censorship, the horrors of war tend to be something that happens to the enemy while one's own state's own war deaths remain "serenely untouched even in death" (Moeller, 1989, p. 152).

Leaking secrets about the reality of war can therefore be seen as a national security issue even in democracies that are supposed to base their decision making on open information. The eagerness of even democratic and peaceful politicians to put Chelsey Manning, Julian Assange, and other whistle blowers behind bars can be understood, within the bargaining structure of security bargaining, as an attempt to safeguard the US national bargaining position, even if it also raises outrage globally as informing about the sorrow of war is clearly necessary for the security of humankind. Silencing truth tellers about war is useful in the structure of coercive bargaining because of the fact that popular consciousness of the suffering of war might make the democratic USA more impatient to end its involvement in wars.

In totalitarian nations, such as Stalin's Russia, institutions facilitated very different means for censoring information that could make soldiers or people more dependent on peace.[13] According to an analysis of Soviet war propaganda and censorship, the centralized control of information about the war was the responsibility of the Soviet Information Bureau and Agitprop — the Directorate on Propaganda and Agitation of the Central Committee of the USSR Communist Party under the close surveillance of Stalin — and its main task was to prevent information about the sufferings of the war from reaching the public. The organization banned "without exception all pieces of information that can call forth a panicky and depressed mood in the army or in the hinterland. Exaggerated data on the results of enemy military action and on its material and technical resources, overestimation of the enemy army's morale and military situation, and so on" (Berkhoff, 2012, p. 35, quotation, is from Berkhoff's translation of documentary sources). As a result, according to Haynes, Soviet fatalities in the war were downplayed or remained unreported (Haynes, 2003). Furthermore, the Soviet control of information downplayed the power of the enemy and accused those who did not stick to the official line of underplaying the suffering of the war of being unpatriotic: According to *Pravda*, the enemy was "not as strong as some terrified panic-mongers imagine" (Berkhoff, 2012, p. 48). Pravda also boosted Russia's patriotic, fearless morale that enabled independence of peace. On January 27, 1942 it carried a story about a certain Tatiana, who was behind enemy lines and was quoted as saying: "I'm not afraid to die, comrades. It's a great joy to die for your people ... Don't fear, Stalin is with us" (Berkhoff, 2012, p. 230).

While the misinformation made it possible for the Soviet Union to continue its fearless, hard bargaining with Germany (due to the fact that the manipulation of access to knowledge made Russians less

---

[13] At the same time, the effect of Russian propaganda was limited by the fact that the state lacked resources and the country lacked a communication infrastructure that could be used for propaganda (Livshin & Orlov, 2012).

dependent on a peaceful solution), it also had its downsides. Given the means afforded him by a totalitarian regime, Stalin was able to limit access to knowledge to such an extent that it sometimes made his own military's ability to make rational decisions difficult (Murphy, 2006; Pleshakov, 2005). By manipulating access to information, Stalin could make the country so insensitive to the sufferings of war that even individually rational decision making on compromises became impossible.

The need for partisan bargaining power also justifies within the structure of bargaining the manipulation of public morality, institutions, and the people. It is necessary to keep peace activists and even activist, pragmatic peace researchers in check. Even in democracies like Denmark, peace researchers have been systematically followed even during peacetime by security and intelligence organizations for the sake of bargaining leverage (Mariager, 2013): if a nation become too attentive of the risks and costs of war, it will have to yield in world politics in order to avoid such risks and costs. By studying the sorrow and destruction of war, and the value of peace, peace researchers affect the national mood *vis-à-vis* conflict by making people more eager to end conflicts and reach a settlement. This, if done on one side of the conflict only, increases the country's eagerness to maintain peace (dependence) and thus reduces the bargaining leverage of the side where peace activists and peace researchers can operate freely. The suspicion of the security apparatus even in democracies with regards to peace activists and peace researchers, critical journalists, and truthful reporting on wars can be understood within the structure of bargaining. The more one suppresses one's own peace groups, the more one treats one's own peacemakers as traitors, the more one declares peaceful communication in one's own country/ethnic group with potential enemies as aiding espionage, the greater one's bargaining power in world politics, be it with governments or ethnic groups.

In addition to suppressing information, the need to reduce a country's need for a settlement requires nationalist norms that play down the suffering of war. The first normative rhetorical strategy to make oneself less eager on coming to a peaceful outcome is to deny moral values in wars by claiming that war is unavoidable, and that one's violent actions are therefore not a free choice that can be morally criticized. According to Fritzsche, this was one of the successful elements of Nazi propaganda among Germans (Fritzsche, 2008).

To the extent that the use of violence is a moral decision, propaganda tries to make it normatively more attractive. The idea of national heroes and heroism is based on a clever conceptual association (conceptual gerrymandering) between self-sacrifice and nationalism. The willingness to sacrifice personal comfort (even life) for fairness, the common good, and justice is seen as a virtue in all normative systems that aim at resisting the temptation to be selfish and prescribe altruistic behavior (Kant, 2005): self-sacrifice for the common good is a virtue. However, in the creation of a mythology about the virtue of national heroes, an assumption is smuggled into the thinking concerning self-sacrifice. While the emphasis in the mythology of national heroism is in the generally accepted virtue of self-sacrifice (the selling point of the myth), this self-sacrifice should be made for the national good, not for the good of humanity, the family, the race, or something else. With this association between self-sacrifice and nationalism, the mythology of national heroes creates a situation in which anti-nationalist actors are not willing to make this sacrifice, although they may well be prepared to do so for humanity rather than for the nation. During the First World War, American war propaganda portrayed those who were not 100% American, and did not buy liberty bonds, which funded the American war effort, as traitors, that is, people who were willing to sell the common good for their own comfort (Brewer, 2009, p. 69). Communists with class solidarity, pacifists with global loyalties, as well as people who simply thought that the war was wrong or somehow not in the interests of the United States, easily fell into the category of traitors. As a result of this particular campaign by the Commission of Public Information about being 100% American, the association between nation and self-sacrifice was additionally built in a way that, in a cultural history context, supported primordial ideas something as absurd as the American ethnicity. These ideas associated an American race to the 100% pureness of Americanness. Consequently, people with other races were not only not 100% Americans, but they risked being traitors as well. An Iowa politician, for example, claimed that "90% of all the men and women who teach the German language are traitors" (Brewer, 2009, p. 70).[14]

The association between people and discourses of peace and dialogue, on the one hand, and treason and espionage, on the other, can be clearly seen in times of tension by following the development of legislation that deals with individuals and organizations that are seen as weakening the partisan morale during wartime. At particularly tense moments during the First World War, Americans enacted the President Act, the Espionage Act, the Trading with the Enemy Act, the Sedition Act, and the Sabotage Act, all of which could be used to deal with the question of cooperation with the enemy (Stevens, 1970). Furthermore, with the support of the Justice Department, the American Protective League, a group of 350,000 private, patriotic citizens spied on their neighbors and workers, opened mail, burglarized homes, bugged telephones, and advocated assaulting dissenters, etc. (Brewer, 2009, p. 70). Yet, no sabotage or cases of German espionage were proven in court during the First World War (Stevens, 1970). In the case of Nazi Germany, dangerous individuals or groups that tried to reach out to the enemy were discouraged by banning communications with foreigners, and making it illegal to listen to foreign radio broadcasts (Kundrus, 2005). In the Soviet Union, one method used to obstruct contact with foreigners and foreign news was the general confiscation of radio receivers (Berkhoff, 2012, p. 269).

Dissenting voices against the general willingness to violence against the enemy are silenced, especially at tense times with

---

[14] It is interesting to see how President Bill Clinton's heroism-rhetoric paid careful attention to this problem. Very often, when Clinton used the word heroism in reference to military matters in his speeches, he made references to the heroism of ethnic minorities, native Americans, or black Americans (William J. Clinton: Remarks Commemorating the 50th Anniversary of Iwo Jima in Arlington, Virginia, 1995, William J. Clinton: Remarks on Presenting the Congressional Medal of Honor to **African–American** Heroes of World War II, 1997). Thereby, instead of sowing seeds of racial intolerance or militaristic nationalism his rhetoric of heroism often aimed at emphasizing the racial inclusiveness of American nationalism.

restrictions, norms, and constructs that delegitimize views that emphasize the value of peace. This is common even in democracies. In the United States before the First World War radical labor unions held that the war was motivated by capitalists, who wanted to protect their loans in Allied countries. This interpretation was clearly dangerous to the partisan individual rationality of US bargaining efforts against Germany and such opinions were seen as treacherous (Brewer, 2009, p. 57). As a result President Wilson's propaganda machine, the Committee for Public Information, instructed the media that this interpretation of the war "as a 'rich man's war' was a lie spread by German propaganda". Pro-peace interpretations were thus tied to enemy propaganda and treason (Brewer, 2009, p. 57). But, in addition to these associations, a link was also built, perhaps surprisingly, between pro-peace interpretations and espionage. "Cartoons that conveyed gossip about a 'businessman's war'" increase discontent and prolong the war. "These lies, started by German spies," the ad explained, "will kill our boys in France" (Brewer, 2009, p. 62).

In addition to moral condemnation, sanctions have been used extensively to discourage critique of war. According to Brewer, a Wisconsin farmer was sent to jail for one year for saying: "This is a rich man's war and we would not have this war if it had not been for rich girls in the US marrying English lords." An Ohio judge sent a farmer named John White to jail for saying that German troops had done the same thing in Belgium as American soldiers had done in the Philippines. The socialist leader Eugene Begs received a 10-year sentence for making an anti-war speech in Ohio. A film producer got 10 years for showing how UK soldiers bayoneted women and children (Brewer, 2009, p. 71).

In addition to taking action against pro-peace interpretations and sentiments, state propaganda always rewards patriotic pro-war sentiments and interpretations regardless of the country or the type of polity. In partisan framing of the suffering in war, sacrifice was sometimes even glorified. In the Soviet media and arts during the Second World War, individual stories of heroism were used to provide models which, it was intended, the people should follow and from which they could be inspired, or they were presented as building blocks of Soviet identity (Hodgson, 1996). In this literature the moral appeal of national heroism was also sought by highlighting "selflessness" (*samootverzhennost*) of heroes who gave a low priority to their own lives and prioritized the national interest (Hodgson, 1996, p. 149). Yet, as in American or any other partisan propaganda, the Soviet idea that the common good was in effect partisan national interest was more or less smuggled into the thinking of the people. Given the Soviet Union's ideological inheritance, and its construction of world politics as a class struggle, nationalism was a peculiar imposition, as, on the face of it, it was in clear contradiction with official Marxist–Leninist ideology. Perhaps therefore, in some cases the association was articulated between self-sacrifice and the saving of comrades (Berkhoff, 2012, p. 68).

In addition to appealing to morality, Soviet propaganda also consciously created an identity that was useful for Soviet bargaining position. Heroism was not only presented as a moral duty, but also as something that was natural to people who were Soviet Citizens: "We Bolsheviks have hearts forged from steel," claimed a famous Russian poem (Hodgson, 1996, p. 149). A *Pravda* editorial claimed that "self-sacrifice was an eternal trait of Russian Soldiers, who had always been acclaimed for it" (Berkhoff, 2012, p. 65). With an identity that was tough, heroic, and unmoved by the thought of personal suffering, expectations of behavior and attitude could be manipulated in a direction that was useful for partisan bargaining leverage. Again though, the casualty was social rationality and peace.

Independence on peace and cooperation is also useful with regards to the question of peace mediation. The problem in many peace processes is that any public expression by the conflicting parties of their willingness to reach a peace settlement is easily interpreted as weakness (i.e. need for peace). This is why conflicting parties might want to conceal their willingness to accept external help in settling their conflicts. In Southern Thailand, the government has been in conflict with Islamist separatists in the southernmost provinces of the country. A Thai negotiation panel that was authorized by two consecutive Thai governments was negotiating under Indonesia's Vice President Jusuf Kalla in Bandung, Indonesia with some of the rebel leaders in a secret process when the negotiation effort was accidentally publicized. As a result the Thai government denied that it had given a mandate to the Thai negotiators while the ones responsible for most of the rebel violence denied that the rebel negotiators in Bogor had been authorized by the rebel side.[15] Both wanted to deny the fact that they were willing to end the war, since this would have reduced their bargaining leverage toward each other. Both wanted to show that they were not too impatient to end the war, and, thus, they were not eager to make compromises to get peace.

Clearly, a readiness to accept the suffering associated with war, a degree of patience with regard to when it comes to an end, and the ability to hurt the opponent in order to make it more eager to seek peace and more willing to make compromises, are useful for individual bargaining power. Yet, a willingness to damage others and a lack of interest in peace are surely individual attitudes that are dysfunctional for the collective good. In other words they are socially irrational orientations.

4.4.3.3. *Making oneself more determined about one's terms of peace*

Whilst bargaining logic pushes potential conflicting parties into constructs and discourses that undermine the value of peace and encourage them to adopt orientations that make punishing their opponents easier, the same logic also makes compromises more difficult. This is simply because of the fact that being committed to one's own terms for reaching an agreement (and being hostile when it comes to the opponents' terms) increases one's bargaining power. The inauguration of the main British organization for the production of shared knowledge/interpretation of the First World War, the National War Aims Committee crystallized this need in its inaugural statutes in the following manner: The two main aims of the Committee were to "counteract, and if possible, render nugatory the insidious and specious propaganda of pacifist publications" and to

---

[15] Anonymous interviews by the author with four of the participants of the negotiation in March 2010, September 2011, and August 2012.

exhort the public to "inflexible determination to continue to a victorious end the struggle in maintenance of those ideals of Liberty and Justice which are the common and the sacred cause of the allies" (Resolution passed at the inaugural meeting of the National War Aims Committee. August 4, 1914, Queens Hall, cited in Haste, 1995, pp. 125–126).

Often the strength of smaller powers in asymmetric coercive bargaining is based on this kind of greater sensitivity toward the terms of cooperation. Superpowers tend to defend globally some of their remote interests when at war while smaller powers, such as Vietnam, when it was at war with the United States, was fighting for her very survival. This is why weaker powers, despite the fact that they cannot hurt their enemies as much as big powers can, still do well in coercive bargaining. This is simply due to their stronger commitment to their objectives in a war (Vital, 1967). Yet, sensitivity toward the terms of cooperation (determination in bargaining), especially if mutual, constitute a contradiction between individual and social rationality. The opposing positions of patriotic allied knowledge production and the "pacifist publication" that the inaugural document of the British National War Aims Commission clearly document points to this conflict between individual and social rationality. While the British people had to be exhorted to an inflexible determination to reach victory, world peace needed compromises.

The most obvious and universal way of constructing bargaining settings that are beneficial for the bargainer is to frame one's own terms in a positive light and create a collective commitment to it. For American bargaining with its opponents during the cold war, the frame that legitimized American determination was the idea of America's role in "making the world safe for democracy". According to the Secretary of State, Dean Acheson, such a formulation can "bring the whole story together in one official narrative" (Acheson, 1969, p. 414). During the First World War, President Woodrow Wilson appealed to the mothers of soldiers that had been killed in action by assuring them that their sons had died to save the "liberty of the world". Before the cold war the US frame for its terms in coercive bargaining was tied to the colonialist discourse of the role of the white man's burden. To justify US coercive interference in the Philippines, President McKinley told the nation that the Filipinos "should be helped . . . to a more scientific knowledge of the production of coffee, rubber and tropical products, for which there is demand in the United States" (William McKinley: Third Annual Message, 1899). In another speech, President McKinley justified US coercion in the Philippines as an effort to bring Christianity to "little brown brothers" (Brewer, 2009, p. 8). In territorial disputes, the conflicting parties often recall or invent histories that highlight the importance of the disputed territory for their national existence and the unity of their state (Kivimäki, 2002). Justifying one's claims as civilized is not, however, just an American or colonialist prerogative. China, too, has boosted its sensitivity towards the terms of peace in the context of territorial disputes, by linking non-acquiescence with nationalism and dedication to civilization: "territory once won for civilization must not be given back to barbarism; therefore, territory which was once Chinese must forever remain so, and, if lost, must be recovered at the first opportunity" (Fitzgerald, 1963, p. 12).

For hegemonic powers, the justification of one's terms of interaction are often related to the common good, and even the preservation of peace. As a result the sensitivity for the terms of peace is rather absolute as peace is *possible* only if the terms of the hegemonic power are accepted. Given this attitude, it is not possible for a coercive bargainer to accept their opponent's peace terms as the opponent's terms *meant* war. According to President Roosevelt, war in the Philippines could not be avoided because without the acceptance of the US's peace terms, the Philippines would not have achieved a real peace. Roosevelt declared that the US task was to make the Philippines "fit for self-government", so that the US would not have to leave them "to fall into a welter of murderous anarchy". Roosevelt explained that "wars with uncivilized powers" ... "are largely mere matters of international police duty, essential for the welfare of the world". Opposition against US troops was illegality and banditry, according to President Roosevelt (Brewer, 2009, pp. 43, 45). The metaphor of police action for military intervention was also used by President Harry S Truman for the US operation in Korea (*ibid.*, 149). However, the idea that US terms for peace are the only terms that could genuinely be called peace terms was also present in global conflicts. According to President Wilson, "The peace of the world cannot be established without America" (September 18, 1919) ... "if the US did not commit to keeping the peace, an even more devastating war would break out" (Brewer, 2009, p. 83). The Soviet Union and China instituted a similar position in their identities as they divided the world between fascist and imperialist powers on the one hand and Peace-Loving Nations on the other (En-lai, 1962; Ro'i & Morozov, 2008, p. 57). During the Second World War, German violation of the neutrality of Belgium was used by the anti-German forces as an event representative of the danger of not committing oneself to one's own positions. Such a representative case helped those mobilizing their countries for war against Germany prove that acceptance of German peace terms was the same as war. In the UK this was even used to counter the anti-War argument of the Liberal Party (Haste, 1995, p. 107), whilst in the US, people were reminded of the fate of Belgium in war posters issued by the Office of War Information (Brewer, 2009, p. 60). Settling for peace on the enemy's terms was also framed as impossible by using the example of the Munich Agreement between Neville Chamberlain and Adolf Hitler, an agreement that bought time for Hitler and made it possible for him to plan for further military advances in Europe. For decades, making peace on compromised terms became plagued by the much used memory of this incident, and the incident was explicitly used for war mobilization by President Ronald Reagan in the 1980s and President Bill Clinton in the 1990s (Brewer, 2009, p. 97; Humpreys, 2013). It was also one of the main rationales for the US involvement in the Korean War and in Vietnam. As Secretary of State, Dean Rusk put it "We are in Korea because we are trying to prevent a world war" (Rusk, 1951).

The association between peace and one's own terms of cooperation for hegemonic powers also associates the hegemon's power with leadership in the world. Emphasizing this serves as a powerful rhetorical strategy in domestic discourse for boosting the determination of the hegemonic state's population. Whilst making peace on the opponent's terms is impossible (since it would only prolong the war), making peace on one's own terms consolidates the country's hegemonic position. According to Brewer, this was also seen as legitimate and moral because of the fact that since the First World War American public opinion started to see world interests and American interests as identical. "For Wilson, the contradictions between the promotion of democratic ideals and the assertion of US power through military intervention were resolved by his conviction that what was best for the United States was best for the world" (Brewer, 2009, p. 47). It was President Wilson's position that "once the Hun was defeated the rest of the world would … embrace an American-led new world order" (Brewer, 2009, p. 85). The legitimacy of this view that US peace terms were best for the world, strengthened and became an idea that could be taken as given as US hegemony matured. As Truman put it "Against the futile and tragic course of dictatorship, we uphold, for all people, the way of freedom — the way of mutual cooperation and international peace. We assert that mankind can find progress and advancement along the path of peace. At this critical hour in the history of the world, our country has been called upon to give of its leadership, its efforts, and its resources to maintain peace and justice among nations. We have responded to that call. We will not fail" (Truman, 1950a).

In addition to framing the consequences of one's own terms of peace as positive, partisan rationality and relative bargaining power also required that the terms suggested by the enemy were framed negatively. The metaphor of slavery has been extensively used during the 20th century in the framing of the enemy's peace terms. During the Second World War, Stalin talked about the Nazi desire to "Germanize the Soviet peoples" and that the aim of "German princes and barons" was to "enslave" Russia. In Russian propaganda, German rule was portrayed as slavery. In Wasilewska's story *Rainbow* a mother explains to her son how German "slavery is worse than death" and that if her son had to choose between German slavery and death he should choose death. The eviction and extermination of the Russian people was also sometimes suggested as the effect of accepting German peace terms (Berkhoff, 2012, pp. 169 & 237).

But the slavery metaphor was also used by Americans. According to the *Armed Force Talk* journal's (No. 340, August 18, 1950) *The Issues at stake in Korea* of the Office of the Secretary of Defense, "if the Communists were successful, you would become the slave, body and soul, of as cruel a band of individuals as ever ranged the earth". According to the vice president, "This is a fight between a slave world and a free world" (Brewer, 2009, p. 104). US propaganda has also framed its opponent's peace terms as extermination and the ending of independence. According to Truman, the Korean War was about US survival. "We are fighting in Korea for our own national security and survival" because the attack upon Korea made it clear to him that "the goal of the communists is to concur independent nations" (Truman, 1950b). At the same time the term extermination was sometimes replaced by the expressions lost, or even rotting. Secretary of State Dean Acheson, for example, declared in Congress that "countries are like apples in a barrel, if one goes rotten the next one is in danger of going rotten, too" (Acheson cited in (Brewer, 2009, p. 146)).

In addition to making one's own terms of cooperation look good and those of the opponents bad, the construction of the bargaining setting in a way that served partisan purposes also attached norms and sanctions to peoples' attitudes towards the terms of peace. The most brutal example is the fact that, in war, states often punish people who surrender or who collaborate with the enemy's government. One of the objectives of Soviet propaganda was to deter Russians from surrendering to the Germans (Weiner, 2001). Thus, punishments could be used to increase resolve towards the terms of peace. Also norms can be constructed in ways that emphasize resolve. Societies under pressure from the outside also tend to develop a fanatic "true believer culture" that emphasizes that refusing to yield is a virtue (Hoffer, 2002). In Aceh, as was the case in the battle for Indonesia's independence, the slogan "*merdeka atau mati*"/"independence or death" also describes the way in which people were indoctrinated to believe in a true believer culture, or simply to be unyielding when it came to bargaining or negotiating.

Finally, in special situations, the determination to stick to one's own peace terms can sometimes be strengthened by intentionally attaching political costs to yielding. Descriptions of the two sides of the Aceh Peace talks (Husain, 2007; Kingsbury, 2006)[16] show that in this peace negotiations both parties made public statements to their constituencies about their most important commitments just before each round of the negotiations. This is a very common practice in peace negotiations and, again, it is good for their partisan purposes, but makes achieving compromises and peace very difficult. Again, partisan individual rationality turns out to lead to social irrationality in the negotiating process.[17]

4.5. Bargaining and Rationality

The above treatment of the elements of bargaining show how a structure gives reasons for action that without the structure seems irrational. Peaceful agents in a bargaining setting have incentives for (1) hurting their opponents (or at least for threatening and preparing for violence), (2) disregarding the value of peace, and (3) taking an unyielding attitude towards peace-enabling compromises. If we follow Hollis and Smith (1990) and try to find a "reason" why purposive agents act as they do, here we can see a structure within which even agents who might want peace also have a reason for continuing the violence, disregarding peace and being unyielding toward compromises that could resolve the dispute behind the conflict. In a structure of bargaining that has been constituted by the preferences of the conflicting parties toward alternative outcomes, the identification of

---

[16] Farid Husain was Indonesia's main pre-negotiator in the Aceh peace process. Kingsbury was an adviser to the rebel negotiation panel. He, too, participated in each round of negotiations.

[17] Of the four elements that determine bargainers' leverage only the opponent's lack of determination to reach the terms necessary for a settlement is one that does not give incentives to manipulation, which then leads to social irrationality. When a bargainer makes it easy for her/his opponent to make compromises she/he is contributing to peace. In fact, doing this is one of the prescriptions proposed by Fisher and Ury for successful negotiations. Putting oneself in one's opponents shoes and thinking how it would be possible for her/him to accept a settlement and consider it a victory is central to "getting to 'yes'" in dispute resolution (Fisher & Ury, 1991).

people involved as collective agents, as well as their interpretations of the strategies available in conflict, socially irrational conflict behavior can be given a perfectly rational reason. The fact that the bargaining setting seems like a very common structure for conflict situations makes the analysis of bargaining very interesting for pragmatic peace research.

While for the prisoner's dilemma there is a solution within game theory that removes the conflict between individual and collective rationality, for the bargaining structure there is none. Moving to a super-game level only makes things more difficult. "The shadow of the future" in bargaining rewards toughness in bargaining: If a terrorist is known to be unconcerned about dying anyone confronted with one has to be sensible and yield in order to avoid casualties. Similarly, if Vietnam was known to the US during the Vietnam War, to be an unyielding bargainer, there was no point in the US trying to persuade it by force (Young, 1991a, 2000). Vietnam's reputation for being unyielding gave her leverage and was one reason for the US to yield and make peace on Victnam's terms. In a similar vein the Speaker of the House of Representatives Tipp O'Neal revealed the meaning of Reagan's intervention in Nicaragua in an interview with Larry King: "It's being a man. (the president believes that) America has to show the firmness of manhood" (Booth & Wheeler, 2008, p. 64). If America acts in a manly manner it gets the respect of a man when it comes to bargaining. A quotation from Bill Clinton after the Somali rebels had humiliated the US by killing one of the US soldiers suggests the same logic: "I believe in killing people who try to hurt you, and I can't believe we're being pushed around by these two-bit pricks." According to Henry Kissinger, a "really strong overt act" by the president, such as bombing North Korea after its military provocation of the US, was "essential to galvanize people into overcoming slothfulness and deta-chment arising from general moral decay" (Haldeman, 1995, p. 65; Young, 2000, p. 365).

At the same time states often fear that yielding in some coercive negotiation situation creates an image about them that will later haunt them. According to Lo, after the 1968 Soviet aggression against Czechoslovakia, China needed to take a more unyielding stand in territorial disputes in the South China Sea, due to the fact that they had wanted to "make a point there of not becoming another Czechoslovakia — ready to compromise its territorial sovereignty" (Lo, 1989, pp. 7–8). A soft cooperative reputation would clearly have been harmful for China. Thus, clearly, the level of super-games does not offer a way out of the contradiction between social and individual rationality in the structure of bargaining. Having a tough reputation is good for bargaining and this just adds to the contradiction between individual and social rationality. In order to deal with the social irrationality, and threat to peace, involved in the structure of bargaining, we will have to go into the constitution of the elements of the structure. We cannot do this within a given game structure. Instead, we will have to move further toward neo-pragmatism and study the consequences for peace research of the fact that social structures, such as the game of the prisoner's dilemma and the game of bargaining, are created in interpretations and constitutions. Thus the social engineering of peace complemented with insights to anti-determinism is not enough. We will have to study what interpretationism and constructivism can teach us, before we can resolve the problem of the social dysfunctionality of individually rational action in coercive bargaining.

Chapter 5
Interpretations as a Conflict Reality

The need for interpretation in peace and conflict research could be understood from the position that rejects determinism. If conflict behavior cannot be understood from its determinants, it has to be understood by understanding the ways in which warriors, decision makers or belligerent constituencies of war politicians understand the world and how they see their own action in this world. The reconstruction of the world according to the warrior or a war president is an interpretation.

5.1. Introduction

For knowledge that can help prevent violence, it is important to understand the opportunities of purposive behavior in principle, but also how a social or a material structure can constrain purposive behavior. So far we have introduced the idea of purposive, free action, and how fundamentally it changes our thinking of knowledge needed for conflict prevention, but we have also introduced a simple structure that can make peaceful actors that are operating under conditions of total freedom of the will end up acting to incite violence. To continue the analysis of the interaction between structures and actions, and to build knowledge that enables us to deal with the type of contradictions bargaining structures imply for national security and world peace, it is time to see how action can transform, not just manipulate (as in the case of dysfunctional bargaining) structures, such as the structure introduced as a bargaining game. It is time to remember how the structure of bargaining is constituted by perceptions of agency and strategic choices and outcomes, as well as by free formulation of preferences. In this way we can open the dilemma of bargaining, not by working inside the model, but by moving outside the model and trying to see how the constitution of the model can be transformed.

According to Blumer and his symbolic interactionism, we can understand people's actions only if we understand the meanings they give to their actions and if we understand what the actors themselves believe about their world (Blumer, 1969). This is a more sophisticated version of the previously presented model by Hollis and Smith of explaining action "from the inside" by understanding the reasons actors give for their actions.

The aim of social science, for symbolic interactionists, is therefore to reconstruct the reality of the actors that social scientists perceive. The worst mistake a social scientist can make, according to Blumer, is to replace the meaning of the actor with the meaning the situation and the acts have for the scholar. This is the mistake most game theoretical analyses make in their insistence that there are objective preferences that scholars can impose on their objects of studies, while the game structure can simply be analyzed from the objective material realities, such as nations and their material resources that automatically give their meanings to the actors in bargaining games (Wendt, 1998, 2001).

This means that fixing conflict problems cannot assume a given conflict setting, but instead it needs to analyze the constructions of the conflict by the conflicting parties (and meanings that exist in language and existing social practices). But what is important, too, is not just how the conflict setting is constructed, but also how it could be deconstructed and reconstructed. The key is not just the symbol, but also the symboling, the manipulation of symbols by active persons, defining and redefining their social situations (Charon, 1995, p. 63). This is one of the basic ideas of critical discourse analysis — critical discourse analysis is not only the analysis of existing interpretations, but also analysis of the production of reality which is performed by discourse (Jäger, 2001, p. 36).

If, as we have shown above, the bargaining setting is the basic structure of conflict and if we realize that the contradiction between individual rationality (partisan security) and social rationality (peace) cannot be reconciled from within the structure, pragmatic peace research cannot avoid broadening the ontology of classical pragmatism toward ontologies that go beyond the empiricism of the classical pragmatists. Otherwise it is not possible for pragmatic peace research to understand how interpretations constitute conflict realities or how their reinterpretations can change social realities.

In West Kalimantan, violent rejection of the local traditions of the "locals" by the migrant community was used as a way to articulate a reality where their own tradition was equally important as the tradition of the local population. For the local population the violent expulsion of the migrant community was a way to articulate the identity of the local population as hosts that could ask the "guests" to leave their home area. Thus, actions had symbolic meanings and only by establishing more cost-efficient means of dialogue between the "migrant" and "host" groups could the region be pacified: Only through understanding the meaning for the conflicting parties of their own actions as arguments and articulations was it possible to design ways of verbally articulating the very same arguments that were articulated in violence (Kivimäki, 2012a). Thus, peacemakers needed to reconstruct the meanings conflicting parties gave to their actions, instead of just empirically observing the behavior and manipulating the exogenous conditions that were associated with violent behavior.

Similarly, the suggested bombing of North Korea was not simply something that aimed at some concrete consequences (North Korea being bombed) in that particular relationship, but if indeed, it was, as Kissinger explain, a symbolic signal that was made to emphasize American resolve and leadership in world affairs, fixing US–North

Korea relations would not prevent this act of violence (Haldeman, 1995, p. 65; Young, 2000, p. 365).

If China's violent arrest of Vietnamese fishermen around Paracel Islands was "exercising of sovereignty" in a disputed territory, and not something related to the fishermen, a peace action would require alternative ways of signaling commitment to considering this area as one's own. The stipulation of the United Nations Convention on the Law of the Seas (UNCLOS) according to which countries can protest officially when their sovereignty in maritime areas is being violated, gave the opportunity and made it at least in theory possible for claimant states to avoid a situation where their inaction toward foreign fishermen would be treated as an admission that the territory does not belong to one's sovereign territory and thus foreign fishermen have the right to use the territory as they please. By instituting mechanisms that were not violent and that did not call for counteraction UNCLOS was able to prevent a process of escalation. Before UNCLOS violent demonstrations were necessary and other claimants of the disputed territories had to defend the rights of their fishermen in order to demonstrate their sovereignty in the area. This often gave rise to instant escalation of the conflict (Kivimäki, 2014b).

Reconstruction of meanings of conflicting parties can also make our understanding of some of the generalizations of behaviorist peace research more realistic. Relative deprivation as a gap between the expected and the experienced level of wellbeing is clearly constituted in interpretations of how things are and how they should be. According to Santos Winarso, the constitution of rights of indigenous people has built up the expectation of how the Malay population of Southern Thailand should be treated, while ideological interpretations of the actions of the Thai government create the reality of experienced wellbeing among the rebellious populations of "Patani". The very same logic characterizes Jamie Davidson's analysis of the Dayak population in West Kalimantan (Davidson, 2007; Winarso, 2014). Similarly, incentives or opportunities of legitimate violence are often created through the constitution of realities that only exist in the head of people who need to be convinced of their existence. The fact that the rebels of Papua are considered "smelly bugs", or that the

Madurese of West Kalimantan are "black dogs" enables their hunting, an action category that is normally reserved for the pursuit of animals not human beings. The fact that fighters are in a trance or possessed by their ancestors enables their violence without moral condemnation, since their action is not a chosen act of violence (Kivimäki, 2012a).

This means that for peace research to be useful for the peacemaker it can no longer explain conflict only as an exogenous relationship between material conditions and conflict behavior as the mainstream behaviorist peace research does. Nor can it simply seek simple reasons for actions of free-willed conflicting parties within a given conflict setting. Instead, peace research has to see how development of thoughts and interpretations, language and social practices constitute game structures within which reason then operates and makes sense of conflict behavior. Conflict structures, collective agency, motives and preferences, strategy choices and their normative implications are generated in social interaction with rules that define who is the West, what is self-defense, what is an intervention, etc. These socially constructed elements of the game structure interact with materially defined elements (a bullet kills regardless of amulets or spells, and regardless of what meaning we give to bullets that kill) and create the game structure within which we can then understand purposive behavior.

The knowledge of constitutive rules that create intervention, self-defense, sovereignty or nation-building as actions, but also the West, peace-loving people, or imperialists as agents and war, security or peace as consequences for agents of actions, is important for a peacemaker. More importantly, a pragmatist will need to know how self-defense, the West or security can be constituted (Smith, 2003). What kind of narratives or violent demonstrative actions are behind the constitutive rule that defines the identity of an agent as "local", and what kind of critique of the narrative or alternative, non-violent action could be offered for the argumentation about or articulation of an identity. The attitude of pragmatist peace researcher to "truths" about institutional facts like arresting fishermen as an exercise of sovereignty, or the reality of local customs, the existence of states, the existence of sovereignty, etc. follows the same logic as the attitude of peace research toward material realities. The peace researcher should consider them real only if they are as realities useful for peace. If acting as if they were real helps peaceful societies, they should be considered real, while if not, they should be rejected. Again, of course, we have to make a difference between the individual's and society's ability to reject institutional facts: an individual who rejects commonly accepted social structures and lives as if an entirely different set of realities and institutional facts existed cannot function in society. At the same time, societies can articulate, adopt and reject social realities as long as they manage to stay conscious of the social origin and existence of their social structures.

5.2. Social Rationality and the Constitution of Bargaining Structures

As we learned in the previous chapter, a bargaining structure is constituted by a perception that

1. There are at least two agents;
2. That their preferences are affected by their actions so that
   a. A cooperative outcome on their own terms would give them most benefits;
   b. A cooperative outcome on their opponent's terms would give them less utility;
   c. A cooperative outcome on terms that are somewhere between these two above-mentioned outcomes gives less utility than an outcome on their own terms, but more than the original terms of their opponent; or that
   d. If they cannot agree on a cooperative outcome, they will both end up in a situation which is worse than either of the two cooperative outcomes.

In other words, agents form preferences and perceive a setting of strategies and outcomes that have both cooperative (to find a cooperative solution) and divisive (to get agreements on terms as close to one's own as possible) aspects.

The partisan manipulation of this structure for the sake of bargaining power already exemplifies the articulation of social realities by means of argumentation. Without constitutive and regulative norms a person who is willing to risk his life at war would not be a hero without the nationalistic constitution of heroism as an identity. Similarly, without the machinery of propaganda it would not be virtuous to hate and kill as part of the nation's coercive bargaining. These social realities are born out of the rather shallow manipulation of narratives and arguments of propaganda. The weakness of such knowledge production is propaganda's weak compatibility with other social norms and constitutive rules. Violence is not normally positively sanctioned, while the framing of people as subhuman contradicts much deeper structures relating to the social constitution of identities. According to Haste, at least the UK had tremendous problems in selling the realities of patriotism during the First World War, and Brewer suggests the same of US propaganda, while Berkhoff testifies to the same in the Soviet Union in the Second World War (Berkhoff, 2012, p. 277; Brewer, 2009, p. 88; Haste, 1995, p. 124). When rules of constitution of realities of partisan propaganda are contradictory to those that are central to our sense-making of our world, realities articulated by propaganda cannot be considered real as that would render some central elements of our interpretation of the world impossible, as we cannot make sense of the world by assuming both A and −A.

If we then think of ways in which a society could reinterpret/create social realities/interpretations that would be useful for peace to consider real, we will have to think of ways to emphasize the cooperative side of bargaining and de-emphasize the divisive element. This, as such, goes against the logic of successful bargaining if we already are players in a bargaining game. However, as outsiders, facilitators of peace, say, peace researchers, we can imagine realities that would be more useful for the social rationality (peace) of the bargainers, instead of having to be concerned about the partisan/individual benefits of the players. Furthermore, conflicting sides can mutually reconstitute a bargaining setting, for example, by mutually giving up some of the harmful ways of manipulation of enemy dependence on peace, our own independence or our own sensitivity toward the terms of peace.

This process of de-escalation is just like the process of escalation; it is dialectical and progressive. It cannot be grasped by looking at isolated causal relationships, as the rationality of one's moves can only be seen in the context of the dialectical process. In each moment in time when it is time for an agent to make a move toward giving up one of his/her methods of partisan manipulation in the bargaining setting, the agent is taking a leap of faith that can only be justified as rational within the context of the dialectical movement toward a more peaceful structure. If analyzed in isolation of the movement or in isolation of the dialectical relationship of reciprocal compromises, each move toward a more peaceful structure of interaction has to be seen as sub-rational. Yet in its right context it is the only rational thing bargainers can do to transform both structures of conflict and destruction and the discrepancy between individual and social rationality.

One way of operating outside the bargaining structure in order to transform it into something else, is by transforming preferences. In order to facilitate compromises bargainers need to have stronger preferences for a peaceful solution. The Harvard Project on Negotiation (PON) has emphasized the opportunities of mutual gains if bargainers focus on expanding the pie rather than focusing on dividing it up (Fisher & Ury, 1991). In a way, the project thus prescribes relational preferences, i.e. attitudes that favor the opponent's welfare. Secondly, the project suggests that in frequent, iterated interaction of the structure of bargaining, there are material benefits for developing cooperative relational preferences. Collaborators can produce more mutual gains if they focus on cooperation rather than on the divisive issue of how to divide up the fruits of cooperation: if negotiators focus on "expanding the pie", rather than dividing it, they will have a bigger pie to divide. If one then factors into the calculus, the transaction costs of bargaining, in many cases it becomes clear that a focus on mutual gains is in line with individual gains too. Yet, one cannot develop an image of a willingness to sacrifice individual gains for the sake of collective gains, because such a weak reputation would make others exploit one's unwillingness to bargain. It seems that in bargaining situations it would be difficult to prescribe strategies for one party only, as has been done in the Harvard project: bargaining and conflict resolution is a dialectical matter where softness pays, but only if it manages to provoke softness on the opposing side too.

In societies with frequent interactions, society creates norms that favor cooperative, relational preferences and emphasize the fact that a higher level of cooperation can indeed be achieved by focusing on the cooperative element of bargaining rather than on the divisive side of it. Such development of norms that promote social rationality can be explained even within the framework of individual rationality as Axelrod and Keohane have done within the model of the prisoner's dilemma (Axelrod, 1985, 1986; Keohane, 1986). When the frequency of interactions increases the social irrationality of hard bargaining leads to the failure of cooperation and peace more often and this eventually becomes intolerable to bargaining actors. As a consequence norms appear as rational remedies to promote "responsible bargaining"; this bargaining tackles the irrational manipulation of dependencies toward an agreement and sensitivities toward the terms of agreements. All this can be seen in the development of international norms. While during the lower level of globalization partisan values of patriotism and national selfishness were considered virtuous or at least a reality of world politics, today more cooperative and cosmopolitan values are becoming a reality in world politics. In international society a responsible cooperative attitude earns prestige and power (Li & Zheng, 2009; Nye, 1990; Yue, 2008), while an uncooperative attitude comes with a risk of isolation. A power that drives a hard bargain risks other states not wanting to cooperate with it, or they might even consider it a rogue state (Tanter, 1999). The status of China, for example, has often been judged on the basis of how cooperative (i.e. responsible) it is as a great power (Ikenberry, 2012; Nye, 2013; Shambaugh, 2013), while mutually beneficial trading with Iran or North Korea has often been limited due to the perception of these two nations' unwillingness to collaborate with nonproliferation regimes (Choi & Shali, 2013). Furthermore, in most of the countries peace and peace research is not treated with suspicion, and peace activists are not followed by the security bureaucracies of true democracies, even if this would be understandable from the partisan logic of rationality in bargaining. A country that mistreats peace activists, whistleblowers of a country's own military abuse, and investigates peaceful interaction with potential opponents and treats it as subversion, is normally not treated as a full democracy among other democracies. The treatment of Chelsey Manning and other whistleblowers in the United States has attracted a lot of negative publicity, and it has eroded the US status as a leading democracy in the world. Thus even if the structure of bargaining in itself encourages partisan behavior and even a partisan reputation and gives rise to partisan norms, heroism, toughness and to true believer cultures, the sense of social rationality has also given rise to socially rational norms. These norms reconstitute a new structure of interaction in which individual rationality is no longer as much opposed to social rationality.

While the development of international norms in support of social rationality in international society will take a lot of time, in individual peace negotiations social rationality can sometimes be negotiated rather quickly by bargainers who see the destructiveness of the bargaining structure. Such negotiation of the normative structure of conflict resolution could be called meta-bargaining. Despite the fact that a bargaining structure is very different from the structure of prisoners' dilemma, on the level of meta-bargaining conflicting parties often seek solutions where they both give up some destructive bargaining tactics in a reciprocal manner (as is done in the neo-liberal institutionalist solution in the iterated prisoners' dilemma). Learning about social conventions often happens quickly in peace processes and negotiations on the modalities of negotiations (meta-bargaining) often takes place before and all through peace negotiation processes. Partly in order to prevent partisan commitments to hard line stances and promises of unyieldingness to constituencies by negotiating parties, many negotiation processes take place in secrecy. The needs of such secrecy in the Aceh Peace pre-negotiation is well described by the main pre-negotiators, Juha Christensen and Farid Husain in the analyses by people close to the pre-negotiation process (Husain, 2007; Merikallio, 2005). Especially the early phases of peace pre-negotiations are almost always kept secret, and while there are many reasons for this, one is the fact that in secret negotiations parties are not able to make public promises that commit themselves to unyielding positions.

In some meta-negotiations conflicting parties make explicit commitments to considering violence on a disputed issue a matter of law enforcement and thereby give up the option of legitimizing coercive moves in bargaining as something unavoidable, mechanistically caused, and outside the regulation of normal laws on violence. In West Kalimantan, for example, the ethnic leaders of the conflicting ethnicities made a public declaration where they gave their authoritative interpretation about the fact that violence between their ethnic groups is not an ethnic matter, but a matter of law enforcement. In this way they made it impossible for individuals in the conflicting ethnic groups to legitimize their violence that aimed at gaining partisan bargaining leverage (see Pontianak Declaration of the West Kalimantan Ethnic Communication Forum, Annex 2, in Kivimäki, 2012a).

Progress in the creation of relational values that counteract hate-propaganda, give normative side payments for socially rational strategies and emphasize the value of non-violence as something socially rational, follows the logic of interaction rather than the logic of one-directional causality. In one-directional causal analysis my transformation of preferences to more relational preferences simply has the effect of reducing my bargaining leverage as revealed above. However, progress can only be achieved by modeling progress within an inter-actionalist framework. In such framework the analysis of violent processes is interactive in a way that my violence constitutes the legitimacy of my opponent's violence, which again legitimizes my violence and causes the escalation in the relationship. Similarly, my concessions with regard to relational preferences have to be negotiated as part of my opponent's similar concessions. De-escalation, just like escalation, has an interactive shape and one-directional causal thinking will not find ways to produce outcomes one wishes to produce. From the point of view of players in the de-escalation game, progress is constituted by small leaps of faith that are performed in turns.

The process of transformation of problematic structures of bargaining into more socially rational structures could be seen as starting from a pure logic of self-interest and individual rationality as explained by Axelrod and Keohane (Axelrod, 1985, 1986; Keohane, 1986).

At this early stage, the transformation of socially irrational bargaining structures, in which partisan manipulation of one's preferences and interpretations makes reaching agreements difficult, is simply a rational adaptation to a changed external situation, mainly to the increased frequency of interaction. At this stage there is no need to assume that interaction changes preferences or identities: the increase of the frequency of interaction is sufficient to explain the evolution of norms that externally affect individual preferences by creating social pressures against behavior that goes against socially rational norms. Thus, so far pragmatic peace research can still follow the theorists of neo-liberal institutionalism and theorists of regimes who claim that rational self-interest is the foundation of transformations of social structures into a more socially rational direction. However, through the interactive logic of this transformation, through leaps of trust, the process of transformation eventually changes both preferences and identities. Eventually cooperative moves change identities and constant social rationality in a society of several actors constitutes social intentionality (Ruggie, 1998) or a we-intention (Tuomela, 2005; Tuomela & Miller, 1985) and eventually the merging of the several collective actors into a single collective actor. To deny this would be inconsistent with the realization that in world politics agencies are collective and instead of individual preferences conflicts are about clashes of tribal, national, transnational (religious) or regional interests.

While individual rationality considerations might be the origin of social transformations from belligerent structures of bargaining into structures that focus more on common interests, eventually relational preferences become internalized and socialized and as a result larger collective identities such as families, clans, city states, nation-states and regions such as the EU emerge (Booth & Wheeler, 2008; Kratochwil, 1989; Wendt, 1998). While individual identities still exist in various issue areas, in security issues historical evidence suggests that norms also affect preferences and identities by transforming individual security preferences into family or clan preferences, which then eventually become the foundation of new "individual, partisan clan/ family rationality" in inter-clan/family security interaction, which then again transforms into state preferences and identities.

Fukuyama, Tilly, Elias, and Pinker have traced this process empirically in a very convincing manner (Elias, 1982; Fukuyama, 2011; Pinker, 2011; Tilly, 1990). While in the beginning the individual's choice to belong to a larger security unit could be seen as a rational individual choice and even if the preference for larger security units originated in the logic of fear and in the fact that larger units could be stronger against smaller security actors, it is historically undeniable that larger security communities will eventually have to win the loyalty of their members. Eventually children will be born into a system of expectations and meanings where collective security units are taken to be as given as the units whose security one needs to be concerned with. To believe in national interests and national agency in security affairs and yet deny the fact that interaction and norms transform preferences and identities, as many realists do, does not make sense as the existence of national identities and preferences logically requires that such identities could have emerged from smaller security units. National identities and interests/preferences necessarily require that somehow interaction and the emergence of norms have transformed individual preferences through clan, city state or other collective preferences and identities into national identities and preferences. Without the possibility of such a fundamental transformation from individual to social preferences and identities national interests could not have been formed.

Despite the fact that Europe is still a union of states and that each state still has its own identity, in security issues Europe is approaching a stage where one could be talking about the merging of previously belligerent agents. Clearly Germany and France disagree on security issues, such as participation in the military operation in Libya in 2011, but when it comes to internal European security, EU members no longer act as separate bargaining agents. To say that Sweden will soon attack Finland because it has a more powerful army and because it could benefit from the natural resources Finland has, is almost as ridiculous as saying that Stockholm will soon attack Gothenburg. When it comes to ice hockey or benefits in Swedish regional policies it is quite clear that Gothenburg and Stockholm are still very much separate bargaining agents, and yet in security issues Gothenburg and Stockholm or Finland, and Sweden are not separate in a way that they could consider war imaginable. The same is true, albeit to varying degrees, for most EU countries, even for former enemies.

While this presentation has used the neo-liberal institutionalist models of Axelrod and Keohane in the description of the process from individual to collective identity, it is clear that the metaphor of meta-bargaining better describes the process. It is true that Gothenburg and Stockholm are now part of a common security identity, but it is also true that Stockholm is the capital city of the nation, while Gothenburg is not. Thus, the process of formation of relational preferences, common interests and common identity is relevant to the terms of common agency: those that have a better bargaining position tend to get their way in the definition of the common interest, and the identity of the common agency. Thus the process, while containing some elements of overcoming a prisoner's dilemma type of security problems, is indeed a process of meta-bargaining, where often niceness and cooperative attitude is not useful for one's bargaining power, no matter how useful it is for the common interests, and the common agency.

To sum up how bargaining structure changes as a result of action by bargainers, we will be able to establish a tentative idea of the levels of peaceful transformation. In order to escape a bargaining setting that puts individual rationality and security at odds with social rationality and peace:

1. Bargainers need to see the interactive, dialectical totality of their relationship, and they have to realize the symmetry of their situation, to appreciate the fact that only their own aggression or concession can legitimize aggression or concession of their opposing bargainers. Once bargainers understand this;
2. Bargainers have to establish rules against the partisan manipulation of the bargaining setting.
3. Then they will have to find ways for each to reciprocally increase positive relational preferences and focus on "getting to yes" rather than on the logic of relative gains.
4. Through positive relational preferences, bargainers need to establish commonness in preferences, in intention, and in collective maximization of utility.

5. Finally, bargainers can establish collective agency in issues of security and thus make security common and move from partisan security to peace.

All of these moves, while intentional on the individual or social levels, are geared by the frequency and regularity of interaction, which makes the conflict between individual and social rationality costly. In each of these transformations the main unit of action is not a single actor but at least two interacting opposed actors within a dialectical structure, where one's move becomes meaningful only once it is reciprocated. However, while it is possible to imagine a reinterpretation of the violent bargaining situation by two parties of a specific conflict on the basis of symbolic interactionalism, we will have to dig deeper into the problematics of social constructs before we can think of broad peaceful transformation of social structures.

5.3. Reconstruction of other Conflict Situations

While bargaining is a very common structure within which peaceful actors act in a belligerent manner, the understanding of conflicts also requires the explanation of behavior which is intentionally belligerent. Such understanding is based on the revelation of the meanings, knowledge and interpretations that make the violent act intelligible. Without such an understanding we cannot know if a fighter committed a violent act by accident, as revenge, as a ritual act or as an effort to articulate his interpretation of justice (or whether the actor of the deed was a fighter or something else and whether the act was indeed violence or a ritual, a means of education or something else). In some cases, violence is instrumental and thus its understanding can be understood through the understanding of the aims that violence is used for. Violence can be an instrument for coercive bargaining, but it can also be a physical defense (repelling invasion, for example), or offence, as in robberies (a criminal act or robbery of territory, for example).

However, violence is often also communication or designed to articulate new social realities. Donald Horowitz has suggested that in deadly ethnic riots murders can become a form of violent demonstrative communication, in some cases they might be the only means available or might even be the most desirable mode of communication (Horowitz, 2003). Frustrated communities demonstrate their frustration by means of violence, while landlords might also demonstrate their superiority over their subjects by using violence (and getting away with it) against them. I. William Zartman and Maureen Berman have hinted that violence is also communication in coercive bargaining situations where conflicting sides demonstrate their commitment to their preferred terms of peace and their dependence on a negotiated outcome by violent means. Before they have experienced enough "mutual hurt" and before the conflict has ripened into resolution they will keep on demonstrating through violence (Zartman & Berman, 1982).

In West Kalimantan the migrant community that was pressured hard to adopt the local norms and habits tried to communicate their rejection of the local norms by violent means, and in the end also eradicate the local norms, as the idea was to bully the locals into not reacting to the violations of their norms. A peacemaker who is able to understand the function of violence in such a social situation can redirect the conflict path to less violent futures if she/he manages to find alternative ways to articulate the same things that violence articulates in this situation. In West Kalimantan the local population reacted to the migrant articulations by simply "asking" the "visitors" to leave the district. Since "migrants" were naturally unwilling to leave their homes, the local militias used violence and terror to expel them, thereby "proving" that they were in a position, as hosts, to require the "visitors" to leave. In this case violence was used to create the agency of locals and visitors/migrants, even if such a construct would otherwise have been difficult to sustain given that many of the "visitors" had stayed in the territory for generations, and since they were actually from the same country (Indonesia), only from another island. The construct was short-lived, though, as after the terror and violence, many people from the migrant community started demanding to be allowed to return to their homes (or at least to be allowed to sell them), and the need for the rearticulation of agency rose from time to time. The way to redirect the path away from conflict in West

Kalimantan was the establishment of a communication forum between ethnic leaders, who could then articulate their claims and debate them in a negotiation process under the Vice President of Indonesia. Violence lost its role in the articulation of positions as verbal argumentation took its place (Kivimäki, 2012a).

A very similar logic can be seen in maritime territorial disputes where claimant states have sent fishermen or oceanic research teams to disputed areas or have built a military or tourism infrastructure there to demonstrate their exercise of sovereignty. While this is not physical violence, it is considered violation of the sovereignty of other claimants, and it is often met with physical violence. If the other claimants do not react to the violations of their sovereignty, this practice constitutes a reality where their claim to sovereignty in this area is less credible and thus less existent. Thus violence (the arrest of the fishermen, or even the sinking of ships, the destruction of tourism infrastructure, airstrips, etc.) by other claimants is a symbolic act in the argument for sovereignty, and a necessary undertaking to counter the social reality that the first country's deed would constitute. Violent acts in many maritime territorial conflicts, certainly in the Sino-Vietnamese conflict in 1974, and in 1995, as well as between Malaysia and the Philippines in 1995 can certainly be made understandable by understanding violence as a construction of social realities or as communication (Kivimäki, 2002; Lo, 1989). This understanding can also be used for the prevention of violence. United Nations Convention on the Law of the Seas (UNCLOS) from 1982 addresses the problem of conflict escalation inherent in sovereignty articulation as it allows states to legally protest to the Secretariat of UNCLOS the illegal use of their territory by other states. This means that if another claimant nation protects its fishermen in a disputed area a nation does not need to send its own navy and risk war to demonstrate its claim and can prevent the emergence of a de facto situation where the claimant nation has an unchallenged sovereignty over the disputed territory. The understanding of the symbolic meaning of a violent act allows the UN agreement to offer other, non-violent means of doing the same thing belligerent nations do with violence.

While the bigger picture of many conflicts can be captured by the logic of coercive bargaining, many violent incidents can still be best understood as a communication or demonstration of social constitutions. Violence against wives of enemies can be performed as a way to humiliate or emasculate the enemy and demonstrate one's superiority, while individual violence can be seen as enacting one's masculinity (Myrttinen, 2010). The fact that at least 90% of fighters in all conflicts are men (Horowitz, 2003) clearly demonstrates the need to understand the ways in which conflicts offer opportunities for young men to demonstrate and enact their masculinities. This understanding leads peacemakers to consider ways of transforming the construction of masculinity (Myrttinen, 2010; Porter, 2013) or ways of channeling masculinity into less violent expressions (Kivimäki, 2012a). The way in which, for example, Japanese or North European males have moved away from machismo toward greater sensitivity offers hope for changes in masculinity: since masculinity has been constructed it can also be transformed. The example of West Kalimantan again shows that competitiveness, heroism and many other characteristics that many cultures associate with masculinity can be demonstrated in non-violent ways, for example in many sports, and thus the channeling of masculinity (without transforming it) also works for the transformation of conflict structures. In West Kalimantan, villages with a volleyball court in a central place affords non-violent modes of enacting somewhat traditional masculinities, and thus redirects young men from violence to sports achievements (Kivimäki, 2012a).

In many cases wars that on the macro level can be modeled as coercive bargaining, are marred on the micro level by acts that communicate interpretations and articulate realities that manipulate the bargaining structure. Heroic violence demonstrates the agent's (masculine) insensitivity in relation to peace (lack of fear, Collins, 2008), while sadistic episodes of violence against the enemy often articulate the special conditions of the warfare (and underline that normal norms against violence do not apply) or patriotic hatred of the enemy (Berkhoff, 2012; Horowitz, 2003). Tackling these types of micro level incidents of violence would on the one hand require an understanding of the function of violence, but also a commitment on the part of the conflicting parties to the de-escalation of the partisan manipulation of the bargaining structure. Men will not stop being heroic in wars until there is a mutual, collective process in the broad consensus (a new masculine identity) against violent heroism; until violent heroism stops being a masculine virtue. In a structure where bargainers interact sufficiently, frequent violent heroism becomes dysfunctional and thus knowledge about the virtues of heroism become unpractical, a false consciousness to borrow from Marx.

Finally, violence in wars can be symbolic on the macro level as conflicting parties bargain about the terms of peace. This kind of structure of violence could be called violent meta-bargaining. Violence can be "acting as if a certain construct of peaceful reality was real" if, for example, a superpower or a colonial master enforces its norms and calls it police action and considers itself a world police. An example of this is the two police actions by the Netherlands during Indonesia's war of independence, 1945–1949. In this war the colonial master re-imposed it colonial order after the collapse of Japan in the Second World War. The Netherlands wanted to emphasize that the colonial norms were in force, and that Indonesian independence-minded people were just violent exceptions to the colonial rule. Thus, the Dutch military actions were called police actions (Kahin, 1952). It would not be difficult to find a parallel from the level of hegemonic global governance. This type of demonstrative violence is like two sporting teams who, however, instead of both playing baseball (negotiation), try to impose their own interpretation of what game they are playing. When one team imposes on an interpretation according to which two teams are playing baseball, but one insists it is playing football, it is clear that the reconstruction of the conflicting meanings is difficult, just as it is clear that the nature of the conflict is confusing.

Chapter 6
Social Construction of Structures of Peace and Conflict

Social constructivism is related to Interpretationism. However, instead of just assuming that human or states' action can only be understood if the world according to those whom we want to understand can be reconstructed, social constructivists say that interpretations do not just make action understandable, but they constitute social realities. Thus, social constructivism, at its core, is a belief according to which social realities are constructed in social interaction. They exist only because the actors in the society believe they are real. Social constructs could be normative (moral rules, traffic rules, norms, etc.) or constitutive (states, ethnic groups, action categories, such as revenge, acts of aggression, or outcomes of interaction, such as capitulation, a goal in football or mediation). Even though social realities did not exist if people or states or other actors did not imagine them, this does not make these realities less real. They can have very material consequences (imagine being labeled a terrorist, it would have terrible consequences), and they might be related to material realities: a member of an ethnic group could claim that her skin color is objective and material as a reality, but the groupness of people with certain material characteristics is created in the imagination of people. Thus, left-handed

(Continued)

> *(Continued)*
>
> people are not a group in conflicts, and yet there is material similarity in people who are left-handed. Social constructs could result in practices, linguistic forms, or institutions that make them look more material and "natural" and they can cause material changes.
>
> In peace research and especially in international studies literature constructivism is often associated with research that takes identities, norms and ideas seriously. One could say that identities, norms and ideas are typically social constructs, and if one shies away from factors in conflict reality that are clearly social, one would obviously not emphasize identities or norms. However, the treatment of norms or identities does not make research constructivist. It would be possible (stupid, but possible) to study identities as causal determinants or natural material realities, and thus focusing on them does not make a study constructivist.

One should not think that classical pragmatists do not recognize the difference between "water" and a "nation-state" as realities. In fact they did note such differences and theorized social structures in a competent manner. Dewey himself has even been read as a constructivist (Neubert, 2009). Yet the fact that systematic thinking about what the difference between social and material structures means for the social sciences was only born with the emergence of constructivism, meaning that the systematic thinking of social facts and social structures is something we will have to incorporate into our pragmatist peace research. In this way the benefits available from investigation that focuses specifically on realities of social origin can be gained. This is the intention with this chapter.

6.1. Social Constitution of Conflict Realities

When we put together many interpretations around us including interpretations about ourselves, we will be able to reconstruct a world of social structures that individuals perceive rather in the same way as they perceive the material world. States are creations of interpretations of all people; they survive and are reproduced by language, practices and material formations that are based on the common interpretation of their existence. As such they appear to individuals as external realities in a rather similar manner as material realities do: anyone who tries to ignore the reality of states will be confronted by them when trying to walk, for instance, from Finland to Russia. Yet states and other social realities are institutional facts, as John Searle points out, which would not exist without our knowledge of them. For Searle, the football reality of "offside" is a good example of an institutional fact, but we could also consider institutional facts, terrorism, states and ethnicity, which would not exist as political facts in conflict realities without our knowledge of and conventions about them (Searle, 1976).

In fact, almost all elements of conflict structures and realities of peacemaking are socially constructed. Conflicting parties in wars are social constructs: there is nothing given or natural about Christians being a collective agent in the conflict in Maluku 1999–2000, nor about states like Finland being an agent in the Winter War of 1939–1940. Some would have liked to consider the local Ambonese a collective agent in Maluku, while others would have liked to see national agency as a "false consciousness" and interpret social classes rather than states as relevant agents in the Winter War. Similarly, most war objectives are socially created. What is sovereignty over a given territory if not a social convention, and the same is true even for such a materially sounding objective as ownership of natural resources. Ownership of a plot of land gives, according to conventions, the right to its exclusive utilization, within certain limits. There might be a convention offering passers-by to pick berries or mushrooms from private forest properties, while in some cases ancient paths or logistics oblige the plot owner to allow the crossing of her/his land. War strategies clearly, too, have social meanings: Without the convention of revenge it would not be possible get even with one's enemies, while protection of civilians, too, is a strategic option that cannot be imagined outside the social convention that establishes the protection of civilians as an act.

6.2. Implications of the Social Constitution of Social Realities on Peacemaking

For pragmatists the interesting thing about constructivism is the strategic notion that changing social structures is fundamentally different from the changing of material realities. Constructivism is interesting for pragmatists only to the extent it can guide them to more freedom to change the world. There is one strategic benefit in peacemaking with the realization that when we acknowledge that some conflict realities are socially created this gives us greater options in transforming them. This benefit is related to the difference in the relationship between knowledge and reality when dealing with material and social realities. When dealing with material structures, knowing is an active, intentional strategy to adapt to external realities. Knowledge is something that reveals that amulets or spells do not prevent bullets from penetrating the body of warriors, as some of the Dayak warriors in Indonesia's West Kalimantan used to believe. Concepts and theories are there to prevent us from being surprised by unexpected events when we interact with the external reality and to put us on top of things when we try to change the world. In this idea of knowledge, truth and theories are instrumental.

However, this idea changes when dealing with social realities. The fact that social structures are a product of the way in which we think, changes our concept of truth and theory. Certainly, things are still real to us through our interests and purposes, and not in terms of some simple correspondence that can necessarily be verified by means of pure sense data. Pragmatists are still between relativists who think that one interpretation is as good as another, and absolutists think that an interpretation of the world can be judged by its empirical correspondence with reality. For the pragmatist, reality offers an element in the judgment of our theories and truth claims, but not in a correspondence sense. Instead, reality offers one element and our purposes another element in the judgment of truth claims.

However, material reality out there is real in the sense that it affects us through our purposes: if we want to avoid being killed in a war, we will have to avoid bullets and explosions. Social realities, at the same time, are not really "out there", but rather inside our consciousness. We could also judge knowledge about social realities from the perspective of its practicality. Then the question is "Is it practical for us to consider money/states/ethnic agency/hegemonic leadership as real?" It would not be possible in any absolute sense to consider states as real or unreal, nor would it be correct to say that any decision to consider states real or not would not rebound on us by blocking some of our opportunities or offering others. Again, the useful question is not to ask whether a sentence claims to be the truth, but what we should consider to be real. Yet "what we should consider real" is not really the same question when dealing with social and material realities. Knowledge about social realities that we create in our minds differs from knowledge about material realities since not believing in social realities simply makes them disappear, while refusal to believe in the hardness of a bullet and a belief in the protective force of amulets against bullets does not change the fact that bullets kill. While the pragmatic knowledge about material realities considers whether material realities will be useful for us if we consider them to be of a certain kind (say, we consider the hardness of a bullet as real), pragmatic knowledge about social realities considers whether it is useful for us to "articulate realities" or "believe something into being". To use Searle's examples of social constructs, or as he calls them, institutional facts, we should consider if football as a game becomes more interesting with the articulation of offside into being, and this is how we judge knowledge about social realities too. This has a strategic relevance for pragmatist peace research: this theory of knowledge yields prescriptions on how we can prevent violence. In principle, while knowledge about material realities helps us adjust to them, knowledge about social realities transforms (Bhaskar, 1997) them and sometimes creates or destroys them (Thurlow & Helms Mills, 2009). When after the Westphalian peace in 1648 people in Europe stopped seeing feudal entities,[1] city states, clans and families as a foundation of political agency, and started

---

[1] Historically this is naturally a simplification, as is shown by Krasner and Osiander (Krasner, 2001; Osiander, 2001).

seeing states as political agents, a new political reality of state agency was created and an old political reality of feudal agency in politics was destroyed. It is important to realize that social realities are in essence like this, and thus whatever has been constructed, can be transformed (Porter, 2013).

Thus social realities are different from material ones and they can be transformed in a different way than material realities. Understanding this gives the peacemaker some new tools for conflict prevention. However, there are at least three things that peace research has to deal with, that limit the opportunities offered by the difference between social and material structures. While it is important for a peacemaker to understand the transformative power of political reinterpretations and critical sense-making, it is also important to know the limits (limits that can also be transformed) of transformation. To make peace requires both an understanding of the socially constructed tools with which one can operate in a conflict situation and of socially constructed limits and restrictions, some of which can possibly be transformed and some which have to be seen as "realities."

The first of the limits is related to the *rejection of idealism and naiveties*. While the articulation of new social realities is possible for a collective, it may not be possible for individual peacemakers. There is a difference between how knowledge about material and social realities offers us opportunities for the transformation of conflict structures. This difference is related to the issue of individual and inter-subjective knowledge. While judgment with regard to knowledge about material realities is similar for individuals and societies (if an individual should consider a stone wall hard, so should a whole society), the same is not true for social realities. Suppose, for example, that our convention of the value of money had created great misery to humankind and our analysis would be that we would be better off without the invention of money. In such a situation the society in question should simply not consider money as real. This would end any further misery that an economic system based on money brings to humanity. However, if only one individual discovered the misery that money causes, and refused to consider that money was real, while all others acted as if it was real, that one person would have problems with his landlord, and he would have difficulties in a grocery store. Thus, an individual critique of knowledge about social realities is not always possible. This is strategically and practically important as it means that the strategy of producing knowledge for peace practitioners about social structures needs to take this into account. In some cases, individuals can initiate a reinterpretation of social structures, such as a leader that declares certain media interventions to be security threats and thus moves parts of publicity into the "realm of security," (Wæver, 1995) or when the head of a powerful nation interprets world politics as a battle between totalitarian powers and the free world. But even in these cases interpretations become social reality only through their acceptance among their audience. If other world leaders, businessmen and people had thought that the idea of terrorism as the main challenge to current security was a joke, while continuing to believe that famine, which kills 10,000 times more people than international terrorism (Kivimäki, 2003c, p. 6), was the main threat, the post-9/11 world would look very different. Also if a leader (or even better, a plumber from a small, distant, rural village) interprets the media as a security issue in an established democracy where media freedom has been among the values security policy tries to protect, this would not change social realities, as collective interpretations would not change. Thus changing social realities in individual interpretations is naive idealism.

We need to define who "we" is when we consider the question of whether we should consider something socially constructed as real. On the one hand, we need to be realistic about social conventions, while at the same time we will have to be careful not to unnecessarily help reproduce realities that are harmful for peace. Neville Chamberlain at the 1938 Munich Conference could not have created a reality of a peaceful Germany all by himself by simply believing in the words and promises of Adolf Hitler, while at the same time he should have worked toward strengthening the sanctity of the convention of promises in world politics. An individualist idealist approach to knowledge about social realities is not useful — my rejection of a social reality does not destroy the social construct, it would only give justification to a cynical realism that ignores the fluidity of social structures, and considers only the commitment to selfish material gain realistic (Humpreys, 2013). At the same time, of course, cynical political realism is not pragmatic either as it reproduces all the harmful and dangerous conventions and social realities of "real politik". Thus, when the WE is just the British, we should not consider a process of de-escalation with Hitler's Germany to be real or possible. However, when the WE is both we British and Hitler's Germany, it would be foolish not to realize the potential of genuine preventive peacemaking in Munich. Events after the Munich Agreement killed 5% of Germans, and made Hitler so desperate that he committed suicide, and thus avoiding war would have been useful for Germany and Hitler too. In the absence of the availability of the option of fooling the naive UK Prime Minister, he could have accepted measures that could have avoided war. To be sure that neither side deceives, such a potential for peacemaking should only have been realized by adding measures that verify and enforce the pacific consensus.

The fact that social meanings and structures are social, not individual, (and hence we need to consider the "we" when considering what should WE consider as real) means more than just the fact that idealism will not be practical. Social constructs also have their own resistance against individual efforts to articulate alternative constructs. Personal structures of meanings that are independent of socially created meanings are diagnosed as mental illness, where our realities fail to interact with the realities that all others in the society recognize. In this way the construction of mental illness has a role in protecting hegemonic social constructs as sane and healthy and isolating alternative constructs as something the society does not need to take seriously. As in the case of marginalization of individual interpretations of social realities by categories of mental illness, it is also clear that social realities sometimes protect themselves against transformation. And the construction of "mental illness" is not the only way in which social constructs protect themselves. Certain alternative interpretations are treacherous, while some should not be considered true belief. A Dayak who tried to promote solidarity toward the suffering Madurese in West Kalimantan, could be "expelled" from the Dayak community for not being true to his roots. Presidential candidates in the US during the Cold War who were "soft on Communism" (and thus articulated realities outside of the Cold War reality) did not stand a chance in elections. Thus, while social constructs that are there before us constrain our consciousness, and create the "us" (and also create the options for us), they sometimes also protect themselves from our transformative actions.

The second limitation to the transformation of socially created conflict realities could be called *structural limitation*. The fact that social structures are just in our heads does not mean that constructivism would not add anything to symbolic interactionalism. We should not think that peace actors can without problem change conflict realities by reinterpreting them. While social structures are more fluid than material realities, since their existence is dependent on our knowledge of them, one should not think that social structures could be created simply by negotiating interpretations. Since in interpretations we are actually talking about meanings that are the tools for our understanding of the external world, and which already existed before our birth, our consciousness is conditioned by, but also facilitated by, already existing interpretations. These interpretations are sedimented in our language and knowledge, which we should be using to make peace (Foucault, 1994). We are born to meanings with which we make sense of the world outside us and ourselves, so, instead of believing in our voluntary ability to create and constitute social structures, we should take a look at how existing social structures limit, but also facilitate, our ability to transform, rather than create, social structures of war and peace (Bhaskar, 1989, 1997).

Given the fact that peacemakers are born already within social structures, in order to be on top of things in peacemaking, actors need to have some kind of a self-understanding about how one's understanding of the conflict situation and preferences are constructed and formed by the historical interaction between interpreting actors (such as President Truman framing world politics as a battle between the free world and totalitarianism), the logic of inter-subjective interaction (such as the logic of bargaining within US foreign policy bureaucracy and among world leaders), social structures (such as the conventions of diplomatic language or the setting in which only nuclear powers can have a veto in the UN Security Council) and material realities (the reality of nuclear weapons or the material constitution of capitalism). The fact that social constructs are only in people's heads does not mean that it would be possible for people always to challenge some constructs that are so central to their understanding of the world.

In addition to the fact that we are born into a structure of meanings, concepts, language, practices and other social structures peacemakers might have positional limitations to their transformation of conflicts. Peace actors can be situated in the social structure in a place where they cannot challenge certain constructs. A German pope, for example, cannot fully address the antagonistic constructs that plague the relations between Muslims and the West, due to the fact that the history of German holocaust prevents him from going against constructs that are useful for the position of the Jews in Palestine. If he does he will be categorized as anti-Semitic or at least given a history lesson.

There is also a limitation to our ability to transform conflict structures that could be called the *rejection of voluntarism*. In addition to the social structures being there before us, "us" (the actors in peace and war) are defined in the existing structures of meanings before we enter the scene. Nations, citizen, women, or Dayaks as actors would not be possible, and the national interests, private interests or ethnic loyalty would not be possible without the existence of the social realities that create "the private", ethnicity, the nation, or gender. The historical social constitution of "the self" and the "interest" interfere in our ideas that were developed in the chapter that criticized determinism. Since social structures are there to be transformed by human, national, ethnic or any other agency, it would be foolish to think that the realization that social structures that constituted us before we were born returns us to determinism. Yet we will have to consider agency in peacemaking as something less than a purely voluntaristic reinterpretation of social realities. Peace actors, and their consciousness are part of a historical process and structure, and yet they are the driving force of future processes and social structures. What genuine agency in the already created structure of meanings requires, though, is that the decision to consider or not to consider something as real requires more than the reflection of one's interests, it also requires a reflection of one's motives and agency as part of a historically conditioned setting.

There are also *material limitations* to what we can achieve in our effort to transform social structures of conflict. To construct cosmopolitan solidarity, or constitute global citizenship or common humanity has required interaction and the physical ability to communicate globally. Otherwise integrating one's own preferences and aims into the preferences and aims of people in far-away countries would not seem useful. The President of the US can, in his speeches, create realities, frame something as security, and thereby create new rules for interaction in the issue area that he defines as a security issue, while a resource-less single mother in Liberia cannot make others treat as security issues even the things that most clearly threaten her life or the lives of thousands of poor people. The difference in material resources and institutionalized social structures that make someone a president and someone else a political non-entity — in our example the Liberian single-mother of five and the President of the US — clearly affects the way in which others are forced to consider their framings as real, and thus the material resources at their disposal do affect their abilities to transform social constructs.

To work constructively for peace despite the limitations given above will require reflection on the categories and conceptions that one is born with in terms of their usefulness for peace and then tackling those that are not useful one by one. To some extent this work might be individualistic in the sense that for my understanding of a conflict situation I will need to self-reflect on the vantage points and the histories and positions that my thinking about the conflict comes from. One needs to be self-reflexive about one's own presuppositions and one's impact on the representation of particular events. But self-reflection is needed also for the collective "self". While it is not possible to study any conflicts without engaging the social meanings of language and theoretical constructs that scholars mobilize in making sense of a situation, one should also be open to a reflexive interaction between experiences of the conflict and the theoretical presuppositions that give meaning to it (Gadamer, 1989). Here pragmatic thinking of what kind of understanding works to aid peace leads to a process of reflection. Theories and concepts that make sense of the conflict in a way that enable peacemaking should survive, while those concepts and theories that represent "false consciousness" in the sense that they do not facilitate knowledge and understanding that could be conducive for peace should be criticized. While all of this is already understood by classical pragmatists, the idea of social construction adds one element to this reflection. If theories and meanings reflect the bargaining process where bargaining power plays a role then power is traceable also in the concepts and theories that make sense of and constitute our world (Foucault, 1994). While the definition of the "we" is important in the judgment of what is pragmatic to consider as real in the context of social realities, the same "we"-specificity can be found in our social constructs. The agents that have most bargaining leverage (US Presidents rather than Liberian single mothers) are those whose practicality has survived in the process of bargaining interpretations of the world. This offers pragmatist peace research opportunities to critically analyze our hegemonic understanding of the social realities that sometimes constitute conflict realities (Bieler & Morton, 2001; Cafruny, 1990; Femia, 1981). In some cases, the power relationships that created the concepts and theories we use to make sense of conflict realities no longer exist, and then we can deconstruct such realities in our reflexive search for practical approaches to conflicts and peace. Furthermore, the constructivist perspective offers opportunities for a democratic critique of the social constructs that structure our conflict realities. Perhaps our sense-making reflects practicalities that are highly elitist, and thus we could challenge such theoretical constructs that give sense to conflict realities by using the norm of democracy as our normative bargaining leverage in our effort to renegotiate social realities of conflict.

Finally, in some cases dominant, undemocratic constructs (perhaps even such that reflect power realities that no longer exist) have been naturalized so that they are treated as real in the same way as water and the hardness of a bullet are real. This treating of social constructs as natural, material realities that can be changed, as social constructs can, is obviously problematic as it closes our eyes to the opportunities we might have to transform conflict realities into peaceful ones, as we fail to realize the availability of transformation through changing our thinking. We cannot change the hardness of a stone by thinking differently, and so, if we think of the political agency of the Dayak ethnic group as natural we cannot realize the potential offered for peace by emphasizing Indonesianness as a source of political agency instead of one's own ethnic origin. In such cases the revelation of how these constructs are created already reveals opportunities for transformation of belligerent, or structurally violent elitist structures into more democratic ones.

If conflict structures are thus transformed and peaceful realities constructed in the consciousness of people, and if these realities are "carried" and reproduced by our social practices, language and institutions then practical peace research seems to have two important missions. On the one hand, it needs to reveal the opportunities for transformation by showing how conflict structures are constituted in constructs that only serve some or no longer serve anybody (but simply stay alive in our language because of the fact that we do not reveal and criticize them) or in constructs that we no longer realize we are in control of (because we think of them as natural). The critical task of revealing our opportunities of imagining realities alternative to the conflict realities is the negative side of practical peace research. It is emancipated from the necessity of conflict structures but does not build new peaceful structures. The other mission of practical peace research would then be positive. It is to build the knowledge for the transformation of social realities into more peaceful ones. It is to reveal what in a current social and material reality needs to be done to achieve progress in peaceful development. On the one hand, the second mission is about the logic of how social realities are created (how to define practicality of knowledge when knowledge becomes reality-creating politics) and on the other it is about what realities the current situation would require to become more peaceful.

The first of these two missions will have to use tools we can find for a neo-pragmatic peace approach from the critical security studies tradition. The second will need some critical social science tools that reveal something about the principles needed for a more democratic and more reflexive and self-conscious construction of social realities. But it also requires analysis of the ways in which the terms of security and peace are bargained and the characteristics of the current stage of development in violence and peace. What are the main challenges and what kinds of steps can be taken in this specific moment in the history of violence and peace? These will be the topics of the last two chapters. The next chapter, Critical Peace Research, will criticize existing constructs that constitute the foundation of conflict structures today. The final chapter of this book will then present alternatives on how and what kind of social structures should be created to allow progress in peaceful human interaction.

Chapter 7
Critical Approaches and Peace

Critical approaches in peace research are essentially approaches that reveal social constructs that people treat as given, natural or materially constituted. For example, people who feel that they need to be loyal to their Malay leader since they are themselves Malay naturalize the socially constructed reality of Malay agency in a conflict. They feel that their Malayness is materially constituted, perhaps it can be seen in the color of their skin, or in the shape of their noses, but they fail to understand that the groupness of their Malay ethnicity is dependent on their collective imagination. In a community of Malays where the idea of natural groupness is a hegemonic interpretation, a critical approach to peace research could try to reveal the social origin of the groupness of the Malays if it seemed that ethnic loyalties were not conducive to peace in the area where Malays lived. In this way a critical approach allows people to "take into their own hands" realities they have considered natural and given, and in this sense critical research is emancipatory.

A critical approach follows logically from social constructivism. If we consider that social realities are constructed in social practices and collective interpretations, and we see violent social realities that people fail to transform due to their belief that these realities are somehow natural and given, it is somehow understandable that social constructivists should engage in critical research, too.

(Continued)

> (*Continued*)
>
> In peace research and international studies critical approaches are often associated with various kinds of criticism of existing orders, capitalism, and hegemonic agents. Associations are also made with all kinds of often leftist projects which aim to change material realities in accordance with ideologies that are often left-leaning. This practice artificially associates an emancipatory scholarly approach with ideologies that it does not necessarily have anything to do with. By pretending that there was a natural association between anti-capitalist ideologies and denaturalization, it rules out emancipatory opportunities from alternative ideological standpoints. This is dishonest and self-contradictory for critical scholars.

If social constructs are realities that people articulate in their interpretations of the world and create and reproduce in their practices and in their language, and if the relevance of this for pragmatist peace research was only found a few decades ago, it is understandable that there are belligerent and violent social realities that people have grown used to treating as if they were somehow materially given and natural. Our stereotypical understanding of masculinity, for example, can push male conflicting parties to unpractical ways of addressing the conflict reality in a "manly manner" by emphasizing power and unyieldingness. If these men do not realize that there is a possibility for a collective reinterpretation of the masculine identity and a masculine way of making compromises and understanding opposing opinions, these men are likely to lose peaceful opportunities simply because they are men (in a stereotypical sense). The dominance of men in the interpretation of realities of world politics can furthermore push us, men and women, make "realistic" decisions and vote people suitable for the dealing with these masculine realities (Tickner, 1992). This is problematic for peace, given that stereotypical masculinity is often violent. At the same time, critical research and the realization that some realities have a social origin opens up opportunities for conflict transformation. The interpretation of the "naturality" of harmful social structures is a political problem for peace, and thus neo-pragmatist peace research has to aim at denaturalizing violent naturalized social constructs. If we do not know that we do not need to consider states or ethnic groups, real in a conflict situation, we do not realize all the options we would have for peacemaking if we knew that the social reality is in our hands (or better, in our heads). To put it in pragmatist language, by naturalizing social structures we cannot reflect if it was useful for peace and for us to consider these structures into becoming real or not as we think that somehow realities like masculinity, the state, money, ethnicity or the national interest are given and something that cannot be challenged.

Denaturalization of social structures is also the main mission of critical peace research. According to Booth, critical security studies aim at identifying opportunities for "immanent critique", i.e. critique that can open options for emancipation (Booth, 2007). Even though Booth often associates emancipation with human survival, and some-times expands the concept to egalitarian, non-repressive conditions between human beings, pragmatist peace research could be more direct in its identification of targets of denaturalization. For pragma-tist peace research denaturalization should be targeted against natu-ralized social structures that are harmful for peace, and that legitimize or constitute categories of actions that result in the loss of life years.

In critical, pragmatic peace research denaturalizing results in the emancipation of people from naturalized, violent, and social struc-tures. As Booth points out, "As a discourse of politics, emancipation seeks the securing of people from those oppressions that stop them from carrying out what they would freely choose to do, compatible with the freedom of others. It provides a three-fold framework for politics: a philosophical anchorage of knowledge, a theory of progress for society, and a practice of resistance against oppression. Emancipation is the philosophy, theory and politics of inventing humanity" (Booth, 2007, p. 112). For practical peace research the objective of emancipa-tion is still to liberate, but it does not need to be as broad and "revo-lutionary" as Booth suggests. Neo-practical peace research aims at liberation from thoughts that reproduce perceived fixed natural struc-tures of violence: here the mission is the same as in any neo-pragmatic production of knowledge, namely to consider what kinds of things we should consider real, and what not. If we have thought that our allegiance to our ethnic brothers is a natural necessity for us, because of the color of our skin, it is useful for us to ponder whether it is useful for peace that we consider ethnicity real in politics and conflict. Ethnicity was considered real in the conflict between Hutus and Tutsis in Rwanda, but it is no longer real in Rwandan politics, and it was not recognizable before the colonial policies of "divide and rule". The construct of ethnicity was created for oppressive political purposes of ethnic rule, and it constituted war agency in the civil war of the 1990s, but it was possible to get rid of once people were ready to consider something else that could more constructively structure political agency. For many democratizing nations these are political visions, which then compete in politics and elections within rules of competition that keep this competition from becoming a violent security issue.

7.1. What Kinds of "Natural" Connotations and Associations Does the Word Security in its Current Practice Smuggle into Our Thinking?

Critical security studies have not often focused on the fact that the whole concept of security has a partisan connotation. Yet, it would be logical for critical, self-reflexive scholarship to start from the reflection of the discipline. Security studies represent an institutional form of thinking of security in a partisan manner, so that someone else's security is ruled out of consideration. A more structural institutional practice of peace research has the opposite connotation as peace, by definition, defines relationships rather than positions of partisan actors. There is peace between two countries, but there is security for one country often in an oppositional way to the other country as theorists of security dilemma have suggested. In this way the institutionalization of security studies has normalized the search for partisan security as an alternative to the practice of searching for reconciliation in relations between actors. To some extent one could claim that security studies is an institutional form that reproduces some of the premises of realist political thinking in which it is realistic for nations not to consider each other's security and wellbeing, but instead to simply consider one's own security. Selfishness and a partisan perspective becomes normal, natural and realistic in the institution of the security studies discipline, while in relations between people and groups in most societies concern for the other is natural and realistic in the sense that it is more common than strongly sanctioned partisan selfishness. Furthermore, while we usually perceive science and scholarship to be universal, security studies is not universal, but national or sometimes regional or ethnic, but always anti-universal in its partisan perspective. The fact that in pragmatic scholarship it additionally represents the kind of definition of utility and practicality that is based on the values, utilities and practicalities of only some people ruling out the practicalities of others, makes a security studies approach very difficult to tolerate. However, most critical research in conflict studies can be found in security studies rather than in peace research. Can it be that critical security studies has been somewhat blind in relation to its assignments as it has failed to criticize the untenable premises of partisanship?

However, critical security studies have contributed to many practical progressive steps in scholarship on peace and war by denaturalizing hegemonic interpretations that peace research has been too affiliated with. One of the core targets of denaturalization in critical security studies resonates with the idea of neo-pragmatist peace research. According to one of the founding members of the critical security studies, Ken Booth, critical security studies has to denaturalize security concepts that obscure the fundamental objective of security as the survival and emancipation of human beings: "At base, proponents of Critical Security Studies argue that the corporeal, material existence of human beings should be the central focus of security studies: that is, security should ultimately be concerned with the real world security of human beings" (Peoples & Vaughan-Williams, 2010, p. 24; Wyn Jones, 1999; Booth, 1991) Whenever powerful definitions of practicality in peace research do not originate from the survival of all people, they do not reflect global democratic practicality. This does not necessarily mean that we should always reject state centrism in security studies or peace research, since states can be instrumental in human survival and human wellbeing. However, autocratic military establishments are often central in countries that emphasize state security over human security, and in those states state security does not always yield safety or wellbeing for the people.

The original critical mission of critical security studies was to reveal the state bias of security concepts. For some scholars of critical security studies such social structures that are naturalized and harmful for security are often related to the concept of nation. Security studies, as Cox puts it, take "prevailing social and power relationship and the institutions into which they are organized (namely states) as the given framework for action" (Cox, 1981, p. 126). Thus, traditional security studies privileges states as referent objects of security and yet it associates state security — and in fact often regime security — with the security of citizens and human beings. By creating theory and concepts of "national security" traditional security studies has naturalized the association of human safety and the order and survival of a nation-state by binding the two into a single category and theory. The mechanism of naturalization here is some kind of conceptual gerrymandering (Rehg & Davis, 2003; Wodak, 2001). While in electoral gerrymandering one tries to define the borders of electoral districts to ensure electoral victory for a certain party, in conceptual gerrymandering one tries to associate two (or several) things — often something that all consider positive (the safety of citizens) and something oneself wants to promote (the nation) by defining borders of referents of concepts so that the two will always remain within the borders of the same concepts. This association is necessary for the legitimation of state security, and it is carried by the confusion between the concepts of state and nation (Krause, 1998). It would be possible to defend this association by referring to causal connections between safety and states: states can be very good instruments for individual safety, and if we look at stateless people or orderless territories, we realize that this is not very farfetched. Yet, individual human beings, such as dissidents, are killed for the sake of national security. In this way "to countless millions of people in the world it is their own state, not 'the enemy' that is the primary security threat" (Booth,

1991, p. 318). In fact, if we compare statistics of conflict and democide, it has been argued that many times more people are killed by their governments than by wars, intra-state and inter-state wars included (Rummel, 1994). While it is clear that the imperative of "national security" has legitimized democidal episodes, especially during the times when there is a clear hegemonic ideology that legitimizes harsh action in the name of national security (such as during the Cold War), it seems clear that national security has been a particularly useful concept for democidal and adventurist regimes during the time of the War on Terror. While during the Cold War eight times more people were killed by democide than wars, the post-9/11 period seems to produce even more extreme ratios (Kivimäki, 2003c, p. 7). As a result, Booth and others criticize the concept of national security and suggest that it should be seen as a derivate or an instrument of human security (Betts & Eagleton-Pierce, 2005; Booth, 1991). One could add to this that in some cases one should be open to considering the possibilities of the creation of order that could safeguard people on the level of smaller or greater units than nation-states. Thus, we have greater preparedness if we do not consider the relationship between security and the state as natural. In some areas of Somalia, for example, where production is based on small units and needs very little help from larger units of governance, one could imagine options where pockets of good governance could be more efficient than nation-states at taking care of the safety of people (Kivimäki, 2001a). Elsewhere, and in some issue areas, safety could be produced regionally or globally. We do not have enough imagination to do that if we associate safety with a nation-state.

The practical implications of our false knowledge about the naturality of security associating national survival with the safety of citizens can be illustrated with an example from the westernmost state of Burma/Myanmar, the Chin State, before the first semi-democratic election in 2010. Historians can tell us that Chin State experiences severe famine about every 50 years due to the intensive flowering of bamboo. In 2009, bamboos flowered in very wide areas of Chin attracting a large number of rats to the area (Sakhong, 2009). These rats managed to destroy a large proportion of the rice harvest in large areas of Chin State, leaving people without food. There were still stockpiles of rice in those areas with fewer or no bamboos and rats, but there were not enough villagers to carry rice from these areas to the famine-stricken areas. This was due to the fact that only national military issues were seen as security issues with the highest priority, and because the Burma/Myanmar army was moving forces between bases, and they needed young strong men to carry ammunition and weapons from one military base to another. Since regime and state security was considered the only high priority security issue, and since it was not considered an instrument of the wellbeing of citizens, it was not possible for the Myanmar military to release villagers so that they could carry rice instead of ammunition and as a result many people in the state died of famine. The association between the regime and state survival and security was so strong that it was not possible for soldiers to judge whether the situation needed a more humane focusing of resources. Interpretations of security created social structures that resulted in the loss of human life: critical reflection on the concept of security — neo-pragmatic peace research that borrowed from critical theory — could have saved these lives.

In addition to state centrism, our use of the word security associates peace with order and stability. Yet, as Rummel has revealed, order has killed six times more people than all wars (challenges to order) (Rummel, 1994), and thus it would not be useful for peace and for us to consider order and peace as somehow naturally linked. "Conflict" and "war" in our linguistic practices associate violence with the lack of national order and a challenge to stability and the *status quo*, while the concept of "peace" associates non-violence with stable national order. For example, in the UCDP/PRIO Conflict Dataset, an armed conflict is defined as "a contested incompatibility that concerns government and/or territory where the use of armed force between two parties, of which at least one is the government of a state, results in at least 25 battle-related deaths". On the one hand, a conflict is a conflict only, if it "concerns the government", and thus if it is about a certain sovereign order in part or the whole of a state's territory. This linguistic practice is naturally useful for the argument for the existing *status quo* and order: the order and *status quo* acquire pleasant associations if they are seen as "naturally associated" with non-violence. Anything that threatens the *status quo* can be fought as a security threat. But at the same time, this naturalized association makes us forget and neglect the conflicts that do not fit into the picture. What if we have violence that we could fruitfully study from the perspective of conflict theory, but which does not threaten order or the *status quo*? In most data sources communal conflicts that do not have the state as one of the conflicting parties are not considered to be conflicts. Uppsala University's Center for Peace and Conflict Research has recently established a new dataset on non-state conflicts as a separate dataset (UCDP/PRIO dataset), but its regular conflict dataset does not consider non-state conflicts to be conflicts. However, such conflicts could be as violent as rebellions, and they could equally well be studied by using the lessons generalized by conflict theory. Or perhaps it could be possible to imagine a one-sided conflict where the order itself is violent, but where the subjects of the order are too weak to violently oppose the violence in the order. This has only relatively recently been added as a category in a separate dataset in the UCDP/PRIO conflict dataset on "one-sided conflicts," and data is now available from 1989 on violence by the order. But in the standard conflict dataset — let alone political and journalistic language which often equates political instability with conflict — conflict is not a conflict unless the popular groups fight back against the order of the government. This authoritarian killing is possible in the name of security and conflict prevention, even though such authoritarian violence tends to produce more casualties than the security threats it prevents, as Rummel suggests.

The violent crackdown on pro-democracy demonstrators in Burma in 1988, and by the Chinese government on Tiananmen Square, as well as the systematic killings of somewhere between 500,000 and 1.5 million Communist suspects during the first years of the term of former authoritarian leader of Indonesia, President Suharto, or the killings of suspected enemies of the state in Cambodia during the terror regime of Pol Pot, or the current drone warfare that kills 10 times more "terrorists" than there are victims of terrorism, were perfect examples of how the effort to defend order and stability components of "security" results in insecurity for citizens. In the case of Suharto's Indonesia, close to 1% (later in East Timor, much more than 1%) of the population was killed for the sake of "security". In Pol Pot's Cambodia, more than 8% of the population was wiped out each year in the name of order, peace and security. In the aftermath of the Civil War in Finland in 1918, close to 2% of the population died in prison camps for the sake of security. In standard conflict datasets these periods are often exceptionally peaceful (in Cambodia especially the deadly years of 1976 and 1977) as conflict statistics often ignore "violence for security reasons".

The linguistic practice of linking order with peace is an important element in the legitimation of "orderly violence". It constitutes violent acts as legitimate law enforcement, stabilization or security measures. The association between order and peace makes orderly violence invisible; "violence in silence" or makes it seem as if the challenger of the violent order is the reason for the violence: if a particular order is part of peace, then the act of challenging it becomes a naturalized cause for the act of returning to order by violent means of government control. In this way a naturalized association between security and order creates a violent social structure, which pragmatic peace research needs to denaturalize and replace with another kind of interpretation and social structure.

Denaturalizing the relationship between security and nation, security and order and security and *status quo* can lead us to the realization that the social realities our practices and language reproduce serve the political elites rather than people, but it does not necessarily lead us to anti-state, anti-order or anti-*status quo* positions. Denaturalization opens opportunities to think things that previously sounded unnatural. Yet certain states can be good instruments of popular survival and wellbeing, and certain types of democratic order are likely to be needed for general survival and wellbeing. As will be investigated later in this book, some of the security practices of ignoring the need for indigenous states and orders in some of the developing (especially Muslim) countries can be a major source of violence and threat to survival as such scholars as Chung-in Moon, Edward

Azar and Muhammad Ayoob have suggested even before the War in Iraq began (Ayoob, 1995, 1997; Azar & Moon, 1988).

7.2. What Kind of Critical Perspectives could be Useful for Peace Research and Peace? Feminine and Third World Critical Perspectives

In addition to being critical toward the language of security, peace and war, critical pragmatist peace research should seek emancipation and the expansion of the menu of choice for peace action by means of self-reflexive search of biases in the interpretations of security realm. Feminist International Relations scholarship points to the dominance of men in the field of security studies. According to Tickner, the theory of international relations "has been constructed without reference to most of women's lived experiences, women have rarely been portrayed as actors on the stage of international politics" (Tickner, 1992, p. xi). From there the Feminist scholarship derives the suspicion that the overall interpretations of "realities" of international relations, security, peace and wars are affected by stereotypical masculinity. The focus of attention in Feminist scholarship is to "seek answers to ... questions by bringing to light what ... (Feminists) believe to be the masculinist underpinnings of the field" (Tickner, 1992, p. xi). The intention of the Feminist perspective in pragmatic peace research is based on "Drawing attention to gender hierarchies that privilege men's knowledge and men's experiences ... to see that it is these experiences that have formed the basis of most of our knowledge about international politics" (Tickner, 1992, p. xi). This way Feminist International Relations scholarship identifies the Feminine critical perspective suspicious of "strength, power, autonomy, independence, and rationality, all typically associated with men and masculinity" (Tickner, 1992, p. 3). These, according to Tickner, "are characteristics we most value in those to whom we entrust the conduct of our foreign policy and the defense of our national interest" (Tickner, 1992, p. 3).

In my critique of the practicality of causal determinism in peace research, I have already taken stock of Tickner's list of suspicious orientations to peace and war. The critique of the idea of viewing international security from the point of view of independent, partisan power play and the suggestion of seeing international relations as interactive, relational and dialectical resonates with Tickner's feminist critique of hegemonic stereotypical masculine interpretations of political realist and neo-realist scholarship. Furthermore, the treatment of partisan bargaining logic in this book relied somewhat on Tickner's characterization of masculine heroism (Tickner, 2004, pp. 43–44).

Feminist scholarship has pointed to the ways in which male-dominated security studies rules out female agency in its discourse of protection (Åhäll, 2012; Åse, 2015; Parashar, 2009). I have discussed this briefly in Chapter 4 in conjunction to the ways in which the legitimacy and mental capacity of punishment of the enemy was constructed in war propaganda by associating violence against the enemy with the protection of women. However, this framing inactivates female identity by making women an object of violence rather than an actor in conflicts or in their resolution. The protection of women in wars gives an opportunity for fighters to enact their (stereotypical) masculinity, but at the same time the myth of heroic protection constructs women as objects (of protection) rather than active actors. This way the myth of protection reinforces connections between state, masculinity and physical force and undermines the potential of female agency in crises (Åse, 2015).

While revealing the connection between the discourse of protection in security studies and the marginalization of feminine agency, Feminist scholarship touches upon a very interesting theme that requires emancipation also from the Third World perspective. Current cosmopolitan thinking[1] on the protection of global civilians has

---

[1] Here we should not necessarily think of cosmopolitan thinking as a scholarly orientation, but also as a political orientation that tends to legitimize many of the wars of the past decade. Western interventions are needed to protect civilians of the world against terrorists and tyrants. There has been analyses that try to distinguish these political discourses aiming at legitimizing violence from the scholarly ideas associated with cosmopolitanism (Bray, 2013). However, others have claimed that cosmopolitan scholarship has also pushed forward an agenda that is uncritical to Third World perspectives and the right to agency of the Third World (Ayoob, 2004).

clearly been blind to the Third World perspectives and the right for agency of the Third World. While China has now started making reports on human rights situation, in the United States, it is still inconceivable to imagine the protection of civilians by a Third World country in a developed country. And not only that, cosmopolitan protection tends to imply unilateralism that excludes Third World agency even when the intention is to protect civilians in the Third World. Cosmopolitan practice, as it is exemplified in the US/UK/France-led operations in Syria, Libya, Afghanistan, Central Africa, Mali or elsewhere can be criticized from the Third World perspective of a colonialist blindness to the asymmetry between the willingness to protect globally and the unwillingness to share the agency of protection globally. This could be, as Åse claims, related to the nature of the man-dominated, Western-dominated discourse of protection, which implicitly puts people and nations into three categories: protectors, perpetrators and victims, denying agenthood from the last category of people/nations. Since the protection of global civilians is getting an important theme in current reality of international conflicts, I will keep this critique of the post-colonial and feminist perspective in mind when I start building positive horizons to practical peace research in the next chapter.

7.3. Positive Critical Perspectives

Critical approaches tend to define their positions with negations: they tend to display non-Masculine or non-Western perspectives. Yet, alternative perspectives could be utilized for positive build-up of alternative, neglected realities. This will naturally risk reifying the female and Third World perspective, and treat it deterministically as something given, as an objective quality of women or citizens of the Third World. Yet, if we seriously try to bring in the Feminine or Third World life-experience to practical peace research, we need to reveal part of the diversity of female or post-colonial perspectives.

Positive feminine or Third World perspectives can be introduced as an alternative to the Western/masculine perspectives, even though one should always remember that as actors of world politics both women and the people of the Third World are free to choose whatever perspective they want rather than being somehow bound to represent perspectives that are reconstructed here. Femininity and agency under the conditions of post-colonial historical phase are perspectives not descriptions of fixed positions in the debate about security and peace.

We could imagine stereotypical feminine identities and life experience and build positive alternatives to security discourse based on strength, power, autonomy, independence and rationality. Instead of portraying enemies as crazy dictators securing them by weakening them with counter-force, a mother would try to influence motives rather than capabilities of conflicting parties, sometimes by tackling the interaction (rather than actors), referring to norms and by working with identities. Naughty children are not destroyed or weakened, but taught with compassion.

Even if we take the feminist approach of criticizing the mainstream of security policies for stereotypical masculinity, it is possible to identify feminine approaches to specific conflicts. This obviously has nothing to do whether such approaches are taken by men or women, as such approaches cannot be deterministically derived from the objective characteristics of men and women. In the aftermath of the collapse of the Soviet Union, a masculinist approach was to utilize the weakness of Russia and expand the NATO to Russian borders. Obviously, this reversed the positive relational trends between the West and the East, and helped give birth to the nationalistic, hostile, Russian sentiment in a weakened country. When mediating in the conflicts of the former Yugoslavia, President Ahtisaari took a more motherly, relational approach that appealed to the common norms and offered identities that could be useful for regional peace. The great-power-nostalgic Russia was invited to the negotiation process offering it a more positive identity to substitute its former militaristic image. Ahtisaari's approach was just like that of a mother that tries to induce more positive behavior from a "naughty child" by offering him/her to see her/himself as a more responsible and good child. Powerful Soviet Union was history, but Russia could be a meaningful force for peace in the world. Just like a mother would try to appeal to a child's willingness to be a "good child", Ahtisaari tried to appeal to Russians and encourage them to constructive engagement in the buildup of a more peaceful Europe, by offering them a positive identity, not as a "good child" but as a great power of peace. Yet in the end, this approach was destroyed by the need for those leaders through which the stereotypical masculine discourse was influencing, to humiliate Russia even in this peace process and deny its role in the designing of the architecture of European security. It was important (for the stereotypical masculine approach) to show who was the crazy dictator, and who had to be defeated. The NATO, as a military organization, and its strength had to be the backbone of security in Europe. Instead of focusing on relationships and approaches and deciding what would be a good approach and what kind of approaches should be avoided, the solution was to identify the guilty party (Milosevic in Serbia, later Putin in Russia) and defeat it with military power or at least with sanctions. Security had to be guaranteed by partisan rather than common action. With a positive feminine alternative approach it would have been possible to identify hypothetical alternative ways of dealing with conflicts and to observe if any efforts in that vain has shown any success.

The similar exercise would be possible to conduct from the postcolonialist perspective. While showing the developed country-bias in the militaristic, state-centric and externally oriented concepts of security, Azar and Moon revealed some of the reasons for the failures to establish stability in the developing world. However, instead of just settling for critique, Azar and Moon defined positive Third World perspectives on security emphasizing intra-state challenges of policy performance, national cohesion and legitimacy of the state (Azar & Moon, 1988). Later, Ayoob complemented this positive critical postcolonialist approach by assuming a subaltern position that emphasized Third World lived experiences. International realities emphasize state-agency in the international interaction, while the formation of state in the Third World has been delayed by colonialism. Thus, the first challenge for the Third World is to tackle the internal threats to state governance in order to take the step that Europe and the developed countries had taken already centuries ago, the process of internal pacification by means of state-formation (Ayoob, 1997). I will use this positive critical post-colonialist perspective by Azar, Moon, and Ayoob in my effort in the next chapter to analyze the material and social historical stage of global conflict, criticize the unpractical knowledge that interacts with the main sources of current violence and to identify positive approaches to the building of practical knowledge for non-violence.

Chapter 8
Intellectual Opportunities for the Creation of a Less Violent World

Security community is a concept coined by Karl Deutsch referring to a group within which large scale violence has become unthinkable. In this book, the concept is used in a way that gives a constructivist understanding to the peacefulness of the group. Security community is considered by its members as the subject of security: the community consists of people or nations whose safety security policies aim to safeguard. This way security within the community is common.

Within the group, there is order that regulates resolution of disagreements, while outside it anarchy prevails. Due to the commonness of security within a security community, there is an identity that is common in security issues. The terms of security and the values to be secured within the community are also common. In general, due to the common security identity, conflict between members of the security community is unimaginable.

What is interesting in this concept is the idea that communities can be issue-specific: thus while in federal regional policies, New York and Washington D.C. are separate entities which can bargain hard against each other, they nevertheless do not consider each other as a security threat. An attack from Washington D.C. against New York is thus unimaginable.

We have so far assessed various features and elements of paradigms of social sciences for the pragmatic value for peacemaking. It would be cowardly to leave our investigation there and not try out the elements of various paradigms that we found useful and compatible with the pragmatist meta-theoretical approach. After the meta-theoretical testing, one simply needs to give some indication about how to fix the world for its vices of violence and war. This chapter will give a taster of neo-pragmatist peace research by looking at the interaction of materially and socially constituted realities our world has and by investigating how they can be transformed to make killing and violence less frequent. I will first look at the ethical issues involved in the fact that knowledge is politics and thus knowledge production involves an exercise of power. From there, I will look at how knowledge-based social realities can be transformed and what kind of transformation should peace research support in the current historical context.

8.1. Normative Considerations in Relation to What to Consider as Real

If our interpretations that constitute social realities are to be judged from their usefulness, then a question arises about whose utility considerations we should take into account. When thinking about what to consider as real in practical peace research, we must therefore remember not only the negative rules of how to avoid taking social realities as natural or how to be more reflexive and self-conscious of the sources of one's understanding of one's social environment. In addition, we will have to know how social realities are transformed, and whose practicality we should consider when assessing what kind of ideas we should make into reality by considering them as real. After all, social reality-creating knowledge is politics and thus some political rules of openness, inclusion, transparency and democracy apply to it (Habermas, 1984; Rorty, 1991; Wilshire, 1997).

While it seems that questions of peace and war could be separated from politics by using measurements of violence (say battle deaths), it seems it would be possible to judge political realities in a pragmatic manner by simply considering their impact on the legitimacy of taking lives and causing conflict-related fatalities, pragmatic peace research cannot be as technical as that. Peace is always defined in relation to specific terms of peace (as learned above) and this means that political evaluations of what should be considered real and what should not always enter into the picture. If everyone accepted terms of peace in which the society was structured by the reality of hierarchical agency of races and the subordination of one race to another, there would not be battle-related deaths, but there would be a violent structure that most people (whoever is not a racist) would not consider as fair. This is why pragmatic constructivist peace research cannot avoid criteria that define how different people should be taken into account and how they should be allowed to participate in the definition of what is practical, and thus how do we construct peaceful knowledge, truths and realities.

The reason why this book is about practical peace research and not practical security studies has something to do with the democratic criteria of constitution of peaceful social structures. As mentioned above, partisan approach to peace has been naturalized in the establishment of security studies. This natural connotation goes against the democratic ideal of practical peace research. Thus, security studies is not only not the only natural option but also not an option at all for pragmatic peace researcher. By seeing security as the starting point of a discipline, scholarship can develop practices where the funder of the science defines the nations whose security one needs to be emphasized in practical security studies. For example, most Anglo-American studies about the possibility of the "battle of titans", the US and China focus on whether China is a revisionist power, whether it is a rogue state that could use its nuclear weapons in an irresponsible manner, and whether it will become a trouble maker for the existing global security order in which the United States has a hegemonic role (Ikenberry, 2012; Mearsheimer, 2001; Ross, 1999; Shambaugh, 2012). This is because of the fact that the starting point of these studies is the security of the current American order and the values it protects. Yet, it is the United States who has used nuclear weapons, not China, and it is the United States whose securing and interference in East Asia's wars has contributed to the 95% of increase in the intensity of those conflicts the United States has participated in (Kivimäki, 2014b). Yet, within an institutional setting that seeks security rather than peace, these practices of investigating only China's propensity to shake the Pax Americana become possible. Talking about the possibilities of peace rather than security would define the values to be secured and the subjects that define peace differently. It is possible to secure the village by killing its people, but we would not call killing villagers peace. This is why the conceptual premises of peace research are more conducive for practical scholarship with global democratic commitment. Peace research has to appreciate everyone's safety equally and everyone's dreams of the terms of peace alike. It needs to speak for the security of all and allow voice and agency for those that have been silent and inactive in the mainstream security studies.

8.2. How are Peaceful Social Constructs Created and Violent Ones Transformed?

Concepts, practices, and social structures might be socially constructed, but this does not really reveal much of the process that constructs them. Somehow people reach agreement on interpretations and their common interpretation on something becomes social reality. The emergence and transformation of social realities is a process where power plays an important role, but so do existing and emerging rules and categories that on the one hand are results of power, but on the other hand, constitute power in the new social setting. To explore this relationship I will first take a look at the power-side of the creation and transformation of social constructs, then look at the principled side, the power of categories (as opposed to brute power), and then look at how the two interact in the emergence of new, or transformation of the old social constructs.

As we realized above, the President of the United States has a louder voice in the creation of common interpretations on conflict realities than the Liberian single mother. Material resources of power are relevant in the constitution of factual or normative conventions. In fact, one could imagine that common interpretations came about in a similar manner as settlements in conflicts: realities are bargained. If the President of the United States acts as if the world was structured by competition between the free world and the tyrannical communism, then the foreign minister of the Philippines has to share this interpretation (or act as if she did) in order to get foreign aid from the United States. In this meta-bargaining of social structures, the position of the US President is of course one of the social realities that historical meta-bargaining processes had created. Similarly, language that has been meta-bargained in social interaction reflects the relationships of bargainers that have created these linguistic constructs. As shown in the previous chapter on critical peace research, peace is understood with existing linguistic conventions in an order-biased, *status quo*-biased and state-biased manner. Thus, even when societies find peaceful order, they cannot escape the logic of bargaining, which defines the terms in accordance with the bargaining leverages of each of the bargainers. This way, new social constructs and civilized rule-governed interaction that is based on such constructs is continuation of war with other means as Foucault has suggested (Foucault, 1994).

In the analysis of Charles Tilly, Steven Pinker, Norbert Elias, and Frances Fukuyama, the beginning of cooperation between former combatants, emergence of common norms and common interests and the emergence of common norms and eventually common identity and common security agency when families merge into clans, clans merge into societies, societies into city states and city states into nation-states, are all processes where military (and economic) power and the consequent bargaining power has played an important role (Elias, 1982; Fukuyama, 2011; Pinker, 2011; Tilly, 1990). None of these scholars model families, clans, societies or different kinds of states as security communities, communities with some common identity and common rules and order for the maintenance of peace, but all of the descriptions of these entities by the main theorists of the long history of violence correspond with the definition of security community, which as a concept offers greater generality and generalizability to the theories of these scholars. Neither do they name the expansion of security communities as a bargaining process with a structure of a bargaining game, but the logic of the process in their analysis clearly likens the model. In this bargain, various actors try to avoid the collapse of cooperation or negotiation and the beginning of war, but nevertheless want to insist on their own terms of cooperation, peace interpretation, norm or common identity.

Coercive bargaining related to the expansion of a security community takes place, on the one hand, between the unifying agents: families when tribes were formed, tribes when larger societies were formed, etc. Those tribes that were strongest and could, with their military power, make others more dependent on peace were the ones who got more of their own norms and terms included in the common security community. Also, those actors of the emerging security community that had something important and unique to offer to the security community could make others more dependent on their contribution, and thus got more of their demands included in the terms of the new security community (Tilly, 1990, p. 83).

On the other hand, bargaining also took place between rulers and the ruled: according to Tilly, "The core of what we now call "citizenship" indeed, consists of multiple bargains hammered out by rulers and ruled in the course of their struggle over the means of state actions, especially the making of war" (Tilly, 1990, p. 102). The dependence of rulers of nation-states on tax money made them also dependent on the taxed citizens (Elias, 1982, pp. 108–109; Giddens, 1985, pp. 181–191; Pinker, 2011). Kaldor also emphasizes the need of men for conscription: "In order to fight wars, rulers needed to increase taxation and borrowing, to eliminate "wastage" as a result of crime, corruption, and inefficiency, to regularize armed forces and police and to eliminate private armies, and to mobilize popular support in order to raise money and men." (Kaldor, 1999, p. 5, see also pp. 13–30.) The modern nation-state's need of the ruled for conscription, taxation and for the acceptance of the norm against private armies made the rulers more dependent on their subordinates and was an important explanation for the rise of democratic ideals in Europe (Tilly, 1990, pp. 115–116). This idea of bargaining in the process of expansion of security communities gets support also from modern times from areas where nation-building is still an unfinished business. In countries with natural resources regimes are less dependent on citizens for tax money. As a result, these regimes are then also less interested in making democratic compromises to their citizens. For such countries, it is more important to have an efficient deterrent against attempts to control government's natural resources than it is to please citizens (De Sousa, 2000; Ross, 2001). Thus the same logic of bargaining with dependence on consensus and determination to defend one's terms rule also the meta-bargaining process that establishes security communities.

But bargaining for new social constructs, for example, those that are needed for the formation of new security communities, is not only focused on relative benefits but also on the question of how beneficial new constructs are in relative terms to each of the agents of transformation of social structures. As discussed in Chapter 5, on the creation and transformation of common interpretations, the construction of new social structures is also about moving toward common benefit in a dialectical process involving trust-building and relative preferences (Baker & DeFrank, 1995; Booth & Wheeler, 2008; Elrod, 1984; Stein, 1990). It is also about a civilizing process (Elias, 1939; Pinker, 2011) and internal pacification (Giddens, 1985) where the use of brute power gives way to adherence of commonly accepted norms and categories. In addition to power, the creation of social realities is then affected by the logic of existing interpretation on what is progress and what is fairness. It is affected by existing general categories and meanings. New meanings that constitute social structures and identities are created in accordance with certain "grammatical rules" of the existing meanings. Structuralist (Saussure, 2006) and post-structuralist (Laclau & Mouffe, 2001; Mouffe, 1996) scholars claim that social identities are articulated by defining their identity in relation to other meanings: "war" gets its meaning from its relationship with "peace", and "justified" war gets its meaning in its relationship with "unjustified" wars, or "peace" can be defined with "stability" and "order", and "war" with "instability" and "chaos". The more politics and bargaining moves from war to civilized, rule-based interaction, the more general categories govern interaction and the less politics is just a reflection of the wartime power balance. While in war and in coercive bargaining process actors can react directly to specific acts of their opponents (by punishing specific offense, yielding to specific pressure, etc.), in a peaceful order, everything has to be more predictable and actors need to know in general terms what kind of sanctions different actions result in. The need to avoid wastage and brute force in governance creates new parameters for bargaining as rules and interpretations become the new sources of dependence and sensitivity, as in coercive bargaining the concrete punishments and rewards were. Inside a security community, rulers cannot impose violent and exploitative rules that are in conflict with the constitution of peaceful order that the whole community is dependent on. At the same time, rulers can be very determined to impose such rules (say pacification of partisan militias of some of the members of the security community) that peaceful order is sensitive about.

Again, an example from the construction of national identities and expanded national security communities with expanded normative communities could help understand this element of the process. After the emergence of nation-states, the institutional parameters of efficient, transaction cost-minimizing governance started restricting the rulers' autonomous sovereign power at the same time as the revolutionary activity of sub-state entities declined. "The monopolist's freedom of decision is restricted more and more by the immense human web that his property has gradually become. His dependence on his administrative staff increases and, with it, the influence of the latter, the fixed costs of the monopoly apparatus constantly rise, and at the end of this development the absolute ruler with his apparently unrestricted power is, to an extraordinary degree, governed by and functionally dependent on, the society he rules" (109–110). Predictability, orderliness and rules that have been defined in general terms imply smaller transaction costs especially to the powerful actors who no longer have to police the order by reacting to specific offenses, but who can only react to exceptional cases of offenses against the commonly known and respected generalized rules (Fukuyama, 1995). Effective peacetime governance also created a web of meanings, identities and norms that required abstract generality.

In a setting where order is based on generalized rules, powerful actors cannot take special privileges as they would not be consistent with the predictable order with generalized rules. Exercise of power becomes bound to the logic of general categories. This is beneficial also to the powerful actors. Even the most powerful clan leader will have to yield to norms that forbid the random acts of violence against weak members of the clan. Otherwise, the category of random action against the weak could be applied to the leader himself, when he is asleep, or against his children, before they get strong, or by a sufficient number of people, who together would be more powerful than the leader. Furthermore, rule by generalized norms is cost-efficient as powerful actors do not need to react to each specific offence, but instead, other actors already know in advance what the rule requires from them. Yet, when the exercise of power has to comply with the norms of generalized orders, powerful actors lose the privilege to use force at their will and react to specific situation the way they want: reactions to specific situations will have to be in line with generalized norms that regulate how one can react to situations of the general category that the specific situation belongs to. Otherwise, powerful actors risk weakening the order and sliding back to the violent and costly rule of coercive bargaining. This way general categories that constitute order and that members of the security community are dependent on become a source of bargaining power, just as ability to hurt others can be a source of bargaining power in coercive bargaining. But instead of someone owning that power resource, this normative or interpretative bargaining leverage is owned temporarily by all those who are in a position to defend it or who can associate their own projects to these normative or interpretative pre-agreements of argumentation in the community.

This "civilizing process" (Elias, 1939) or "internal pacification" (Giddens, 1985, pp. 181–191) from brute power to power by legitimacy has been analyzed in the historical context of the formation of nation-states by Elias and Pinker. In addition to the dependence of rulers on the ruled in the new regime of the enlarged security community, legitimacy and acceptable rules also helped the expansion and the complication of the state administration: as mentioned above, rules needed to be the foundation of order, rather than *ad hoc* punishments and rewards (Elias, 1939, 1982, pp. 106–110). Binding of the rulers to legitimate rules and the elevation of those rules over the power of the rulers especially in Europe was assisted, according to Fukuyama, by the independent power of the Catholic Church, which represented "the power of principle" over the brute power of secular rulers (Fukuyama, 2011). The idea of the law as something that also concerns the rulers, and that is above the political elite (the principle of the rule of law), is the most clear example of the power of normative categories over the one with brute power resources. The fact that rulers were dependent for their legitimacy on a common rule of religious norms is a concrete example of the power of general categories of ethical and constitutive (=something that constitutes interpretations of the reality) thinking.

Just as the invention and the use of money made possible the expansion of feudal states into national-states,[1] so has the invention of cheap means of global communication facilitated a momentum that on the long run could make steps toward the emergence of a global security community possible. Due to the regularity of international and transnational interaction, it is understandable that there is a need and a process toward the emergence of an international community. This was visible already in the 1930s when Norbert Elias drafted his theories of international cooperation: "We see the following movement: First one castle stands against another, then territory against territory, then state against state and appearing on the historical horizon today are the first signs of struggles for an integration of regions and masses of people on a still larger scale. We may surmise that with continuing integration even larger units will gradually be assembled under a stable government and internally pacified, and that they in their turn will turn their weapons outwards against human aggregates of the same size until, with a further integration, a still

---

[1] The use of money made it possible for rulers to tax larger communities. When taxation meant that people had to work for the ruler certain days a week, it meant that the number of people that could be taxed was limited by logistics. The use of money enabled rulers to tax people who were too far away to be called to work for the ruler. Thus, money afforded the expansion of feudal states into national-states.

greater reduction of distances, they too gradually grow together and world society is pacified" (Elias, 1982, p. 88).

However, even while waiting for a world society that Elias speculated about, it is possible to see how civilizing processes also take place in world politics, and sideline the use of brute power and give space to authority, legitimacy and principles. Also, abstract new common meanings, identities, and norms created new parameters for bargaining that we can even see in different phases of peaceful hegemonic periods of world politics. In addition to the fact that Finland had to consider the strength of the Soviet Union in its diplomacy, as its strength obviously made Finland dependent on peaceful relationship, in a peaceful international society, Soviet Union also had to consider its dependence on the norm of non-interference or non-aggression. Dependence on such norms weakened the Soviet hand *vis-à-vis* Finland, as despite its strength it could not casually punish Finland with its military might. This would have damaged the social order that was useful not just for the world, but for the Soviet Union too (Kivimäki, 2015).

When the United States bargained a leadership position in the developing world after the decline of European colonial powers, it was able to create a situation where it did not have to demonstrate its physical strength constantly. This was because there was a liberal economic order with an interpretation of the world in which the US was leading the protection of the free world. This hegemonic order was useful for the US, but in order to generalize the rule, the US had to generalize the norms. It could not say that the UK and France could not rule Malaya and Indo-China because the US wanted to do that, but instead, the rule had to be defined on levels of generalized principles. The new hegemony could only be defined by means of generalized rules that were anti-colonial. While the new anti-colonial set of generalized rules could establish norms and expectations that consolidated US leadership, these generalized rules constrained the new hegemon by making it impossible for the United States to act in a colonial manner without risking the legitimacy of the US hegemony in the West (Cafruny, 1990; Femia, 1981). Considerable manipulation of history and twisting of concepts were needed, for example, to adjust the long US colonial rule in the Philippines to the generalized rules of the new times, and yet, the US role in the Philippines often became a reason for doubting the consistency of the US post-colonial rule in Southeast Asia. For example, the way in which the United States ensured military bases in the Philippines by simply not decolonizing the areas of these bases, making it impossible for the Philippines to deny US those bases, was not criticized and resisted in the Philippines as a specific act. Instead, it was resisted as something that went against the general norm of post-colonial US leadership — something that was making the rules of US hegemony less consistent, coherent and credible. This is because of the fact that orderly US hegemony required consistent rules and these rules constrained the US hegemony (Kivimäki, 1995).

After revealing the power side and the civility side of the construction of new social realities, it is time to see how these two sides interact. When interpretations and constructs are questioned and renegotiated, both questions of power and the logic of generalized categories have relevance. Power can affect renegotiation directly as we could see in the Philippine adoption of the cold war interpretation of world politics. Declassified documents of correspondence between Philippine officials (letters by a foreign minister and by a trade negotiator) reveal how the Philippines adopted some of the norms of anti-communist cooperation with the US in anticipation of aid, i.e. brute power (Laurel, 1954; Serrano, 1954). The Philippines was not afraid of communism, and was especially undeterred by the global threat of international communist infiltration. However, the country was dependent on US aid and trade, and if trade and aid could only be received if the Philippines managed to argue for it in a way that was consistent with the US world view, it was tolerable for the Philippines to act as if it accepted the cold war interpretation of the world. Here, the brute power of US economy affected the Philippine world framing in a direct manner: dependence on US aid made the Philippines accept the concession of accepting cold war framing of world politics (which then became socialized within the Philippine political elite) as a "payment" for the US aid and trade (Kivimäki, 1995).

However, bargaining leverage also affects through the logic of general categories. If both the powerful nation and the weak party are very dependent on certain normative principles of cooperation, deviation from this principle in the reconstitution of the cooperative regime is costly. This cost affects the equation of bargaining, reducing the utility value of the terms of peaceful new structure on the terms of the greater power, $u(A, c')$, reducing the determination of the powerful agent, A, on his own terms of reconstitution, $u(A, c') - u(A, c'')$ as well as making the weaker power, B, more determined to oppose the power agents terms of reconstitution of the structure of interaction, $u(B, c'') - u(B, c')$. Even relapse to the old destructive bargaining structure would not be as bad for the weaker party if its alternative was a morally repulsive peaceful structure imposed by the stronger agent. Once the US had meta-bargained its leadership, and paid developing countries the price of opposing colonialism for the recognition of the US hegemonic role, developing countries were prepared to use force, even if they were clearly weaker than the United States, rather than accepting another hegemonic period of colonial rule. This is the way in which normative considerations enter the bargaining equation and affect it just as material gains do. This is the way in which normative costs of yielding to a repulsive normative regime (and thus weakening the normative principles of society that this repulsive regime contradicts) can be calculated in the same meta-bargaining logic as brute economic rewards and military punishments. Meta-bargaining is often very much concerned about arguments that aim at showing how proposed regimes of cooperation and peaceful interaction are associated with moral principles that bargainers have common commitment to (Pre-agreement of argumentation, Kuusisto, 1999, pp. 24–27; Perelman & Olbrechts-Tyteca, 1968). To pursue an argument in favor of a specific set of cooperative regime means to associate its norms with mutually acceptable moral principles that both bargainers are maximally dependent on. If the argument about the association is convincing, the dependence of these principles becomes dependence on a certain terms of cooperative regime. This way of seeing normative bargaining reduces "the logic of appropriateness" into the "logic of consequences" (these terms, and the idea of the two logics being separate can be found in Wendt, 1998): just as a bargainer can be dependent on an agreement on the opponent's terms in order to avoid a military attack, a bargainer can also be dependent on an agreement on one's own terms in order to avoid the damage to a normative institution that going against one's own terms would imply.

As empirical evidence of the coexistence of norms and material benefits in one meta-bargaining equation, Kapstein has shown how weaker bargainers often refuse cooperation that they deem exploitative, even if doing so would be harmful for them in terms of material gains (Kapstein, 2005). This way comparing of material dependence and normative dependence clearly happens in real-life bargaining situations. A similar empirical test result has been found in tests by Ned Lebow (Lebow, 2009b). Lebow tested pairs of students who were given out 10 dollar notes if they could agree on their division between the two. The first student was allowed to divide the money between the two students while the second student was allowed to decide whether the division of the money was acceptable. The students were not allowed to communicate with one another. In most cases, the latter student refused to accept free money unless she could get at least 40% of it. While this could be understood as a way of gaining a tough reputation as a bargainer (which according to the logic bargaining game was useful), the more likely interpretation was that the latter students were more dependent on norms of distributive justice than on the money they could get for free if they accepted exploitative terms of receiving it. Thus, they were more dependent on the normative principles than this amount of money. Yet, it is clear that if the students were more in need of money, and if the normative principle to be compromised was not so important for their lives, they would have yielded and taken the money. Normative costs and material costs are thus similar in nature, and the result of a bargain that puts normative principles and material gains at odds follows the normal logic of bargaining where the things that bargainers are most dependent on are decisive for the decision. Whenever something is so important for the society (say resistance to corruption) that a normative principle is elevated above material consideration, this just justifies the treatment of morality as a bargain: a society that is very dependent on the principle of anti-corruption has to create normative pressures to its members so that they could resist the temptation of corruption.

Thus, the society tries to make its members more dependent on the principle than on the money corruption could gain them.

There is a similar tradeoff between material consideration and interpretative principles as there is between material and normative considerations. World politics shows cases where the interpretation of the world is affected by material bargains. Greece yielded to Marshall aid and a membership in the Western alliance even if that was against the moral principles majority of the Greek population while the Philippines accepted the cold war interpretation of world politics both because of their material dependence on the United States. This shows that interpretations (not just normative principles) depend on the logic of bargaining. Yet, it seems that the material gains and normative or sometimes even "interpretative" costs impact the bargaining logic of meta-negotiation on peaceful cooperation in very similar ways despite their qualitative difference (Kivimäki, 2002).

Yet, the relationship between constitutive facts and material power resources in meta-bargaining is a bit more complicated. Principles of verifying realities in the minds of people are part of the buildup of peoples' world view, and this is why people grow very dependent on these principles. Argumentation in favor of a specific cooperative regime relying on specific ontology and principles of verification of interpretations is about association of these ontologies and principles with such ontologies and principles that both bargainers are maximally dependent on. To sell a cooperative regime that is very clearly based on something political lives of the opponent bargainer is dependent on (such as the belief on the existence of states, for example) requires less material incentives and persuasion than selling of a regime that contradicts with the foundational principles of verification and interpretations that the political lives of the opponent bargainer is very dependent on. During the war in Ukraine (2014) and the war in Georgia, Russia has tried to sell an interpretation of world politics in which ethnic agency of Russians is more real than the agency of states. This has been in sharp contrast with the almost 400 years old conventions of the primacy of states in world politics. As a result, no coercion has managed to justify, for the international community or Ukraine and Georgia, the Russian right to interfere with military force in the internal affairs of these two countries. If cooperative common identity is based on the claim that the collaborators are all part of the "free world", selling such cooperative regime and identity is easier and requires less coercion or side-payments if the countries involved in the regime can be observed as free using the same principles of verification that countries have grown dependent on. Thus, the promotion of common security agency of the free world (as opposed to the communist dictatorship) is easier in Europe than it is in the Persian Gulf or in Latin America in the 1960s. This way compromises on the world view can also be reduced to the logic of consequences: just as a bargainer can be dependent on peace in order to avoid a punishing war, a bargainer can also be dependent on the logic of interpretation of political realities. Going against such a logic that the bargainer needs in its own politics causes costs. These costs will have to be factored in the calculus of bargaining.

Yet, in asymmetric situations, material benefits can buy interpretations of the reality, just as long as the material incentives are strong enough for the opposing bargainers to be sufficiently dependent on. Countries have, for example, been perfectly willing to join cooperative regimes that interpret world politics as fight against terrorism, and assume that this danger from terrorists was primary security concern for people and states in the world even though hunger kills roughly 10,000 times as many people in the world as international terrorism.[2] Quite obviously, they are prepared to accept the costs of this inconsistency to the usefulness of their worldview. If in our world politics, we value the 700 people, some of which might be western, killed by international terrorists more than we do the seven million people who die annually of hunger in the developing world, our foreign policy might not have as good chances of getting legitimacy within the developing world (and in fact to build collaborative regimes in the global South might require more side-payments or

---

[2] This calculation was presented in my work for the Danish and Finnish governments, and it was based on long-term averages of fatalities of international terrorism given by the Pentagon, and data on hunger by the WFO (Kivimäki, 2003c, 2005; DoD 1993–2006; WFO, 2002).

coercion from us). The more dependent bargainers are on the truths and ways of verifying truths that their opponent bargainers associate to their terms of cooperative regimes the less strongly they can insist on their own terms of collaborative regimes. Thus, norms and truth-claims act in the same manner in a structure of meta-bargaining as material incentives do.

While the bargaining aspect can be found in reinterpretation or reassessment of social structures, it has one fundamental difference with the bargaining logic that is directly dependent on agent's power. While due to sanctions, for example, South Africa had to accept that apartheid is not a God's order, or system of the free world, South Africa was dependent directly on bargaining actors. However, when meta-bargainers are dependent on factual or normative pre-agreements of argumentation, the power is in the pre-agreement, not with the bargainer who tries to link her own project with the pre-agreement of argumentation. Surely, pre-agreements have been negotiated in a setting where power has some relevance, but then, in argumentation games, the power is in discourses and principle. Even if these pre-agreements were the creation of the dominance of strong powers, these principles can occasionally go against great powers. After criticizing the United States for not respecting Westphalenian principles of non-intervention in the conflict of Iraq and Libya, Russia got its own arguments at itself when invading the Crimean Peninsula (Homel, 2014). This became clearly costly for Russia and it prevented the country from referring to the principle of sovereignty in a credible manner for some time to come. Thus, Russia paid for the invasion by weakening a convention that was useful for it. Thus, Russia could not flexibly change its arguments in accordance with its own interests, but instead, Russia did not have the power, the power was with the principle, not with the one that argued for it (Foucault, 1994).

8.3. What Kind of Social Transformation should Peace and Conflict Studies Support?

In various conflict situations, it is possible to identify several truth regimes and norms that should not be considered correct. For West

Kalimantan, it was not useful to consider ethnicities as hierarchically organized political actors (so that "local" ethnicities are actors that have more political authority than "visiting" ethnicities that nevertheless had stayed in the territory for centuries). Such thinking led the province to wars. In many conflicts, the interpretation of masculinity is problematic for social rationality and peace. Associating male identity with violent competitiveness often constitutes masculine behavioral patterns that are socially harmful and violent. Furthermore, truth regimes and norms that are highly autocratic and emphasize the wellbeing and power of a few powerful actors at the cost of others are difficult to justify in many conflict situations. However, this chapter will focus on the mega-structures that are most crucial, not for some type of a normative order, but to global peace and reduction of lives lost in conflicts and violence. Focusing on such mega-structures does not mean that only such structures are interesting for practical peacemakers. On the contrary, it is likely that the tools developed in this book for peacemaking could most fruitfully be used for various types of conflict prevention situations rather than trying to find one formula that fits all of them. There is likely to be more variation than generality between different conflicts. Yet, it is possible to look at some mega-trends that need fixing before conflict violence can decline on a large scale.

In order to reconstruct realities that need fixing, we will have to take a recap of the premises we have reached in our investigation of paradigms and their value for peace. While we recognized the value of the analysis of materially given causal processes, we acknowledged that social processes are also about purposive action that interacts with material realities and with structures that emerge out of several actors influencing the social space simultaneously and over time.

While we realized that the purposes of people bring an element of instability to any reconstruction of social structures as people can change their purposes, we also realized that there are certain preferences that we can consider relatively stable, not because people would not have the power to change them, but because only those with a certain preference matter for the development of social structures. The preference for survival is such a preference that we can assume, since those who do not have that preference will die and stop influencing the society (yet, as we know from the phenomenon of suicide terrorism, we cannot fully rule people with a deadly preference outside our focus).

When trying to understand how conflicts and peace emerge, we realized that structures are more than just a sum of their elements, and that even with a general preference for survival and peace, we can have structures of interaction where everybody's peacefulness can lead to belligerence. Of such structures, we realized that the structure of bargaining (rather than prisoner's dilemma) is the more general and common. Conflicts and the emergence of cooperative social structures are not about forces of peace fighting forces of war, or about someone defecting from commonly accepted rules while others enforcing the rule. Instead, conflicts are most often about battles between several versions of peace or terms of cooperation and co-existence in a structure of bargaining. As discussed in Sec. 4.4.2, bargaining as a structure provokes rational peaceful actors to violence against their opponents in bargaining, insensitivity about peace and the marginalization of the internal lobbies for peace. This way the partisan constructs of national-states in the international system has a mechanism that defends itself against further expansion of the security order into greater security communities.

While within given identities and preferences, bargaining structure has some material characteristics that make it vulnerable to belligerent social irrationality, Chapter 5 revealed that such structures are constituted by elements that depend on our common interpretations. We can construct agency in conflict situations in different ways, in interaction we can develop relational preferences, and we can interpret the strategies and outcomes of episodes of interaction in various ways. Thus, while the structural characteristics of interaction are given, the premises of structures are socially constructed in the interpretations of agency, norms and values, and truth regimes. Thus, such characteristics have to be understood before we can understand why people end up in wars despite the fact that they generally prefer survival and peace. Through understanding the structural qualities of bargaining structures, and the fact that the premises of such structures are socially constructed, even if often seen as natural and given, we will eventually be able to challenge dangerous bargaining structures and the partisan norms and truth regimes that they give rise to. To do this we will, however, have to be able to identify the historically specific bargaining structures.

The long history of violence suggests that bargaining structures have emerged in several settings during the history of humanity: Families have been internally peaceful security communities but bargained against each other in security matters, then clans, societies, feudal states and finally national-states. A closer look at the current international system shows that there have been efforts to go beyond the security communities of nation states and form common identity and among "the free world", among the "peace-loving socialist countries", as well as within the European Union.

For the expansion of peace, the creation of greater security communities has been seen as important in several analyses of the long history of governance and politics. Expansion does not only mean the inclusion of more people under one security community but also expansion of qualitative inclusiveness of already existing security communities. According to Pinker, violence was not only reduced by the merging of small feudal states into a modern national-state or a nation-state[3] but also when these states started treating all people, not just elites and not just majority populations as subjects and objects of security (Pinker, 2011).

The experience of the expansion of the city states into nation-states has been an important case for many scholars who have seen the "inside" of the order as the zone of relative peace, while the outside as the zone of belligerence. According to Giddens, the process of the formation of the nation-states was a process of "internal pacification" (Giddens, 1985, pp. 181–191). Such pacification was contrasted by the belligerence of the interaction between states, the divide "between

---

[3] Most theorists of the modern state call it a nation state (Elias, 1982; Fukuyama, 2011; Giddens, 1985; Pinker, 2011; Tilly, 1990), even though this term misleadingly associates territorial ethnicity to the concept of state (Ayoob, 1995). While acknowledging the misleading connotation of the concept nation state, I use it as a synonym of Ayoob's concept of national-state.

domestic non-violent legal intercourse and external violent struggle, between civil society and barbarism" (Kaldor, 1999, p. 20). According to Kaldor, "The rise of the modern state was intimately connected to war (between states). In order to fight wars (against other states), rulers needed to increase taxation and borrowing, to eliminate "wastage" as a result of crime, corruption and inefficiency, to regularize armed forces and police and to eliminate private armies, and to mobilize popular support in order to raise money and men" (Kaldor, 1999, pp. 5, 13–30). Thus, outside the security community belligerence reigns, while inside it there is relative peace. This suggests that the expansion of security communities could be useful for peace. In fact this could be one of the main conclusions of many analysts of the long history of violence (Ayoob, 1995; Elias, 1982; Kaldor, 1999; Pinker, 2011; Tilly, 1990).

If there is a lot of interaction outside security communities, the irrationality of brute coercive bargaining pushes security communities that clash with each other into closer cooperation and eventually into a single security community. The process of expansion of security communities (and the internal pacification, and civilization process as Giddens and Elias would say) is "very closely related to growing interviewing and interdependence of people" (Elias, 1982, p. 52). This was also the conclusion of Karl Deutsch, who focused on interaction as the measurable variable of security communities (Deutsch *et al.*, 1955). However, interaction as such does not constitute a security community as interaction can also be coercive. However, it creates the material conditions for the reinterpretation of preferences, identity, agency, as people lear from socially irrational forms of bargaining. If the previous expansion from feudal city states to nation-states was materially afforded by the invention of money (which allowed broader interaction, broader taxation, and thus larger security forces), then the step to a global security community could be afforded by a row of innovations in communication technology as well as the growing costs of wars due to military innovations. Social rationality and the common interest of peace in a setting of growing communication and interaction enables greater cooperative attitudes, recognition, respect and common identities between former opponents in bargaining. Thus the mega-trend we must observe is the regionalization and globalization of security communities. If all the steps to greater security communities created a major decline in violence as more of the everyday interactions between individuals and groups moved to the realm of regulated interaction among all actors that have common security identity, then the step toward cosmopolitan world community, or a "pacified world society", as Elias calls it, could be the mega-trend neo-pragmatist peace research should be especially interested in. This conclusion comes close to the conclusions of the Palme Commission report on common security: "Our alternative is common security. There can be no hope of victory in a nuclear war, the two sides would be united in suffering and destruction. They can survive only together. They must achieve security not against the adversary but together with him. International security must rest on a commitment to joint survival rather than on a threat of mutual destruction." (The Independent Commission On Disarmament and Security Issues, 1982, p. ix).

Since rule-based interaction among people with a common security identity is likely to be less violent (at least when it comes to direct violence) than interaction that uses brute force to strangers, it seems reasonable that peace research should consider the expansion of security communities toward a more cosmopolitan direction as something worth supporting. Even if social processes cannot be seen as deterministic and thus expansion of security communities does not necessarily lead to peace as purposive agents have many alternative paths to choose while the logic of many other processes might be entangled with the logic of expansion of security communities. Yet, if peace has expanded with the expansion of security communities, then surely peace research should consider such progress possible in the future, too, rather than believing in the naturalized realities of realist theory of international relations. It would seem reasonable for peace research to advise in favor and support the process toward a pacified world community. Since the transformation of social constructs is both a matter of power and general categories, scholarship, peace research can have a role in the process of the next transformation into more cosmopolitan normative order. But normative and factual arguments that peace research can serve, exposure that peace research can offer to naturalized hegemonic social constructs and the intellectual alternatives it can offer to global cosmopolitan social constructs are just a part of the process, while brute power necessarily interferes into it.

The cosmopolitan process is progressing. The move among leading industrial states beyond national-state is exemplified by certain identitive changes. The creation of world organizations, such as the League of Nations and the United Nations, by the development of the international law and regimes, as well as by regional, sub-global security entities, such as "the West/the Free World", "the peace-loving socialist countries" or the European Union, where states are no longer as able to imagine internal wars, say between Germany, and Belgium, or between the United States and Canada, no matter how asymmetrical military balance between these states might be, are examples of identitive developments beyond the nation-states, even if they do not reach all the way to the establishment of a "pacified world community".

Slow emergence of global security loyalties can also be seen in the development of normative order beyond the national-state. Unlike identities, loyalties tend to reach all the way to the global level imagining the security of all civilians. The idea of human security that could cover all humanity is one of these normative expansions of the security community. In this concept, the thrive for security is no longer nationally bound but something that reaches to all humanity: we want to protect human beings not only from military but also from all threats that compromise their survival and safety. The relationship between this globalist loyalty with national loyalties and the security of states differs in the Western and the Eastern discourse, the former confronting the state priorities much more aggressively than the latter.[4] The UN declaration of the Responsibility to Protect (International Commission on Intervention and State Sovereignty, 2005) and the several wars that have recently been legitimized by using the need to protect civilians against brutal dictators or terrorists

---

[4] For the relationship between state and global loyalties in human security discourse, (see Kivimäki, 2014a).

(interventions and drone warfare in Afghanistan, Libya and Iraq, and drone warfare in Somalia, Pakistan, and Yemen) clearly show the fact that cosmopolitan ethics have penetrated international normative order, and created global loyalties.

In addition to norms and identities, global loyalties can also be identified in linguistic practices. The discourse on terrorism is one of the examples. Within national discourse, "sacred hatred" was justified against anyone killing our nationals, especially the elitist symbols of our nation. Modern terrorism was born as activity that was targeted against national leaders, the Tsar and his relatives that symbolized the nation. According to Fridlund, the first incident of modern terrorism took place in January 1878 in St. Petersburg when a Governor of the Russian state, Feodor Trepov, was shot with a revolver by a social revolutionist Vera Zasulich (Fridlund, 2012). However, the concept of terrorism reemerged at the latter half of the 20th century in a new meaning, where the killing of civilians of any nationality, rather than national politicians, was highlighted as exceptionally repulsive act of violence. This tells how politics of the definition of the concept has changed, and how norms and loyalties behind the definition of terrorism had changed. Clearly, the killing of innocent civilians as a tactic of hitting political enemies had received new normative meanings from the times of the emergence of terrorism, or even from the times of areal bombings during the Second World War, or from the times of the emergence of Mutual Assured Destruction doctrine (both of which exemplify the very same tactics as terrorism).

It seems that in this historical situation when the world is moving beyond an order where national-states are the main security community, it seems, given that in the expansion of security communities lies great opportunities for the pacification of the world, that peace research should prescribe progress in this process and try to offer tools and social construct for it as well as expose naturalized constructs that hold this progress back. The deconstructive program in support of this progress is still massive. Discourses of nationalism and state centrism are still strong and hinder progress toward the expansion of security communities. We still have strong discourses of national heroism that naturalize the linkage between self-sacrifice and national interest. At the time when life in a globalized world is threatened by global collective environmental threats, global nuclear holocaust and many other planetary security threats, this naturalized association between heroic self-sacrifice and the partisan national security interests should be revealed. Heroism's linkage with partisan interests of national coercive bargaining should be exposed as suggested in Secs. 4.4.2. and 5.1. Immanent critique should also be directed against the other naturalized social constructs that served national bargaining power, but are becoming increasingly dysfunctional in the globalizing world where states should be more dependent on peace and less stubborn about their own terms of it. Denaturalization and exposure of expressions of nationalist true-believer-cultures, dehumanizing discourses about national enemies, discourses and practices that undermine the costs of war, patriotic "sacred hatred" should be included into the deconstructive program of pragmatist peace research of this time.

At the same time, it would seem logical that in addition to critique of the truth regimes and norms of partisan nationalism, there should be norms and truth regimes that could positively build up cosmopolitan constructs and norms. There is a reconstructive and constructive agenda for the neo-pragmatist peace research too. Such agenda includes at least identitive and normative elements. Rule-based world order needs the type of human-based normative agenda-setting that Ken Both and others set in motion more than 20 years ago (Booth, 1991; Cox, 2001; Wyn Jones, 1999).

It would also need normative research on the rules of great power interaction, rather than predictions on the future behavior of the rising China, for instance. China's future behavior is being negotiated while China presents new visions of anti-hegemonic world order (Beng, 2014; Hu, 2005; Xi, 2013), and students of China still keep on predicting China as if the future was determined by external conditions (Lampton, 2005; Nye, 2013; Shambaugh, 2013) and was not in the making by purposive actors and genuine interaction that creates the new realities.

Research should also be able to imagine new types of rule-based opportunities for international practices and order. If we look at how power operates inside security communities through generalized principles and anonymous rules, and how it operates outside and between security communities as brute bargaining among self-interested agents, it seems that positive construction of norms and truth regimes of cosmopolitan order should be directed at the study of global normative opportunities for anonymous generalized rules. Instead of thinking of norms strategically and agent centrically, we should construct anonymous global rules. Thus, the repulsion our loyalty to global civilians should direct us to resisting terrorism, rather than waging a war on terrorists (since wars are directed against enemies, not against principles, thus the current war is not on terrorism, but on terrorists). If the focus was on terrorism as a rejected strategy, we would not be able to use terroristic means to fight those who we consider terrorists, as such a strategy would possibly bring victories against those who we define as terrorists, but also to the tactics of terrorism, as our own action starts reminding of terrorism.[5] Similarly, if the lesson from the Holocaust was taken in a manner that gives rules rather than bargaining agents in the center, it would be possible to promote cosmopolitan orders that reject human rights violations, rather than justifying human rights violations on the basis of claim for victimhood. Inside a global security community lessons from Holocaust would prevent human rights violations of all (even of Palestinians) by all (even by Israel), while outside such an order Holocaust is used just to justify policies of the victims of Holocaust, regardless of how violent they might be. Outside order violence on

---

[5] The high civilian body count in the so-called War on Terror clearly testifies to the propensity to ignore resistance against terrorism, and focus on terrorists. The fact that Al Qaeda rhetoric has changed from the critique of American occupation and infidel order in the Middle East to the critique of American indiscriminate drone targeting (Powers, 2014) clearly demonstrates the mechanisms in which the perceived legitimacy of terrorist tactics is constituted by terrorist actions in this agent-centered dialectical escalation process: both sides fight terrorists and justify their terrorist, anti-civilian actions as necessary means to defeat the opposing terrorist agents.

some justifies violence of the victim against the perpetrator, introducing the conflicting parties into a slippery slope of escalation. However, within the realm of order and security community, violence raises the question of how to prevent it, not how to avenge it as rules are the same for all, and if violence is unacceptable for the perpetrator, it is equally unacceptable for the victim.

The world is changing, it is moving beyond a structure that is purely organized by order within states, and disorder and anarchy between states. This change offers opportunities as the long history of violence suggests. This section has offered some elements to the program of neo-pragmatist peace research in this historical moment. However, as discussed before, despite the fact that our ability of transform structures of war and peace are conditioned by the historical moment, we should not read the long history of violence in a deterministic manner. Even if previous enlargements of security communities offer hope of opportunities for a new drastic reduction of violence, the conditions specific to this time could interfere in the process of transition. The transition from feudal states was a messy one and lasted for a long time. Today, long transitions with unpredictable twists and turns could lead into a nuclear holocaust or an environmental disaster and the ending of the world in a way that was never possible during the previous transitions. Furthermore, despite options and possibilities, people could fail to cease them or they could want to opt for something else than the enlargement of the security communities beyond the national-state. On the basis of existing historical experience, however, the main threat in current transition is the asymmetry between the willingness to protect globally and the unwillingness to share the agency in protection. While there is an increasing global loyalty and solidarity, civilians have to be protected, especially from terrorists and dictators, there is still precious little willingness to engage all societies, including developing countries let alone Muslim countries in the decision-making and implementation of global protection. Global organizations are not getting stronger, cosmopolitan agency is not emerging despite the clear indications of global solidarity and the effort to implement global norms and rules. This asymmetry seems to create problems and the transition of security order has so far produced more wars than peace. This is a dilemma that the next section will be dealing with.

8.4. Problems in the Transition to a Cosmopolitan Security Community

While the prescription for a pacified world community sounds tempting for peace researchers, one should qualify this support on the basis of a more careful analysis of the current historical situation.

After the Second World War, the most intensive conflicts, the Vietnam War, Korean War and the Chinese Civil War were fought in East Asia. Two thirds of East Asian conflict fatalities were produced in conflicts that started as domestic, but which were then interfered by outside powers, mainly the United States, but also China and the Soviet Union (Kivimäki, 2014b). Conflicts were fought as cold war conflicts and the main purpose of foreign interference was the protection of people of East Asia from global communism or imperialism. Still in the analyses of East Asian security, most analysts consider the presence of US balancing as a contribution to peace and stability (Duffield, 2001; Goh, 2008; Ikenberry, 2012; Shambaugh, 2011). However, if one looks at the correlations of US power and decline in conflict fatalities, one fails to find any positive association between the two. Furthermore, it seems that US power served the security of East Asia's allies worst: the relationship between US power and conflict fatalities was positive in most of them (Kivimäki, 2010). Protection had a tremendously poor record if one looked at those 2/3 of East Asian conflict fatalities that were produced in domestic conflicts where others participated in to protect their friends and allies. Up to an average of 98% of conflict fatalities in these wars were produced after the conflict had been escalated by foreign "protection" (Kivimäki, 2014b) and thus the international interference in the domestic conflicts caused 50 times as many fatalities as the original domestic conflict. Clearly, protection was more deadly than the threats it protected East Asians from. Furthermore, the East Asian post-world war history also offers variation in the willingness to accept foreign interference and that variation, too, suggests that cosmopolitan protection has failed so far. After the Vietnam war, the United States became unwilling to get militarily engaged in East Asian domestic wars, after the establishment of the Association of the Southeast Asian Nations (ASEAN), Southeast Asia became unwilling to accept such involvement, and after the victory of the Deng Xiaoping faction in Chinese politics, China became unwilling either to offer interference or accept it in its own wars. As a result, starting in 1979, East Asia transformed from world's most belligerent region into a region more peaceful than Europe, Americas and any other continent in the world. Up to 95% of the regions average annual conflict-related fatalities disappeared, and this was mostly due to the fact that conflicts no longer escalated into wars as foreign interference into domestic conflicts disappeared (Kivimäki, 2014b). Thus cosmopolitan global organization of security failed at least in the context of cold war.

However, cosmopolitan protection also seems to fail in its current context. The horror of sadistic violence in Bosnia and Herzegovina in the beginning of the 1990s, and in Rwanda in 1994 gave rise to the conclusion that cosmopolitan norms have to be imposed globally to end what was called New Wars. According to Mary Kaldor, for example, "The analysis of New Wars suggests that what is needed is not peacekeeping, but enforcement of cosmopolitan norms, i.e. enforcement of international humanitarian and human rights law." (Kaldor, 1999, pp. 124–125). Yet, it seems that the decade after the cold war — the time after the ending of the cold war rationale for the protection of people from communism/imperialism and before the need to protect people from terrorism and tyranny — was the time of constant decline in conflict-related fatalities (Harbom & Wallensteen, 2009; Lacina & Gleditsch, 2005). Despite Rwandan genocide, the post-cold war period was also time of exceptionally low numbers of fatalities of authoritarian violence. While during the cold war, authoritarian violence killed eight times as many people as conflicts did, the number of authoritarian violence after the cold war went down to a fraction of the number of conflict fatalities while at the same time also conflict fatalities were lower than during the cold war period (Eck & Hultman, 2007; Kivimäki, 2005, pp. 24–44).

However, once the terror strike on September 11, 2001, forced the United States to seriously consider the question of terrorism and the autocracy that was seen at the root-cause of such terrorism as a global problem, the costs of international protection started to emerge. After September 11, there was a new rationale for the "enforcement of international humanitarian and human rights law" for the protection of civilians against terror and autocracy, violence started to rise. The world moved from New Wars to New International Wars, or indeed, to Cosmopolitan Protection Wars. This can be demonstrated with the help of statistics of conflict-related battle deaths. I will use a battle deaths dataset produced at Uppsala University, in Sweden (UCDP, 2012), which is based on a meta-analysis of media reporting in conflicts (Sundberg, 2008). The Uppsala data is useful (despite the fact that it is accused of systematically underreporting the number of fatalities in conflicts) for this argument as I am interested in the relative share (which is not affected by systematic underreporting) of fatalities in conflicts that are motivated by global policing. In Graph 8.1, we can see that the costs of protection has increased dramatically over the past decade. We can see that conflicts that are initiated by a US intervention with various coalitions of the willing or interventions with drones that constitute part of the global war on terror are now responsible for 40–75% of all fatalities of wars and conflicts in the world.

8.4.1. *The problem of asymmetry of solidarity and agency*

If we look at how cosmopolitan protection has failed and how it has been different from a genuine expansion of a security community, we could compare the East Asian cold war period of protection wars, and the current anti-terrorist and anti-tyrant protection with the expansion of security community in Western Europe. There the establishment of the European Community and the European Union genuinely reduced the number of fatalities of conflict. It seems that the solidarity of Europeans toward each other in the European security community was matched by the current solidarity of civilians or the solidarity among the Free World during the cold war. There is no

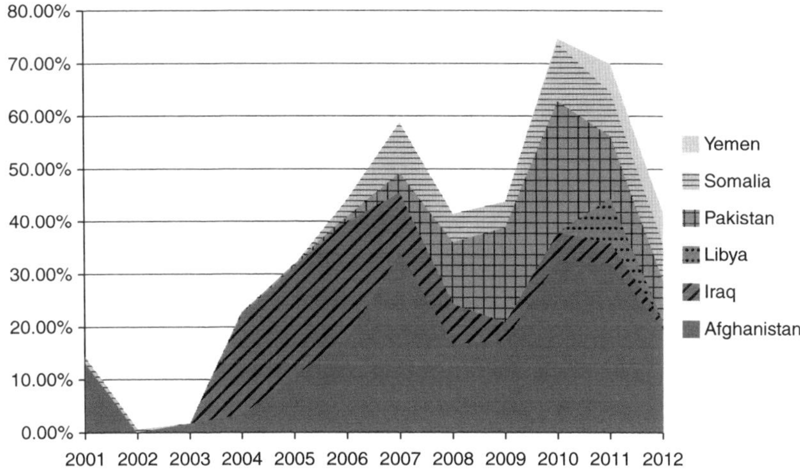

Graph 8.1.   Fatalities of international protection wars as a share of global conflict fatalities

reason to doubt the genuine solidarity that motivates and legitimates operations to protect civilians from their violent autocrats or from fanatic terrorists. Yet, it is clear that security agency for protection was different in the European Union than it was in the current protection wars or in the cold war proxy wars to protect people from communism or imperialism. While in Libya, Iraq, Afghanistan, Pakistan, Yemen as well as in Vietnam and in Korea, protection was mainly implemented from Washington (and in the case of Vietnam and Korea, also in Beijing and Moscow), in the European Union, the protection of civilians is a common European affair. Democratic terms of the security community are commonly accepted, and the organization of intra-European security is a matter, where nobody imposes protection against another permanently against the will of the other. Clearly, the European security community is symmetrical in the sense that solidarity toward each other is matched by the willingness to implement protection together. Outside European Union, in the protection wars, cosmopolitan solidarity exists in the absence of willingness to implement protection together. Thus, the asymmetry.

The mechanisms in which this asymmetry produces challenges to peace can be traced from the failures of protection both during the cold war and during the current anti-terrorist/anti-dictator framing. It seems that three things prevent solidarity from translating into genuine protection:

1. First, the refusal to share power in the agency in the production of security results in legitimacy problems in the implementation of protection. It often delegitimizes the effort to protect and legitimizes autocratic or radical religious nationalist rule against the "invaders".
2. Second, due to the decision-making structure where the constituencies of the security providers are not in the areas where security is produced, selfish, ulterior motives are unavoidable in the protection of civilians.
3. Third, administering security in another, far-away country is difficult. Actions do not produce the intended consequences as their political contexts are unknown to the people implementing the protective security.

I will shortly discuss these problems and show the evidence of their contribution to the failure of cosmopolitan protection of civilians.

On the political side of asymmetry, selling principles of human security and human rights as means to protect civilians is difficult unless there is a feeling that both the one exercising protective influence and the target of influence are "on the same side" together solving problems. If the areas where civilians are protected are themselves simple objects of security action and not allied actors of civilian protection, the question of agency emerges as an obstacle of ownership and support of protection. In Iraq, for example, according to a secret UK ministry of defense poll in 2005, 82% of the people felt strongly opposed to the presence of the coalition forces, while only 1% felt that these forces were responsible for the improvement of the security situation in the country (Rayment, 2005). Due to this legitimacy problem, the coalition activity in the protection of civilians could at best have been of limited success especially as a majority of Iraqi civilians felt that armed attacks against US forces were legitimate (Program on

International Policy Attitudes, 2006). There are no comparable opinion polls in Afghanistan, but developments there and the poorer success in Afghanistan suggest that legitimacy problems rendered the Western efforts inefficient there too. According to Polity IV, Afghanistan is still a failed state, while Iraq has already left that category of states (only to return to it). The problem of legitimacy and ownership was clear even among the ones the Western coalition wanted to take over good governance and protection. The trainees of the Afghan force that were lifted into an elite position by the US-led intervention in the country tended to complicate the pacification of Afghanistan by shooting their American trainers. In Yemen, it would be even more difficult to imagine the emergence of a democratic, protective system, out of a transitional order where a majority of population would be willing to support handing over the decision about who is to be killed as a terrorist to Washington D.C. as has happened in drone warfare. In Pakistan, while no such good governance is in sight, the unpopularity of US protection has already reached the highest echelons and prevented much of US operations there. Furthermore, protection wars are largely run outside the mandate of the United Nations, the only body even theoretically able to represent cosmopolitan agency of protection. This erodes the legitimacy of protection even internationally.

The problem of legitimacy and ownership of protection can be empirically shown on the basis of the experience since the ending of the First World War (mainly after the second though). Coercive economic and/or military efforts (sanctions) have systematically failed if they were not attempted by a group of nations belonging to the same security community of Western nations. At the same time, they have never fully failed if efforts were made by nations that belonged to the same security community (Kivimäki, 2008; data from Hufbauer *et al.*, 2007).

According to Pedersen, pressure from outside sometimes mobilizes a nationalistic siege mentality, which justifies autocratic measures, and even a tougher repression of deviance or disloyalty toward the regime "in defense the nation" against "foreign pressure" (Pedersen in Kivimäki & Pedersen, 2008, pp. 39–50). Statistical evidence (again based on Hufbauer *et al.*, 2007) supports a more general

Table 8.1. Security community membership and successfulness of protective influence[6]

Cases related to Human Rights and Democratization	Totally successful cases	Modestly successful cases	Modestly unsuccessful cases	Totally unsuccessful cases	Total
Allies	2	4	6	0	12
Neutral	0	2	1	6	9
Enemies	0	1	0	4	5
Total	2	7	7	10	26

interpretation of Pedersen's Burma-specific conclusions. Again, when nationalism becomes an issue in an effort to push protective governance changes, chances of successful economic and military coercion become minimal (Kivimäki, 2008, see Table 8.1).

Asymmetry between solidarity and agency implies that the constituency that decides who is in power is outside the area where protection is implemented. This necessarily creates a political reality in which too much and too genuine consideration for the interests of the people in the area where people should be protected by a big power politician implies risking political mandate. This way even if a president was genuinely interested in the promotion of democratic political system in an area marred by terrorism or autocracy, genuine efforts are not sufficient if they are not sustainable in the domestic political context. As protection for the past decade has mainly focused on the greater Middle East area and as this is an area where selfish hidden agendas could be most understandable due to the energy resources in the area, the problem of selfish agendas could fruitfully be observed there.

United States has generally declared a strategy that is legitimized by the interest in the promotion of democracy and freedom in the

---

[6]Table 8.1 is based on data on sanctions and their successfulness (Hufbauer *et al.*, 2007). Coding for alliance status has been added by the current author in accordance with formal alliance membership. Enemy status has been coded if the target of sanctions was a member of the Warshaw Pact or Soviet alliance or was China before 1972 and the sender of sanctions was a member of a US-led alliance.

Middle East, first against the threat of communism and later against tyranny and religious terrorism. According to my previous research, based on the study of correlative relationships between US support of regimes and US opposition of regimes in the Muslim states of the greater Middle East (North Africa, Turkey, and Iran included) and the democratic and autocratic qualities of regimes based on Polity IV data (Eckstein, 1975; Marshall & Jaggers, 2000), US support is very weakly linked to competitive executive recruitment. However, measuring with almost all other Polity IV indicators, US support is associated with autocratic qualities of regimes (Kivimäki, 2013). US opposition of autocracy in the Middle East has often been more speech than action as many of the countries criticized have actually been among the least autocratic, while many of the most autocratic states are close allies. When George W. Bush gave his speech on US opposition of tyranny and about the Axis of Evil in 2002, the highlighted tyranny, Iran, was actually the second least autocratic Muslim state in the Middle East after Turkey according to the US-based authoritative polity data Polity IV. Even the much-condemned Iranian and Sudanese governments of today are less autocratic than the average Muslim regime supported by the United States. After the Second World War, the two most autocratic regimes the United States has opposed were Saddam Hussein's Iraq and the socialist, pro-Soviet regime of Algeria of the mid-1960s. Yet, even these regimes were less autocratic than seven regimes that the US has supported loyally for almost the entire post-WWII period or during their emergence (altogether for 176 country years). If one looks at the types of autocratic regimes the United States has supported, it seems clear that the US has wanted to support stable pro-US regimes that have wanted to cooperate with US energy companies. Stability of oil supply has clearly twisted the interest of protection of civilians in the Middle East (Kivimäki, 2013).

An investigation of the relationship between regime changes, US support and punishment further reveals the mechanism in which selfish interests corrupt the interest of protection in areas where the protected nations and peoples are not empowered to substantially participate in their own protection. Only once did the US increase its support after progress toward democracy: in Bahrain in 1973. There obviously, the US was already supporting more autocratic Bahrain before the turn toward greater democracy. Both the more autocratic and the more democratic regimes were supporters of US oil and military interests in the area, and thus in the absence of corrupting selfish interest, the US support did indeed reflect the interest of the protection of Bahraini civilians. However, in Sudan (1986) and twice in Syria (1950, 1954), democratic progress was met with greater US hostility. According to Polity IV data, these were the moments of greatest democratic progress in the Middle East after the Second World War. Needless to say, in all three cases, democratization brought to power people less supportive of the US strategic interests in the region. During the 1950s, popular pressures toward socialism and closer ties with the Soviet Union made the US hesitant to support the empowerment of people, while from the 1980s until now strategic interests that prevented popular empowerment were often related to positive attitudes toward Iran or Islamism or against Israel. However, most fierce opposition to the empowerment of the people the US was declaring to protect took place when popular pressures were pushing politicians critical toward US oil interests in power. Democratization of Iran in 1952–1953 with the consequence of rise to power of Prime Minister Mohammed Mosaddegh, and the nationalization of US and UK oil assets in the country led to the most radical US punishment of democracy in the region and the CIA-supported instalment to power for 26 years of an absolute dictator, Mohammad Reza Shah Pahlavi (with highest autocracy score and lowest democracy score according to Polity IV data). The toppling of the Shah in 1979 and the subsequent slow and insecure democratization process after that was another example, this time strategically motivated, of US punishment of democratization (Kivimäki, 2012b).

The United States has three times punished Middle Eastern countries for increased autocracy (Egypt 1952, Syria 1963, and Sudan 1989). However, in each of these cases, the United States also had a strategic motive for doing this. Again in the 1950s and the 1960s, this interest was related to the Soviet Union and socialism, while in the 1980s, it was about Islamism. However, in addition to the Iranian case in 1953, the US-backed autocratic coup of Husni al-Zaim in Syria in 1949 also constituted a major democracy relapse. In other cases of democratic relapse, the US reaction has been either supportive or neutral. The cases of US increasing support after an increase of autocracy were those of Morocco in 1965 and Algeria in 1991. Again the case in the 1960s was related to US strategic competition with the Soviet Union, while the case in the 1990s was related to a civilizational competition with Islamist power. In Palestine, the fight against Islamism has lead the West into an absurd situation where after the elections of 2006, it has been able to support the rule of the loser of the elections (Fatah) in the West Bank, while opposing the rule of the winner of the elections (Hamas) in Gaza (Kivimäki, 2012).

Thus, it seems that American-led Western foreign policy elite has not been able to support the protection of people in the Middle East against autocracy due to the fact that this support has had to be matched with selfish interest that appealed to the constituencies of these politicians. Even though one could say that fight against socialism and Islamism have been fights against autocracy, the Middle East specific cases have shown, at least if we measure democratic and autocratic qualities by using Polity IV data, that such fight against socialism and Islamism has resulted in the support of moves toward autocracy. The need to suppress popular pressures that go against the Western support of Israel, or the Western energy interests again is an even clearer example of the problem that asymmetry and the lack of common cosmopolitan protection of civilians has caused: if democracy as an institutional guarantee of the popular will does not allow voice and agency to the people it protects, protection gets corrupted by partisan, selfish hidden agendas and ulterior motives.

Finally, externally imposed protection has suffered from competence-related problems. Security governance outside one's own territory has been challenging and many operations have turned out to produce unexpected consequences. The history of US empowerment of its future enemies, Al Qaeda, Saddam Hussain, Muammar Gaddafi, Ngo Din Diem, and so many others testify to this. In military matters, incompetence has been related to the problem of reliance of big power's own domestic priorities. As could be seen in the Vietnam

War, American fatalities made the war effort untenable, and thus in order to avoid fatalities, the United States attempted to make warfare more clinical and moved the focus to the use of air power and away from fighting on the ground (Lyall & Wilson III, 2009). This was not helpful as differentiating between the targets of protection and military targets became more difficult from the air. As a result, there were more unintended fatalities, thus escalating the motive for anti-American military operations and the consequent conflict (Mack, 1975; Merom, 2003). The extremely unpopular drone warfare in the current protection wars testifies to the same problem of military myopia: the inability of the external protectors to function effectively due to domestic political problems.

8.4.2. *The problem of asynchrony of collective security agency in the Global North and Global South*

So far when talking about the expansion of security communities, we have made an untenable generalization assuming that the move from families to tribes to societies, feudal states and national-states has taken place simultaneously in the world or that the differences in the phase of progress are somehow meaningless for the global development of peace. Asynchrony in such progress has very important consequences on the feasibility of the cosmopolitan program.

As we have learned, the consolidation of the national-state was an important step in the development of a more peaceful world. The fact that most of the wars of today are domestic wars, and that they take place almost exclusively in the developing world where nation-building has not been finished, suggests that we cannot yet talk about global preparedness to global protection. Even national security communities have not emerged for a majority of global citizens. According to Azar and Moon, the main security challenge for the global majority is therefore in development of national legitimacy, national integration and state's policy capacity (Azar & Moon, 1988). Rules inside a national security community are hollow if the state cannot impose law and order. If the state then does not perform and offer security, it does not have a unifying, integrating force or legitimacy as an organizer of a security community. Thus, interaction within the nation is as anarchic as it is between nations and hence the prevalence of intra-state wars in the developing world.

Since the creation and transformation of social structures in the international system involves bargaining, it is clear that the interests of the developing world are not reflected in international social structures as there are no strong actors, no genuine strong national-states to bargain for the interests of these areas (Ayoob, 1991, 1995, 1997). At the same time, pressures for cosmopolitan order tend to hamper the development of bargaining states in the developing world (Ayoob, 1995, pp. 139–163). To avoid corruption and inefficiency, development cooperation, in its interests of protecting global civilians, often sidelines states of the developing world, and operates in a parallel structure that it can control. By doing this, it often does a good job in the individual operations to help civilians of the developing world. At the same time, such parallel structures compromise the development of state's policy capacity, integration and legitimacy and thus complicate the consolidation of the nation-building process (Akech, 2005). Thus, unintentionally cosmopolitan development efforts hamper the progress toward the previous step in the ladder to greater security: the emergence of the national-state. Similarly, security efforts to protect civilians against tyrants and terrorists also erode the nation-building process. They undermine the state's legitimacy and capacity as well as nation's integration as help to civilians comes from outside the nation. This makes the national unit less meaningful in the production of security (Ayoob, 1995, pp. 139–163). This is where the problems of asymmetry and asynchrony interact, as the poor quality of asymmetric protection clearly underlines the need for states in developing countries, while at the same time it is difficult to imagine an emergence of a legitimate state in, say Yemen, under conditions where the highest judicial power on crimes of security is used by the United States who authorizes drone strikes. If acceptance of such "cooperation" is an international reality for a developing state, it is difficult to imagine the emergence of state structures. Under such conditions, it is easier to imagine the emergence of anti-US anti-state groups that would in interaction with the US war on terror constitute the legitimacy of US drone strikes and anti-state terror. At the same time, in the absence of states in developing countries, it is difficult to imagine improvements to the bargaining situation of the developing world. In the absence of functioning states, developing world cannot bargain against the hidden agendas of distant protection by powerful developed countries. At least to some extent, the asymmetric cosmopolitanism of today is a product of the poor bargaining position of the Global South. Developing countries have had to give in the requirement of symmetry of sovereignty between the North and the South. Sovereignty in cosmopolitan protection is only for the former: Sweden can interfere in Sudan's human rights situation, but Sudan cannot protect Swedish civilians. As a result, the security order of today lacks the feature of general categories that could be the same for all. Instead, asymmetry rules because asynchrony creates the bargaining setting for it.

8.5. How do We Proceed from Here: Can Paradigms Give Prescriptions for Peace Action?

As we know from history, previous enlargements of security communities have been violent. Peace research could have a role in pacifying the transition from asymmetric sense of global solidarity and from the asynchrony in the progress of the enlargement of security communities toward symmetrical and fully global cosmopolitanism. It has been shown how inadequate modeling of structures of purposive behavior by the neo-liberal institutionalists can lead to the inability to avoid conflicts between "rogue nations" and the global leading nation, the United States, and even between China, who in the American eyes, is often seen to irresponsibly defend and help the rogue nations.[7] There the development of more appropriate models could help us

---

[7] Shambaugh accuses China of leading the "coalition of the unwilling" (Shambaugh, 2013), and thereby assisting dictators in avoiding the Western sanctions, while Zoellick lists sanctions and policies of coercion that China has to participate in order to be responsible, hinting that unless China does, it is not responsible as it waters down regulative measures of global governance (Zoellick, 2005).

understand that world politics does not yet have clear, commonly accepted legitimate rules, and that therefore, such rules should be first negotiated and bargained. This would be more constructive than simply enforcing partisan interpretations of norms by using reciprocal sanctions against those who refuse to join the normative or truth regime.

Furthermore, peace research can reduce violence in the process of making cosmopolitan progress more symmetrical and synchronized by revealing the functions of violence in the process, and seeking for less violent alternatives for the things nations do with violence. It would be possible to go further with the analysis of the two obstacles of security cosmopolitanism and look at what kind of symbolic functions violence has when violence erupts between the cosmopolitan North and the nation-building South. This way by understanding the arguments that violence articulates, it would be possible to invent alternative ways of bargaining on the rules of global security community in a less violent manner.

Engaging interpretationist paradigm, it seems clear that violent support of the right of a nation to decide on its path is often used to insulate states from external critique on human rights. A strict interpretation of sovereignty not only allows for nation-building, but also helps autocrats to avoid external critique of exploitative practices of citizens that are themselves too weak to resist such practices (Ayoob, 1997; Krause, 1998). The threat of external interference is also being used to defend the regimes from internal critique: if there is an external threat, the nation has to unite in front of it, and this way even if external critique or action was to protect citizens and human rights of the criticized nation, it is often successfully securitized internally, making any collaboration with such critique treacherous. Critical research has attacked this epistemic practice and interpretation by showing that there is a problem with its logic as it naturalizes the primacy of state security over the security of people and assumes the identity of state security and regime security (Booth, 1991; Krause, 1998). Critique of human rights practices is clearly targeted against the regime and its relationship with the people. This seems positive for security of the state even if it is a threat to the regime. This critique has actually exposed much of autocratic nationalist rhetoric, and in some cases, it has also delegitimized the violent arguments of nationalist autocrats and nationalist Islamist movements. The hidden agenda of selfish authoritarianism exposed is much less useful as a tool for legitimation of autocratic violence.

However, the fact that critique often comes with coercive action — action that actually kills a lot of the humans whose rights it aims at protecting — has weakened the critique and made autocratic rhetoric more credible. It has been claimed that the war in Iraq has made the position of the former regime of Myanmar (Pedersen in Kivimäki & Pedersen, 2008, pp. 39–50; Pedersen, 2011) much stronger internally, while giving the leaders of North Korea more reasons not to yield on nuclear weapons (Baer, 2013): external pressure in Iraq was followed by action in support of democracy and human rights, which actually destroyed not only the regime but also the nation and the state, and so, autocratic leaders as well as radical anti-Western groups could legitimize their violent action internally by referring to an external danger to the nation and the state, not only the regime. This is something that protection wars have made credible. The critical deconstruction of legitimate autocracy would have been possible only if human rights critique was not followed by military action that actually binds regime survival with national survival.

Violence by the global North is used for signaling moral condemnation of autocracy and terror. The father of modern protection wars, President George W. Bush, made this very explicit in his own way when he explained the US action in Iraq: "And by acting, we will signal to outlaw regimes that in this new century, the boundaries of civilized behavior will be respected" (Bush, 2003). However, empirical measurement of success of asymmetric protection shows that distant protection does not work, and that it is considered illegitimate by the people it intends to protect. Thus, other ways of signaling disapproval should be invented. Signaling disapproval with military means is no longer acceptable.

Furthermore, democracy enforcement is given a meaning that is positive for democracy: enforcing democracy signals democratic commitment. George W. Bush's explanation of the war in Afghanistan exemplifies this logic and links it to the old narrative of US role in the making the world safe for democracy: "Because we acted, Afghanistan is a rising democracy ... Because we acted America and the world are safer" (Remarks in St. Paul, Minnesota, August 18, 2004, in Bush, 2004, p. 1724). Yet, in the international system, it exemplifies power of the rich and powerful against those with less money and weapons. Coalitions of the willing get their right from their own constituencies and as long as security production is not extended to the area where security is produced, it will never be democratic. The logic that shows this is one that democratic states are very dependent on: democracy means accountability to the people who decisions affect, and as long as Iraqi people are not able to vote in US, UK, or other coalition force country elections, operations to enforce democracy in Iraq should not be interpreted as expressions of democratic commitment. If we do, consistency would require us to change our definition of democracy rather drastically, and since we are rather dependent on some of the core conventions of democratic thinking, we would not be able to do that.

In order to get closer to conflict resolution in the current protection wars between Western coalitions and Muslim states and groups, it would also be essential to see what kind of meanings are given to conflict realities by actors that we label as autocratic or terroristic. It seems clear that Islamist violence is sometimes used against Western coalitions for signaling disapproval of the external imposition of rules to Muslims. Soon after the September 11th strikes, loyalty to and association with Osama bin Laden was very common. According to PEW opinion polls, Osama bin Laden was seen in the Muslim world as one of the people "doing the right thing in world politics." In Indonesia, 58% felt so, in Pakistan 45%, Jordan 55%, Palestine 71%, and Morocco 49% (Pew Research Centre for People and the Press, 2003). This puts countries and populations into a camp that was difficult to reconcile with: the West could not negotiate with terrorists or people with the terrorist position. But if one looks at the perceptions of such countries where majorities felt Osama bin Laden was doing the right thing, we can see that there he was not seen as a terrorist and he was not perceived as the perpetrator of strikes against civilians (Pew Research Centre for People and the Press, 2003). Instead, support for him signaled opposition to the US-led imposition of rules. Just as research on the consequences of protection wars could criticize the democratic meaning-giving, so would exposure in the Muslim world of the real consequences of terrorism criticize this interpretation of Osama bin Laden: expressing opposition to the lack of US respect to the popular sovereignty of the Muslim world by sympathizing America's terrorist enemies is a product of escalation of antagonism between the West and the Muslim world.

Similarly, violent, Islamist opposition to democracy was taken as a position often in opposition to the Western type of democracy and democracy enforcement, rather than to democracy itself. Osama bin Laden opposed democracy several times as a manmade system that replaces the laws of god with manmade laws. At the same time in his critique of Saudi Arabia (and support of Spain), he also supported accountability of regimes to their people and the idea of equal right to the interpretation of God's will (Laden, 2005). Yet, the word democracy in political reality of conflict between the West and the Muslim world is reserved to the Western type of democracy, and thus, radical Islamism is usually associated with opposition to democracy. This, again, could be traced back to the influence of the hegemonic interpretation of the West according to which meddling in the domestic affairs of the Muslim world constitutes support of democracy, even if from the point of view of Muslims, US meddling constitutes limitations to local popular sovereignty rather than expansion of it. If drones are operated from the United States and thus Iraqi or Yemeni death sentences are handed down by foreigners, they are a threat to local popular sovereignty rather than an instrument of democracy enforcement. Thus, opposition of democracy as a means of protesting American or Western influence is a product of false consciousness, caused by the hegemonic interpretation of the West about protection as democracy support. This false consciousness constructs antagonistic opposition and helps the legitimation of protection wars as measures to support democracy and popular sovereignty.

In addition to understanding the functions of violence and blocking or diverting violent demonstrative action that aims at articulating interpretations and arguments, peace research can also strengthen the civilized mode of international interaction and sensitize world politics to a greater dependence on principles and norms global actors are dependent on in their "normal politics". The normative logic of democracy in itself helps resist asymmetry in the promotion of democracy in the world: if in domestic politics, democracy means a system that regulates political power so that it is distributed evenly among the citizens (one woman/man one vote-principle), then civilized international interaction that respects general categories and normative consistency cannot pretend to promote democracy by doing the exact opposite (expanding the right of powerful nations to use all political power with no regard to the rights of weaker nations). Asymmetry in our current cosmopolitan praxis in world politics could, thus, be criticized by means of normative analysis that emphasizes normative consistency and civilized normative principles rather than simple interests of agents of world politics.

Chapter 9
Conclusions and Missions
for Pragmatist Peace Research

This book has assessed paradigms of social science from the point of view of the pragmatic value for peace research and peace. On the basis of that assessment, it has developed a diagnosis and prescriptions for peace research. It is clear that pragmatist analysis of paradigms of social science could also identify a different set of useful elements from the same paradigms that I have scrutinized. However, it would be even more probable that the analysis of the mega-challenges to peace in today's world could have ended up in different ontological, epistemological, and praxiological conclusions. This is not a problem for the credibility of my analysis just as long as other credible conclusions are not contradictory to my conclusion. Since pragmatism is not based on the idea of truth in which the reality simply expresses itself and allows to be interpreted in just one way, alternative interpretations are not falsifying evidence to one's conclusions. Thus, the development of pragmatist peace research can proceed to several fruitful directions. The intention in this conclusion chapter is not only to summarize the main finding of this book but also to pose a challenge to the reader for further research and study that utilize the logical development of paradigms of peace and move the pragmatist program further.

A systematic analysis of the ways in which different types of theories can be used instrumentally in peacemaking, as well as the analysis of how peaceful are the social realities the truth regimes of different paradigms constitute has led to conclusion that several paradigmatic elements can be used within a consistent set of ontological, epistemological and praxiological assumptions in the creation of tools for peacemaking as well as in the creation of truth regimes that are conducive to peace.

Even if social realities of peace and war are ultimately mostly constructed in the consciousness of people — free individuals and groups — for much of the time when these realities are not actively a target of reflexive scrutiny, social realities are almost like material realities. Furthermore, even if all game structures are socially constituted, their internal logic is given and it has material causal powers: once conflicting parties have engaged in a structure of bargaining, the logic of bargaining dictates the context and outcomes of their actions all the way until they understand their collective power to transform the structure of their interaction by adopting relational preferences, common identities or norms that re-define the rules of the interaction game. Finally, despite the fact that individual and collective human action is partly underdetermined and follows the free will, there are existential preferences that can be assumed constant for those people and those groups that we will have to consider in the future, i.e. individuals and groups that prefer survival to self-destruction and act in a way to survive. All these premises give us positive predictability for conflict developments and justify careful empirical observation of regularities and realities between conditions and conflict behavior. The pattern of internal pacification as security communities expand is based on voluntary (and thus unpredictable) behavior, but since survival is a common preference, and since rules to regulate interaction are instrumentally related to survival, it is rather predictable that the expansion of security communities produces pacification within the new enlarged security community. Once people no longer deal with strangers in a context of anarchy, but with members of "our group" (group whose preferences we are socialized to maximize) in a context of regulated interaction, peacefulness is almost like a natural consequence from the condition of enlarged security communities. This can be verified in the study of the long history of violence even if its explanation requires the anti-deterministic understanding of purposive human behavior. Thus, positivistic search for regularities is useful despite the fact that understanding of the process of enlargement of security communities requires its modeling with anti-deterministic game models that make strategic choices understandable on the basis of an analysis of the structural contexts in which they take place. This way empirical studies of the relationship between the enlargement of security communities and peace are needed, and they can be made compatible with post-positivist, anti-determinist understanding of purposive action and structural constraints to such action. Furthermore, quantitative methods common to positivistic empiricist studies are tremendously helpful for the grasping of mega-processes of social transformation. Despite protests from some post-positivist circles, quantitative investigation can also be made compatible with the post-positivist world view of non deterministic processes and social construction of realities of war and peace. In fact, measuring and numbers help us criticize naturalized constructs that defy empirical evidence. For example, drone strikes are justified by labelling something exceptional (say, collateral damage) and something regular (the targeting of civilians by a specific group) even when numbers suggest that victims of war on terror greatly outnumber victims of terror in many areas. Without measurements, it would not be possible to argue what is regular and what is exceptional.

Positivistic, responsible approach to the substantiation of claims and its methods of grasping large phenomena by using quantitative methods can offer instrumental utility for peace praxis. However, while responsible in its empirical substantiation of claims, positivist approaches do not consciously reflect on the social realities positivist scholarship constitutes, as positivist scholarship is committed to classical scientific realist assumption of the unrelatedness of the reality from the ways of understanding and communicating truths about the social reality of peace and war. Correlative regularities can also exist because people think associations between things are natural, and thus, these regularities exist only because they are believed in. Thus, prevention of violence could in some cases require revealing naturalized regularities, and suddenly people can be emancipated from knowledge that create belligerent realities. Furthermore, positivistic scholarship in its belief in deterministic or probabilistic determinism assumes that conditions of war cause violence by necessity, even if only with a probability, and thus it rejects the reality of alternative futures. If we reject this determinism, we will also have to give a lesser value for historical evidence: what has happened was possible but not necessary. This is why sharp observations by positivist scholars need a reinterpretation before they can be made useful sense. In order to understand conflict behavior and the opportunities for a peace action, one needs to see the opportunities social agents have in choosing strategies and interpretations of the premises of the structure where strategies operate. But we cannot overlook the positivistic evidence of correlations and try to force reality to comply with our theories. When there is a correlative regularity, we should take it seriously and see if there are material necessities that cause it (material power resources in a given interpretation of a power relationship), or whether there are preferences that logically force certain consequences (anarchy that offers more actors to challenge a peaceful order, for example), or whether there are naturalized social constructs that have certain regular consequences. In either of these cases, the correlative regularity is an important starting point for the identification of the diagnosis and the development of the peaceful prescription for the situation.

In peace research that abandons determinism, understanding of conflict behavior from the inside of the logic of action is important. However, since it seems that most people want peace and yet we see so much violence around us, it is important for us to understand structures of interaction that lead peaceful actors to belligerent strategies. I have shown that the logic of bargaining comes closest to the structure where agents of world politics make decisions between peaceful cooperation of various kinds and warfare. I have also shown that this structure of interaction is impervious to measures taken within the structure to rescue socially rational peaceful outcomes. Bargaining structure can only be made safe for peace by changing the premises of the structure of interaction: by introducing socially rational rules, relational preferences, common preferences and collective utility maximization, and finally by creating common security identities. This path to peace seems both theoretically and in the light of historical analysis the main road to peace and cooperation: peace seems to emerge from bargaining and the creation of foundations for such security communities that eventually encompass the bargainers. In this kind of a reading of the development of security in the world, it seems that the increased global interaction is pushing the world into a single security community, a peaceful world society. The way security is constructed today, with the referent object moving toward the community of global civilians, and the way in which security operations have been motivated, suggests that such a transformation of security communities from a national state-based system into a global cosmopolitan system, is on the way. Thus in the long run (centuries), the current bargaining process the world is involved in is one in which national state-based security communities are bargaining for a transition into a more cosmopolitan security order.

However, quantitative observation of the trends of violence, and the analysis of the rhetoric of the most powerful leaders of the world suggest that there is an asymmetry in the cosmopolitan preparedness to a world society. On the one hand, there is preparedness for the global protection of civilians, but on the other, there is no preparedness for a joint production of global security. Furthermore, there is a lack of synchrony in the development of preparedness for cosmopolitanism between the Global North and the Global South. While global interaction has been pushing the North into greater global loyalties, the Global South is still struggling with the problems of nation-building. These two problems create the medium-term (decades) challenges to world peace which are then expressed in conflicts related to state-building in the global South, escalation of such state-building conflicts by external "protection", and the potential of major conflict due to the incompatibility of priorities of sovereignty (national state framing) and protection (cosmopolitan framing) in global governance ("The battle of titans": China and the US).

For the identification of the opportunities for the cosmopolitan transformation into greater security communities, and for the identification of remedies for asymmetry and asynchrony, constructivist and critical paradigms are necessary. I have suggested ways in which post-positivist paradigms could not only offer tools for the promotion of the cosmopolitan turn but also ways in which post-positivist knowledge as such could constitute realities that were more conducive to such a turn.

The next challenge is to make these abstract opportunities concrete and real. After the paradigmatic development proposed in this book, pragmatist peace research has to define concrete research projects that could advance cosmopolitan transition and help remedy the problems of asymmetry and asynchrony and prevent the conflict problems: domestic wars in the Global South, protection wars, and the battle of titans. Since this is book is not only a study but also a textbook, it would be possible to suggest post-graduate and doctoral projects that could be part of the pragmatist "activist science" that does not compromise the lessons of earlier paradigms, but takes into account the logical development of the discipline of peace and conflict research.

Thus, the first main challenge for peace research for the next decade is to tackle the problem of mainly domestic type of warfare and genocidal violence (which sometimes spills over to inter-state conflicts in areas where transnational ethnic groups reside) related to the problem of state-building. Peace promoting research projects should identify the ways in which international interaction and the cosmopolitan fever of the Global North in its development cooperation and security and democracy promotion affect the consolidation of the domestic rule, national agency and the national identity necessary for the creation of security communities out of developing national states. How the aid and security operations affect the legitimacy of the state, national cohesion and the capacity of the state to lead policies of the national state is an important one for many specific territorial and historical contexts. It would be possible to study the compatibility of the important project of nation-building and the practices of development cooperation and security cooperation.

It would be possible to look at how the practices of aid and protection with their short-term focus on solving immediate problems of prosperity and security can be reconciled with the long-term priorities of expansion of the security communities in the Global South from ethnic and tribal into national and perhaps eventually also regional and global levels.

There are many opportunities for quantitative scholarly interventions into political conflict realities of today. There is a need to expose the medicines that are deadlier than the diseases they are meant for. The costs of protective security operations should be revealed by peace and conflict studies. At the same time, it would be important to study how much positive effect there is in the partisan international effort to protect civilians against dictators and terrorists. My studies on the Middle East that I have used in this book have revealed only part of the picture. What have coercive programs to enforce democracy and security really achieved, how much have they influenced ordinary people, their security and their voice in politics?

It would also be possible to design post-graduate and doctoral projects that look at the inconsistencies and naturalized social constructs in the rhetoric and praxis of big power protection of developing countries and especially Muslim countries in strategically important places. This could mean projects that could reveal hidden agendas, and colonial language and mindset in the Western dealing with developing countries and follow the consistency of the normative logic of the ideas (such as democracy, development or good governance) that legitimize Western protection and aid in the developing world on the level of national as well as global governance.

It would be possible to investigate how the process of escalation of tension has modified knowledge and interpretations of global security. How the definition of terrorism is moving from determinants of tactics into determinants of objectives: How ISIS is being defined as terrorist not only due to the tactics it uses in its governance but also due to the Islamist objectives it sets for its political program.

In the case of global governance, there is a need for normative research projects that analyze the content of normative arguments of the US and China, as well as for projects that study the kind of social realities different governance concepts constitute for world peace. I have previously looked at the social realities that the East Asian concept of human security constitute (Kivimäki, 2014a), but the main focus with regard to the pacification of global governance should be in the clarification of conceptions of what is offensive or defensive, what is *status quo* oriented and what is not, what is hegemonic and what is not and what would be the relationship between such identified threats that can be seen threatening the human kind and the various formulas of global governance.

Pragmatist peace research should try to do interpretative hermeneutical work to enhance understanding of the Chinese and US normative ideas about global governance, and these ideas should also be criticized against the findings about the long-term (cosmopolitanization) and medium-term challenges (asymmetry and asynchrony) of peace. All in all peace research does not really have a fruitful mission in trying to predict whether there will be a battle of titans between the two global powers, the US and China. Instead, peace research should understand that the future cannot be predicted, it has to be made. Normative research on the value rational principles of global governance would be of utmost importance for the avoidance of a global war between the old ideas of national state sovereignty, and the premature ideas of asymmetric cosmopolitanism.

All of these and many other alternatives lie ahead for peace research. However, it is not the task of this study to proceed to any of these options. Instead, it is the task of the reader to take the challenge defined by this book and continue the development of pragmatist peace research.

Bibliography

AA, Informant. (2006). Party Activist 2, Fijian Labor Party, Interview by the author in Suva. Fiji.

Acheson, D. (1969). *Present at the Creation: My Years in the State Department*. New York: W.W. Norton.

Åhäll, L. (2012). Motherhood, myth and gendered agency in political violence. *International Feminist Journal of Politics, 14*(1), 103–120.

Akech, J. M. (2005). Development partners and governance of public procurement in Kenya: Enhancing democracy in the administration of aid. *New York University Journal of International Law and Politics, 37*, 829.

Arendt, H. (1970). *On Violence*. San Diego, CA: Harcourt, Brace, Jovanovich.

Åse, C. (2015). Crisis narratives and masculinist protection. *International Feminist Journal of Politics, 17*(4), 1–16.

Auvinen, J. & Kivimäki, T. (2000). Somalia: The Struggle for Resources. In *E. Wayne Nafziger, F. Steward and R. Väyrynen, eds., Weak States and Vulnerable Economies: Humanitarian Emergencies in the Third World*. Oxford: Oxford University Press.

Axelrod, R. (1985). *The Evolution of Cooperation: Revised Edition*. New York, NY: Basic Books.

Axelrod, R. (1986). An evolutionary approach to norms. *American Political Science Review, 80*(4), 1095–1111.

Ayoob, M. (1991). The security problematic of the third World. *World Politics, 43*(2), 257–283.

Ayoob, M. (1995). *The Third World Security Predicament: State Making, Regional conflict and the International System.* Boulder, CO: Lynne Rienner.

Ayoob, M. (1997). Defining Security: A Subaltern Realist Perspective. In *K. Krause and M. C. Williams, eds., Critical Security Studies: Concepts and Cases.* London: UCL Press.

Ayoob, M. (2004). Third World perspectives on humanitarian intervention and international administration. *Global Governance: A Review of Multilateralism and International Organizations, 10*(1), 99–118.

Azar, E. H. & Moon, C., *eds.* (1988). *National Security in the Third World: The Management of Internal and External Threats.* College Park, Md: Center for International Development and Conflict Management, University of Maryland.

Baer, R. (2013). Viewpoint: North Korea's Gaddafi Nightmare. *TIME.com.* Retrieved from http://world.time.com/2013/04/05/viewpoint-north-koreas-gaddafi-nightmare/.

Baker, J. A. III & DeFrank, T. M. (1995). *The Politics of Diplomacy: Revolution, War and Peace,* 1989–1992. New York: G.P. Putnam.

Bamba, J. (2003). Interview with the Executive Director of the Institute of Dayakology.

Beng, K. K. (2014). Xi offers vision of; "Asia-Pacific Dream." Retrieved from http://news.asiaone.com/news/asia/xi-offers-vision-asia-pacific-dream. [November 17, 2014].

Bentham, J. (1890). *Utilitarianism.* London: Progressive Publishing Company.

Berkhoff, K. C. (2012). *Motherland in Danger: Soviet Propaganda during World War II.* Cambridge, MA: Harvard University Press.

Bernardinus, B. (2006). Ketua Benua (Head of the regional cultural order of six villages). Dayak fighter–chief, Sanggau Ledo. Interview by the author.

Berger, P. (1963). *Invitation to Sociology.* Garden City, N.T.: Doubleday.

Betts, A. & Eagleton-Pierce, M. (2005). Editorial introduction "Human Security." *Stair, 1*(2), 5–10.

Bhaskar, R. A. (1989). *Reclaiming Reality: A Critical Introduction to Contemporary Philosophy.* London: Verso.

Bhaskar, R. A. (1997). *A Realist Theory of Science.* London: Verso.

Bieler, A. & Morton, A. D. (2001). The Gordian Knot of agency — structure in international relations: A neo-gramscian perspective. *European Journal of International Relations, 7*(1), 5–35.

Blumer, H. (1969). *Symbolic Interactionism: Perspective and Method.* Englewood Cliffs, N.J.: Prentice Hall.

Booth, K. (1991). Security and emancipation. *Review of International Studies, 17*(04), 313–326.

Booth, K. (2007). *Theory of World Security.* Cambridge: Cambridge University Press.

Booth, K. & Wheeler, N. J. (2008). *The Security Dilemma.* New York: Palgrave Macmillan.

Boulding, K. (1978). *Stable Peace.* Austin, TX: University of Texas Press.

Bray, D. (2009). Pragmatic cosmopolitanism: A Deweyan approach to democracy beyond the Nation-State. *Millennium Journal of International Studies, 37*(3), 683–719.

Bray, D. (2013). Pragmatic ethics and the will to believe in cosmopolitanism. *International Theory, 5*(03), 446–476.

Breakspear, A. (2013). A new definition of intelligence. *Intelligence and National Security, 28*(5), 678–693.

Brewer, S. A. (2009). *Why America Fights: Patriotism and War Propaganda from the Philippines to Iraq.* Oxford: Oxford University Press.

Brown, M. E., Lynn-Jones, S. M., & Miller, S. E. (1996). *Debating the Democratic Peace.* Cambridge, MA: MIT Press.

Bush, G. W. (2003). Full text: George Bush's speech to the American Enterprise Institute. *The Guardian.* Retrieved from http://www.the-guardian.com/world/2003/feb/27/usa.iraq2.

Bush, G. W. (2004). Public Papers of the Presidents of the United States, George W. Bush, 2004, Book 2, July 1 to September 30, 2004. *National Archives and Records Administration, Office of the Federal Register.* Washington D.C.: Government Printing Office.

Bush, G. W. (n.d.). "We will hunt down terrorists", Mail Online. Retrieved from http://www.dailymail.co.uk/news/article-71888/Bush-We-hunt-terrorists.html. [December 5, 2013].

Busse, N. (1999). Constructivism and Southeast Asian security. *The Pacific Review, 12*(1), 39–60.

Butterfield, H. (1949). *Christianity and History.* London: G. Bell.

Butterfield, H. (1951). *History and human relations.* London: Collins.

Cafruny, A. W. (1990). The Gramscian Concept of Declining Hegemony: Stages of US Power and the Evolution of International Economic Relations. In *David P. Rapkin, ed., World Leadership and Hegemony. International Political Economy Yearbook*, Vol. 5, pp. 97–118. Boulder, CO: Lynne Rienner.

Charon, J. M. (1995). *Symbolic Interactionism. An Introduction, Interpretation, and Integration.* Prentice Hall, Englewood Clifffs, NJ: Simon & Schulster.

Choi, S.-W. & Shali, L. (2013). Economic sanctions, poverty, and international terrorism: An empirical analysis. *International Interactions, 39*(2), 217–245.

Christensen, T. J. (2002). The contemporary security dilemma: Deterring a Taiwan conflict. *Washington Quarterly, 25*(4), 7–21.

Clinton, W. J. (1995). Remarks Commemorating the 50th Anniversary of Iwo Jima in Arlington, Virginia, February 19, 1995. Retrieved from http://www.presidency.ucsb.edu/ws/index.php?pid=51005&st=Heroism&st1=African--American. [Accessed date December 18, 2013].

Clinton, W. J. (1997). Remarks on Presenting the Congressional Medal of Honor to African--American Heroes of World War II, January 13, 1997. Retrieved from http://www.presidency.ucsb.edu/ws/index.php?pid=53972&st=Heroism&st1=African–American. [Accessed date December 18, 2013].

Colapietro, V. M. (2005). Charles Sanders Peirce. In *J. R. Shook and J. Margolis, eds., A Companion to Pragmatism.* Blackwell Publishing. Blackwell Reference Online.

Coleman, J. S. (1966). Individual interests and collective action. *Public Choice, 1*(1), 49–62.

Coleman, J. S. (1990). *Foundations of Social Theory.* London & Cambridge MA: Belknap.

Collier, P. & Hoeffler, A. (2004). Greed and grievance in civil war. *Oxford Economic Papers, 56,* 565–595.

Collier, P., Elliott, V. L., Hegre, H., Hoeffler, A., Reynal-Queral, M., & Sambanis, N. (2003). *Breaking the conflict trap: civil war and development policy.* Washington D.C. and New York: World Bank and Oxford University Press.

Collins, R. (2008). *Violence: A Micro-Sociological Theory.* Princeton: Princeton University Press.

Cox, R. W. (1981). Social forces, states and World orders: Beyond international theory. *Millennium — Journal of International Studies, 10*(2), 126–155.

Cox, R. W. (2001). The Way ahead: Toward a New Ontology of World Order. In *R. W. Jones, ed., Critical Theory and World Politics,* pp. 45–59. Boulder, CO: Lynne Rienner.

Darwis. (2009). Head of Sambas Malay Organization (Ketua Dewan Adat Malay Sambas). Discussion with the author in Sambas.

Davidson, J. S. (2007). Culture and rights in ethnic violence. In *J. S. Davidson and D. Hendley, eds., The Revival of Tradition in Indonesian Politics*, pp. 224–246. London and New York: Routledge.

De Sousa, I. (2000). The resource curse: are civil wars driven by rapacity or paucity? In *M. Berdal and D. M. Malone, eds., Greed and Grievance: Economic Agendas in Civil Wars*, pp. 113–135. London: Lynne Rienner.

Deif, M. (2012). Interviewed in "Hamas gunmen execute six 'Israeli spies' as Netanyahu hints at cease-fire". *Associated Press*. Retrieved from http://news.nationalpost.com/2012/11/20/hamas--gunmen--execute-six-israeli-spies-on-busy-gaza-street-corner/.

Dessler, D. (1991). Beyond correlations: Towards a causal theory of War. *International Studies Quarterly, 35*(3), 337–355.

Dessler, D. (1999). Constructivism within a positivist social science. *Review of International Studies, 25*(01), 123–137.

Dewey, J. (1917). *Creative Intelligence: Essays on the Pragmatic Attitude*. New York: Henry Holt & Co.

Dewey, J. (1993). *The Political Writings*. In *D. Morris and I. Shapiro eds.*, Indianapolis/Cambridge: Hackett Publishing Company.

Diehl, P. F. (1983). Arms races and escalation, a closer look. *Journal of Peace Research, 20*(1), 205–212.

Diplomatic Push for Assad to Give up Chemical Weapons Could Prevent Military Strike. (2013). *Foreign Policy Morning Brief*. Retrieved from https://mail.google.com/mail/u/0/?ui=2&shva=1#inbox/14107acb5 1b2cb81.

Doty, R. L. (1997). Aporia: A critical Exploration of the agent-structure problematique in international relations theory. *European Journal of International Relations, 3*(3), 365–392.

Deutsch, K. *et al.* (1955). *Political Community and the North Atlantic Area*. Westport: Greenwood Press.

Duffield, J. (2001). Why is there no APTO? Why is there no OSCAP? Asia-Pacific security institutions in comparative perspective. *Contemporary Security Policy, 22*(2), 69–95.

Dumbrell, J. (2009). *Clinton's Foreign Policy: Between the Bushes, 1992–2000*. London: Routledge.

Eck, K. & Hultman, L. (2007). Violence against civilians in War. *Journal of Peace Research, 44*(2), 233–246.

Eckstein, H. (1975). *Eckstein, Harry 1975. Patterns of Authority: A Structural Basis for Political Inquiry.* New York: John Wiley & Sons. Retrieved from http://www.systemicpeace.org/polity/polity4.htm.

Elias, N. (1939). *The Civilizing Process. Sociogenetic and Psychogenetic Investigations.* Cambridge, MA: Blackwell.

Elias, N. (1982). *Power and Civility: The Civilizing Process,* Vol. 5. New York: Pantheon.

Ellsberg, D. (1968). *The Theory and Practice of Blackmail* (Rand Study P. 3883). Los Angeles, CA: Rand Corporation. Retrieved from http://www.rand.org/pubs/papers/P3883.html.

Elrod, R. (1984). The Concert of Europe. In *R. O. Matthews, A. G. Rubinoff and J. G. Stein, eds., International Conflict and Conflict Management: Readings in World Politics,* pp. 411–420. Scarborough, Ontario: Prentice-Hall.

En-lai, C. (1962). Report on Government work, April 18, 1959. In *Communist China 1955–1959: Policy Documents with Analysis,* pp. 503–529. Boston, MA: Harvard University Press.

Fearon, J. D. (1995). Rationalist explanations for War. *International Organization, 49*(3), 379–414.

Femia, J. (1981). *Gramsci's Political Thought: Hegemony, Consciousness and the Revolutionary Process.* Oxford: Clarendon Press.

Fischer, J. M., Kane, R., Pereboom, D., & Vargas, M. (2007). *Four Views on Free Will.* New Jersey: Wiley.

Fisher, R. & Ury, W. (1991). *Getting to Yes: Negotiating Agreement Without Giving in.* Boston: Houghton Mifflin Harcourt.

Fitzgerald, C. P. (1963). The Chinese view of foreign relations. *World Today,* 9–17.

Former Drone Operator "Haunted" By His "1600 Hits" Scorecard. (n.d.). Retrieved from http://crabbygolightly.com/wordpress/former-drone-operarator-haunted-by-his-1600-hits-scorecard/83418009/?google_editors_picks=true&goback=%2Egde_116981_member_247993778. [Accessed June 11, 2013].

Foucault, M. (1994). *The Order of Things.* New York: Vintage Books.

Fridlund, M. (2012). Affording terrorism: Idealists and materialities in the emergence of modern terrorism. In *M. Taylor and M. P. Currie, eds., Terrorism and Affordance,* pp. 73–92. London: Continuum. Retrieved from http://www.academia.edu/1229781/Affording_terrorism_Idealists_and_materialities_in_the_emergence_of_modern_terrorism.

Fritzsche, P. (2008). *Life and Death in the Third Reich*. Cambridge, MA: Harvard University Press.

Fromm, E. (1973). *The Anatomy of Human Destructiveness*. New York: Holt, Rinehart & Winston.

Fukuyama, F. (1995). *Trust: The Social Virtues and the Creation of Prosperity*. London: Hamish Hamilton.

Fukuyama, F. (2000). *The Great Disruption. Human nature and the reconstitution of social order*. London: Profile Books.

Fukuyama, F. (2011). *The Origins of Political Order from Prehuman Times to the French Revolution*. New York: MacMillan, Farrar, Straus and Giroux Paperbacks.

Gadamer, H.-G. (1989). *Truth and Method*, 2nd edition. London: Sheed & Ward.

Galtung, J. (1964). An editorial. *Journal of Peace Research*, *1*(1), 1–4.

Galtung, J., & Höivik, T. (1971). Structural and direct violence: A note on operationalization. *Journal of Peace Research*, *8*(1), 73–76.

Gelpi, C. (1997). Democratic diversions: Governmental structure and the externalization of domestic conflict. *Journal of Conflict Resolution*, *41*(2), 255–282.

Giddens, A. (1985). *The Nation-state and Violence: Volume Two of a Contemporary Critique of Historical Materialism*. Berkeley, CA: University of California Press.

Gleditsch, N. P. (1995). Geography, Democracy and Peace. *International Interactions: Empirical and Theoretical Research in International Relations*, *20*(4), 297–323.

Gleditsch, N. P. & Hegre, H. (1997). Peace and democracy: Three levels of analysis. *Journal of Peace Research*, *41*(2), 283–310.

Goh, E. (2008). Hierarchy and the role of the United States in the East Asian security order. *International Relations of the Asia-Pacific*, *8*(3), 353–377.

Goulden, J. C. (1982). *Korea: The Untold Story of the War*. New York: Times Books.

Gurr, T. R. (1970). *Why Men Rebel*. Princeton, N.J.: Princeton University Press.

Gurr, T. R. (1993). *Minorities at Risk*. Washington D.C.: United States Institute of Peace Press.

Habermas, J. (1984). *The Theory of Communicative Action: Reason and the rationalization of society*. Boston: Beacon Press.

Haldeman, H. R. (1995). *The Haldeman Diaries: Inside the Nixon White House*. New York: HarperCollins.

Harbom, L. & Wallensteen, P. (2009). Armed conflicts, 1946–2008. *Journal of Peace Research, 46*(4), 577–587.

Harré, R. & Madden, E. H. (1975). *Causal Powers: The Theory of Natural Necessity.* Oxford: Blackwell.

Harsanyi, J. (1956). Approaches to bargaining problem before and after the theory of games. *Econometrica, 24*, 144–156.

Haste, C. (1995). The machinery of propaganda. In *R. Jackall, ed., Propaganda*, pp. 105–136. London: MacMillan.

Haynes, M. (2003). Counting soviet deaths in the great patriotic War: A note. *Europe-Asia Studies, 55*(2), 303–309.

Heidegger, M. (1962). *Being and Time.* Oxford: Blackwell.

Hempel, C. (1965). *Aspects of Scientific Explanation.* New York: Free Press.

Hermanus, B. (2005). Interview by the author with a Dayak activist from Malawi, West Kalimantan, Indonesia.

Hertz, J. H. (1950). Idealist internationalism and the security dilemma. *World Politics, 2*(1), 157–180.

Hertz, J. H. (1959). *International Politics in the Atomic Age.* New York: Colombia University Press.

Hodgson, K. (1996). *Written with the Bayonet: Soviet Russian Poetry of World War Two.* Liverpool: Liverpool University Press.

Hoffer, E. (2002). *The True Believer. Thoughts on the Nature of Mass Movements.* New York, NY: HarperCollins.

Hollis, M. & Smith, S. (1990). *Explaining and Understanding International Relations.* Oxford: Clarendon Press.

Homel, J. D. (2014). "Russia's top 20 lies about Ukraine", Examiner.com, June 5, 2014. Retrieved from http://www.examiner.com/list/russia-s-top-20-liesabout-ukraine. [Accessed date June 9, 2014].

Hopf, T. (1998). The promise of constructivism in international relations theory. *International Security, 23*(1), 171–200.

Horowitz, D. L. (2003). *The Deadly Ethnic Riot.* Berkeley, CA: University of California Press.

House Republican Leaders Endorse Military Action in Syria. (2013). *Policy Morning Brief of the Foreign Policy Magazine*, Wednesday, September 4, 2013.

Hu, J. (2005). Written Speech by H. E. Hu Jintao President of the People's Republic of China at the High-level Plenary Meeting of the United Nations' 60th Session. Retrieved from http://www.fmprc.gov.cn/eng/wjdt/zyjh/t213091.htm. [Accessed date October 29, 2013].

Hufbauer, G. C., Schott, J. J., Elliott, K. A., & Oegg, B. (2007). *Economic Sanctions Reconsidered*, 3rd edition: *Database*. Washington D.C.: Peterson Institute for International Economics.

Humpreys, B. (2013). *The Battle Backwards: A Comparative Study of the Battle of Kosovo Polje (1389) and the Munich Agreement (1938) as Political Myths*. Helsinki: Publications of the Department of Political and Economic Studies 12.

Husain, F. (2007). *To See the Unseen (Edited by Salim Shahab and E. E. Siadari)*. Jakarta: Health and hospital Indonesia.

Ikenberry, G. J. (2012). The Rise of China, the United States, and the Future of the Liberal International Order. In *D. L. Shambaugh, ed., Tangled Titans: The United States and China*. Lanham, MD: Rowman & Littlefield.

International Commission on Intervention and State Sovereignty. (2005). Responsibility to Protect Report. Retrieved from http://www.cfr.org/humanitarian-intervention/international-commission-intervention-state-sovereignty-responsibility-protect-report/p24228. [Accessed date October 31, 2013].

Israel launches retaliation strikes against Hamas rocket attacks. (2012). *Fox News*. Retrieved from http://www.foxnews.com/world/2012/11/15/3-dead-after-gaza-rocket-strikes-southern-israel.html.

James, W. (1910). Does consciousness exist? *Journal of Philosophy, Psychology and Scientific Method, 1*(18).

James, W. (1913). *Pragmatismi* (Translated from lectures by K.W. Silfverberg). Helsinki: Otava.

James, W. (1977). *The Writings of William James, (Edited by John J. McDermott)*. New York: Random House.

Jervis, R. (2001). Was the Cold War a security dilemma? *Journal of Cold War Studies, 3*(1), 36–60.

Jutila, M., Pehkonen, S., & Väyrynen, T. (2008). Resuscitating a discipline: an agenda for critical peace research. *Millennium: Journal of International Studies, 36*(3), 623–640.

Jäger, S. (2001). Discourse and knowledge: Theoretical and methodological aspects of a critical discourse and dispositive analysis. In *R. Wodak and M. Meyer, eds., Methods of Critical Discourse Analysis*, pp. 32–62. London: Sage.

Kahin, G. M. (1952). *Nationalism and Revolution Indonesia*. Ithaca, NY: Cornell University Press.

Kaldor, M. (1999). *New and Old Wars. Organized Violence in a Global Era*. Stanford, CA: Stanford University Press.

Kamatsiko, V. V. (2014). Pcia theory in field practice: World vision' pursuit of peace impact and programming quality across sectors. *Journal of Peacebuilding & Development, 9*(1), 26–43.

Kane, A. (2014). 4 Ways the U.S. Is Violently Meddling In the Syrian Civil War. *AlterNet*. Retrieved from http://www.alternet.org/world/how-us-violently-meddling-syrian-civil-war.

Kant, I. (1999). Toward Perpetual Peace. In *Practical Philosophy — Cambridge Edition of the Works of Immanuel Kant. Gregor MJ (trans.)*. Cambridge: Cambridge University Press.

Kant, I. (2005). *Groundwork for the Metaphysics of Morals.* Broadview Press.

Kapstein, E. B. (2005). Power, fairness, and the global economy. In *M. Barnett and R. Duvall, eds., Power in Global Governance,* pp. 80–101. Cambridge: Cambridge University Press.

Kaufmann, C. (1997). Possible and Impossible Solutions to Ethnic Civil Wars. In *M. E. Brown, O. R. Coté, Jr., S. M. LynnJones and S. E. Miller, eds., Nationalism and Ethnic Conflict: An International Security Reader,* pp. 265–304. Cambridge, MA: The MIT Press.

Kaufmann, S. J. (2001). *Modern Hatreds: The Symbolic Politics of Ethnic War.* Ithaca, NY: Cornell University Press.

Kaufmann, S. J. (2006). Symbolic politics or rational choice? Testing theories of extreme ethnic violence. *International Security, 30*(4), 45–86.

Kekkonen, U. K. (1967). Naapurisopu "perivihollisen" kanssa (Neigborly peace with an archrival). A speech in Stockholm on December 7, 1943. In *T. Vilkuna, ed., Urho Kekkosen puheita ja kirjoituksia (Speeches and writings of Urho Kekkonen) 1, Puheita vuosilta (Speeches from years)* 1936–1956, pp. 122–137. Helsinki: Weiling & Göös.

Keohane, R. O. (1986). Reciprocity in international relations. *International Organization, 40*(1), 1–27.

King, G., Keohane, R. O., & Verba, S. (1994). *Designing Social Inquiry: Scientific Inference in Qualitative Research.* Princeton: Princeton University Press.

Kingsbury, D. (2006). *Peace in Aceh: a personal account of the Aceh peace process.* Jakarta: Equinox Publishing. Retrieved from http://dro.deakin.edu.au/view/DU:30000430.

Kissinger, H. A. (1973). *A World Restored: The Politics of Concervatisvism in a Revolutionary Era.* London: Victor Gollancz.

Kivimäki, T. (1995). *Conditions of Hegemonic Order and Strategies of National Development: The Philippine Experience.* Helsinki: Institute of Development Studies.

Kivimäki, T. (2001a). *Explaining Violence in Somalia*. Helsinki: CTS–Conflict Transformation Service, Studies in a Nutshell, No. 4.

Kivimäki, T. (2001b). The long peace of ASEAN. *Journal of Peace Research*, *38*(1), 5–25.

Kivimäki, T. (2001c). *Valtio viidakkoveitsen terällä. Analyysi Indonesian konflikteista.* (*A Nation on the edge of a jungle knife. An analysis of Indonesian conflicts*). Tampere: Tampereen Rauhan — ja konfliktin tutkimuksen instituutti, TAPRI.

Kivimäki, T. (2002). Reason and power in territorial disputes: The South China Sea. *Asian Journal of Social Science, 30*(3), 525–546.

Kivimäki, T. (2003a). *US-Indonesian Hegemonic Bargaining: Strength of Weakness.* Adlershot: Ashgate.

Kivimäki, T. (2003b). Notes on a field trip to Tanjung Keracut, Sambas, West Kalimantan, Indonesia, Interviews with a government official trainee (Zul Alqadrie), village head of Tanjung Keracut and a Malay youth leader.

Kivimäki, T. (2003c). *Development Cooperation as an Instrument in the Prevention of Terrorism.* Copenhagen: Ministry for Foreign Affairs.

Kivimäki, T. (2005). *Islam, the West and Violence between the Civilizations.* Helsinki: Finnish Foreign Ministry.

Kivimäki, T. & Pasch, P. (2009). *Peace and Conflict Impact Assessment Country conflict-analysis studies. The Dynamics of Conflict in the Multiethnic Union of Myanmar.* Berlin: Friedrich Ebert Stiftung.

Kivimäki, T. & Pedersen, M. (2008). *Burma/Myanmar: Mapping the Challenges and Opportunities for Dialogue and Reconciliation.* Helsinki: CMI — Crisis Management Initiative (Office of President Martti Ahtisaari).

Kivimäki, T. (2008). Can the international community help prevent conflict in Burma/Myanmar. In *J. Lagerkvist, ed., Between Isolation and Internationalization: The State of Burma.* Stockholm: Swedish Institute of International Affairs.

Kivimäki, T. (2010). The Jeju process and the relative peace in East Asia. *Korean Journal of Defence Analysis, 22*(3), 355–370.

Kivimäki, T. (2012a). *Can Peace Research Make Peace? Lessons in Academic Diplomacy.* Farnham: Ashgate.

Kivimäki, T. (2012b). Democracy, autocrats and U.S. polices. *Middle East Policy, XIX*(1), 64–71.

Kivimäki, T. (2013). United States and the Arab Spring. *Journal of Human Security, 9*(1), 15–26.

Kivimäki, T. (2014a). Can the Pragmatic East Asian approach to human security offer a way for the deepening of the long peace of East Asia? *Journal of Human Security, 10*(2), 76–88.

Kivimäki, T. (2014b). Regional Cooperation and Joint Development: Speech That Acts And Action That Speaks, In *S. Wu and K. Zou, eds., Non-Traditional Security Issues and the South China Sea: Shaping a New Framework for Cooperation.* Farnham: Ashgate.

Kivimäki, T. (2014c). Soft Power and Global Governance with Chinese Characteristics. *The Chinese Journal of International Politics, 7*(4), 421–447.

Kivimäki, T. (2014d). *The Long Peace of East Asia.* Farnham: Ashgate.

Kivimäki, T. (2015). Finlandization and the peaceful development of China. *The Chinese Journal of International Politics, 8*(2), 139–166.

Kratochwil, F. V. (1989). *Rules, Norms and Decisions.* Cambridge: Cambridge University Press.

Krause, K. (1998). Theorizing security, state formation and the "Third World" in the post-Cold War world. *Review of International Studies, 24*(01), 125–136.

Krause, K. & Williams, M. (1997). *Critical Security Studies: Concepts and Cases.* Minneapolis: University of Minneapolis Press.

Kriesberg, L. (1988). *Constructive Conflicts: From Escalation to Resolution.* Lanham, MD: Rowman & Littlefield.

Kundrus, B. (2005). Rezeptionen der medialen Meinungs — ud Gefühlslenkung. In *Jörg Echternkamp, ed., Das Deutsche Reich und der Zweite Wltkrieg,* 2nd edition, Vol. 9. Munich: DVA Sachbuch.

Kurki, M. (2008). *Causation in International Relations. Reclaiming Causal Analysis.* Cambridge: Cambridge University Press.

Kuusisto, R. (1999). *Western Definitions of War in the Gulf and in Bosnia: The Rhetorical Frameworks of the United States, British and French Leaders in Action.* Finland: Finnish Academy of Science & Letters.

Lacina, B. A. & Gleditsch, N. P. (2005). Monitoring trends in global combat: A new dataset of battle deaths. *European Journal of Population, 21*(2–3), 145–165.

Laclau, E. & Mouffe, C. (2001). *Hegemony and Socialist Strategy: Towards a Radical Democratic Politics.* London & New York: Verso.

Laden, O. B. (2005). *Messages to the World: The Statements of Osama Bin Laden.* London & New York: Verso.

Lake, D. A. & Rothchild, D. (1997). Containing Fear Cambridge. In *Michael E. Brown, Owen R. Coté, Jr., Sean M. Lynn-Jones and Stephen*

E. Miller, eds., *Nationalism and Ethnic Conflict: An International Security Reader*, pp. 97–131. Cambridge, MA: MIT Press.

Lampton, D. M. (2005). China's Rise in Asia Need Not Be at America's Expense. In *D. Shambaugh, ed., Power Shift: China and Asia's New Dynamics*, pp. 317–319. Berkeley, CA: University of California Press.

Lasswell, H. (1995). Propaganda technique in the World War. In *R. Jackall, ed., Propaganda*, pp. 13–25. London: McMillan.

Laurel, J. P. (1954). Laurel's letter to President Magsaysay, Laurel–Langley Papers, Series 5, Correspondence File. Laurel Memorial Library, Manila.

Lebow, R. N. (2009a). Constitutive causality: Imagined spaces and political practices. *Millennium — Journal of International Studies, 38*(2), 211–239.

Lebow, R. N. (2009b). *Forbidden Fruit: Counterfactuals and International Relations*. Princeton, NJ: Princeton University Press.

Lenin, V. I. (1980). *Imperialismista ja Imperialisteista (On Imperialism and Imperialists)*. Moscow: Progress.

Levy, J. S. (1989). The Diversionary Theory of War: A Critique. In *M. Midlarsky, ed., Handbook of War Studies*, pp. 259–288. Boston: Unwin Hyman.

Li, H. Y. & Zheng, Y. (2009). Re-interpreting China's Non-intervention policy towards Myanmar: Leverage, interest and intervention. *Journal of Contemporary China, 18*(61), 617–637.

Lichbach, M. I. & Gurr, T. R. (1981). Forecasting Domestic Political Conflict. In *J. D. Singer and M. D. Wallace, eds., To Auger Well: Early Warning Indicators in World Politics*. Beverly Hills, CA: Sage.

Lindley, D. (2007). *Promoting Peace with Information: Transparency as a Tool of Security Regimes*. Princeton: Princeton University Press.

Livshin, A. & Orlov, I. (2012). The Soviet propaganda state during World War II: Resource constraints and communication capabilities. *Soviet and Post-Soviet Review, 39*(2), 192.

Lo, C.-K. (1989). *China's Policy Towards Territorial Disputes: The Case of South China Sea Islands*. London: Routledge.

Lyall, J. & Wilson III, I. (2009). Rage against the machines: Explaining outcomes in counterinsurgency wars. *International Organization, 63*, 67–106.

Mack, A. (1975). Why big nations lose small Wars: The politics of asymmetric conflict. *World Politics, 27*(2), 175–200.

Madison, G. B. (1988). *Hermeneutics of Postmodernity*. Bloomington, ID: Indiana University Press.

Marchetti, V. & Marks, J. D. (1974). *The CIA and the Cult of Intelligence*. Hodder and Stoughton: Coronet Books.

Mariager, R. (2013). Surveillance of peace movements in Denmark during the Cold War. *Journal of Intelligence History, 12*(1), 60–75.

Marsellino. (2005). Interview in Pontianak, West Kalimantan, Indonesia with a Dayak student from Bengkayang.

Marshall, M. G. & Jaggers, K. (2000). Polity IV Project. Political Regime Characteristics and Transitions, 1800–1999, Dataset User Manual. Retrieved from http://www.systemicpeace.org/inscr/p4manualv2012.pdf.

Marx, K. (1990). *Capital Volume 1*. London: Penguin Books Limited.

McDonald, P. J. (2009). *The Invisible Hand of Peace: Capitalism, the War Machine, and International Relations Theory*. Cambridge: Cambridge University Press.

McKinley, W. (1899). Third Annual Message, December 5, 1899. Retrieved from http://www.presidency.ucsb.edu/ws/index.php?pid=29540. [Accessed date December 9, 2013].

Mead, G. H. (1934). *Mind, Self and Society*. Chicago: University of Chicago Press.

Mearsheimer, J. J. (2001). *The Tragedy of Great Power Politics*. New York: W.W. Norton.

Merikallio, K. (2005). *Making peace — Ahtisaari and Aceh*. Helsinki: WSOY.

Merom, G. (2003). *How Democracies Lose Small Wars: State, Society, and the Failures of France in Algeria, Israel in Lebanon, and the United States in Vietnam*. Cambridge: Cambridge University Press.

Moeller, S. D. (1989). *Shooting Wars: Photography and the American Experience of Combat*. New York, NY: Basic Books.

Morgenthau, H. J. (2006). *Politics among Nations: The Struggle for Power and Peace*, 7th edition, Revised by *Kenneth W. Thompson & W. David Clinton*. New York: McGraw Hill.

Mouffe, C. (1996). *Deconstruction and Pragmatism: Simon Critchley, Jacques Derrida, Ernesto Laclau and Richard Rorty*. London & New York: Routledge.

Murphy, D. E. (2006). *What Stalin Knew: The Enigma of Barbarossa*. New Haven CT: Yale University Press.

Myrttinen, H. (2010). Masculinities, Conflict and UNSCR 1325 — UN Resolutions — Gunda Werner Institute. Retrieved from http://www.gwi-boell.de/en/2010/09/30/masculinities-conflict-and-unscr-1325.

Nash, J. (1950). The bargaining problem. *Econometrica, 18*, 155–162.

Nash, J. (1953). Two person cooperative games. *Econometrica, 21*, 128–140.

Neubert, S. (2009). *John Dewey between Pragmatism and Constructivism*. Bronx, NY.: Fordham University Press.

Nye, J. S. (1990). Soft power. *Foreign Policy*, (80), 153–171.

Nye, J. S. (2013). What China and Russia don't get about soft power? *Foreign Policy*, April 29, 2013.

Olson, M. (2009). *The Logic of Collective Action*. Cambridge MA: Harvard University Press.

Osiel, M. (2009). *The End of Reciprocity: Terror, Torture, and the Law of War*. New York: Cambridge University Press.

Parashar, S. (2009). Feminist international relations and women militants: case studies from Sri Lanka and Kashmir. *Cambridge Review of International Affairs*, 22(2), 235–256.

Pareto, V. (1897). The new theories of economics. *Journal of Political Economy*, 5(4), 485–502.

Pareto, V. (1971). *Manual of Political Economy*. (English edition, translated by *A.M. Kelley*). Paris: Marcel Giard.

Patomäki, H. (1996). How to tell better stories about world politics. *European Journal of International Relations*, 2(1), 105–133.

Patomäki, H. (2013). *Why Do Social Sciences Matter? From Explanatory Critique to Concrete Eutopias in the Study of World Politics*. Jyväskylä: University of Jyväskylä.

Patomäki, H. & Wight, C. (2000). After postpositivism? The promises of critical realism. *International Studies Quarterly*, 44(2), 213–237.

Pedersen, M. (2011). The politics of burma's "Democratic" transition. *Critical Asian Studies*, 43(1), 49–68.

Peirce, C. S. (1931). *Collected Papers of Charles Sanders Peirce*. In *C. Hartshorne, P. Weiss, and A. Burks, eds.*, Vol. 5. Cambridge, Mass.: Harvard University Press.

Peoples, C. & Vaughan-Williams, Ni. (2010). *Critical Security Studies. An Introduction*. London & New York: Routledge.

Perelman, C. & Olbrechts-Tyteca, L. (1968). *The New Rhetoric: A Treatise on Argumentation*. Notre Dame, IN: University of Notre Dame.

Pew Research Centre for People and the Press. (2003). 2002 *Global Attitudes Survey*. Retrieved from http://people-press.org/reports/display.php3?ReportID=165: PEW.

Pinker, S. (2011). *The Better Angels of Our Nature. The Decline of Violence in History and its Causes*. London: Allen Lane/Penguin.

Pleshakov, C. (2005). *Stalin's Folly. The Tragic First Ten Days of World War II on the Eastern Front*. New York, NY: Houghton Mifflin Harcourt.

Popper, K. (2012). *The Open Society and Its Enemies*. Oxon: Routledge.

Porter, A. (2013). What is constructed can be transformed: Masculinities in post-conflict societies in Africa. *International Peacekeeping*, 20(4), 486–506.

Poulton, R. E. & Youssouf, I. (1998). *A Peace of Timbuktu: Democratic Governance, Development and African Peacemaking*. Geneva: UNIDIR.

Powers, M. (2014). Sticks and stones: The relationship between drone strikes and al-Qaeda's portrayal of the United States. *Critical Studies on Terrorism*, 7(3).

Program on International Policy Attitudes. (2006). *The Iraqi Public on the US Presence and the Future of Iraq*. WorldPublicOpinion.org: World Public Opinion.

Rasyid, B. A. (2008). Interview with the leader of the district (Bubati) of Sambas, West Kalimantan, Indonesia by the author.

Rayment, S. (2005). Secret MoD Poll: Iraqis Supports Attacks on British Troops. *Telegraph*. Retrieved from https://www.globalpolicy.org/component/content/article/168/37188.html.

Rehg, W. & Davis, D. (2003). Conceptual gerrymandering? The alignment of Hursthouse's naturalistic virtue ethics with Neo-Kantian non-naturalism. *The Southern Journal of Philosophy*, 41(4), 583–600.

Rios, D. (2004). Mechanistic explanations in the social sciences. *Current Sociology*, 52(1), 75–89.

Risen, J. & Mazzetti, M. (2012). U.S. Agencies See No Move by Iran to Build a Bomb. *The New York Times*. February 25, 2012, p. 1.

Rivlin, A. F. (2008). *The Diversionary Theory of Foreign Policy? American Presidents and Public Opinion*. US: ProQuest.

Ro'i, Y. & Morozov, B. (2008). *The Soviet Union and the June 1967 Six Day War*. Washington, D.C.: Stanford University Press.

Rorty, R. (1991). *Objectivity, Relativism, and Truth: Philosophical Papers*. Cambridge: Cambridge University Press.

Ross, M. L. (2001). Does oil hinder democracy? *World Politics*, 53(April), 325–361.

Ross, R. (1999). The geography of the peace: East Asia in the 21st century. *International Security*, 23(4), 81–118.

Ruggie, J. G. (1998). Introduction. What makes the world hang together? Neo-Utilitarianism and the social constructivist challenge. In *Constructing the World Policy. Essays on International Institutionalization*, pp. 1–39. London: Routledge/Taylor and Francis Group.

Rummel, R. J. (1983). Libertarianism and international violence. *Journal of Conflict Resolution*, 27(1), 27–71.

Rummel, R. J. (1994). *Death by Government*. New Bruswick, N.J.: Transaction Publishers.

Rummel, R. J. (1995). Democracies ARE less Warlike than Other Regimes. *European Journal of International Relations, 1*(4), 457–479.

Rummel, R. J. (1997). Is collective violence correlated with social pluralism? *Journal of Peace Research, 34*(2), 163–175.

Runciman, W. G. (1966). *Relative deprivation and social justice: a study of attitudes to social inequality in twentieth-century England*. Berkeley: University of California Press.

Ruohomäki, O. & Kivimäki, T. (2001). *Navigating Conflict Prevention and Mitigation. Guidelines for Finnish Development Cooperation*. Helsinki: Finnish Foreign Ministry.

Rusk, D. (1951). Statement to the media. *NBC Battle Report*.

Russell, B. (1984). *Theory of Knowledge: The 1913 Manuscript*. London: George Allen and Unwin.

Russett, B. (1990). *Controlling the Sword: The Democratic Governance of National Security*. Cambridge, Mass.: Harvard University Press.

Russett, B. (1993). *Grasping Democratic Peace*. Princeton NJ: Princeton University Press.

Russett, B. (1996). Why Democratic Peace. In *Michael E. Brown, Sean M. Lynn-Jones and Steven E. Miller, eds., Debating Democratic Peace. An International Security Reader*, pp. 82–115. Cambridge, Mass.: MIT Press.

Sakhong, L. (2009). Bamboo famine of Chin State. Interview of the Vice Chairman of the drafter of the federal constitution proposal of the Ethnic Nationalities Union of Burma in Stockholm.

Sales, L. (2012). Israeli spokesman explains attacks on Gaza militants. *Australian Broadcasting Corporation Broadcast*. Retrieved from http://www.abc.net.au/7.30/content/2012/s3633929.htm.

Sartre, J.-P. (1984). *Being and Nothingness* (Translated by *Hazel B. Barnes*). New York: Washington Square Press.

Saussure, F. de. (2006). *Writings in General Linguistics*. Oxford: Oxford University Press.

Scheffler, L. (1974). *Four Pragmatists: A Critical Introduction to Peirce, James, Mead and Dewey*. London & New York: Routledge & Kegan and Humanities Press.

Schelling, T. C. (1980). *The Strategy of Conflict*. Cambridge, Mass.: Harvard University Press.

Searle, J. (1976). *The Construction of Social Reality*. New York: Free Press.

Serrano, F. (1954). "Guide to the SEATO," memorandum written by the Philippine Foreign Secretary, Serrano Papers, Lopez Memorial Library, Filippiana Collection. Manila.

Shambaugh, D. (2011). Introduction. In *D. Shambaugh, ed., Power Shift, China and Asia's New Dynamics*, pp. 1–15. Berkeley, CA: University of California Press.

Shambaugh, D. (2012). *Tangled Titans: The United States and China*. Lanham, MD: Rowman & Littlefield.

Shambaugh, D. (2013). *China Goes Global: The Partial Power*. New York: Oxford University Press.

Sil, R., & Katzenstein, P. J. (2010). *Beyond paradigms: analytic eclecticism in the study of world politics*. Palgrave Macmillan.

Singer J. D. (1969). The Incomplete Theorist: Insight without Evidence. In *K. Knorr, and J. N. Rosenau, eds., Contending Approaches to International Politics*, pp. 62–86. Princeton: Princeton University Press.

Singer, J. D. (1976). The Correlates of War Project: Continuity, Diversity, and Convergence. In *F. W. Hoole and D. A. Zinnes, eds., Quantitative International Politics: An Appraisal*, pp. 21–24. New York: Praeger.

Singer, J. D. (1979). The Historical Experiment as a Research Strategy in the Study of World Politics. In *J. D. Singer, ed., The Correlates of War I: Research Origins and Rationale*. New York: Free Press.

Singer, J. D. (1980). Conflict Research, Political Action, and Epistemology. In *T. R. Gurr, ed., Handbook of Political Conflict*, pp. 490–499. New York: Free Press.

Sisodia, N. S. & Behuria, A. K. (2007). *West Asia in Turmoil: Implications for Global Security*. New Delhi: Academic Foundation.

Smith, A. (1996). Diversionary foreign policy in democratic systems. *International Studies Quarterly, 40*(1), 133–153.

Smith, A. (2001). *Wealth of Nations*. Raleigh NC: Hayes Barton Press.

Smith, R., M. (2003). *Stories of Peoplehood. The Politics and Morals of Political Membership*. Cambridge: Cambridge University Press.

Reardon, B.A. & Snauwaert D. T. (2015). *Betty A. Reardon: A Pioneer in Education for Peace and Human Rights*. Heidelberg: Springer.

Sovacool, B. K. (2010). The political economy of oil and gas in Southeast Asia: Heading towards the natural resource curse? *Pacific Review, 23*(2), 225–259.

Starr, H. (2000). *Anarchy, Order, and Integration: How to Manage Interdependence*. Ann Arbor, MI: University of Michigan Press.

Stein, A. A. (1990). *Why Nations Cooperate: Circumstance and Choice in International Relations.* Cornell University Press.

Stevens, J. D. (1970). When sedition laws were enforced: Wisconsin in World War I. *Transactions of the Wisconsin Academy of Sciences, Arts and Letters, 58,* 39–60.

Suganami, H. (1996). *On the Causes of War.* Oxford: Clarendon Press.

Sundberg, R. (2008). Collective Violence 2002–2007: Global and Regional Trends. In *H. Lotta and R. Sundberg, eds., States in Armed Conflict.* Uppsala: Universitetstruckeriet.

Svensson, I. & Lindgren, M. (2013). Peace from the Inside: Exploring the Role of the Insider-Partial Mediator. *International Interactions, 39*(5), 698–722.

Tanter, R. (1999). *Rogue Regimes: Terrorism and Proliferation.* Palgrave Macmillan.

The Independent Commission on Disarmament and Security Issues. (1982). *Common Security: A Blueprint for Survival.* New York: Simon and Schuster.

Thoha, A. (2005). Interview by the author with a successful Madurese businessman (large scale construction) in Singkawang.

Thucydides. (1972). *History of the Peloponnesian War* (Translated by *Rex Warner*). London: Penguin Books.

Thurlow, A. & Helms Mills, J. (2009). Change, talk and sensemaking. *Journal of Organizational Change Management, 22*(5), 459–479.

Tickner, J. A. (1992). *Gender in International Relations.* New York, NY: Colombia University Press.

Tickner, J. A. (2004). Feminist responses to international security studies. *Peace Review, 16*(1), 43–48.

Tilly, C. (1978). *From Mobilization to Revolution.* Reading, MA: Addison Wesley Publishing Company.

Tilly, C. (1990). *Coercion, Capital and European States, AD 990–1990.* Cambridge, MA: Basil Blackwell.

Tilly, C. (1993). *European Revolutions,* 1492–1992. Oxford: Blackwell.

Tomz, M. R. & Weeks, J. L. P. (2013). Public opinion and the democratic peace. *American Political Science Review, FirstView,* 1–17.

Truman, H. S. (1950a). Radio and Television Report to the American People on the Situation in Korea. Retrieved from http://www.presidency.ucsb.edu/ws/index.php?pid=13604&st=&st1=.

Truman, H. S. (1950b). *Text of Truman's statement.* NewYork: Herald Tribune.

Tuomela, R. (2005). We-intentions revisited. *Philosophical Studies, 125*(3), 327–369.

Tuomela, R. & Miller, K. (1985). We-intention and social action. *Analyse & Kritik, 7,* 26–43.

Van Parijs, P. (1981). *Evaluationary Explanation in the Social Sciences: An Emerging Paradigm.* London & New York Tavistock.

UCDP. (2012). Battle-Related Deaths Dataset v.5-2012, Uppsala Conflict Data Program. Retrieved from http:www.ucdp.uu.se, Uppsala University.

Vital, D. (1967). *The Inequality of States.* Oxford: Oxford University Press.

United States, Russia Begin Discussing Syrian Chemical Weapons Disarmament in Geneva. (2013). *Foreign Policy Morning Brief.* Retrieved from https://mail.google.com/mail/u/0/?ui=2&ik=d48928b4eb&view=pt&search=inbox&th=14111f9ed10f2db6.

Wæver Ole (1995). Securitization and desecuritization. In *R. D. Lipschutz, ed., On Security.* New York: Columbia University Press.

Wallace, M. D. (1979). Arms races and escalation: Some new evidence. *Journal of Conflict Resolution, 23*(1), 3–16.

Waltz, K. N. (1968). *Man, the States and War: A Theoretical Analysis.* New York: Columbia University Press.

Waltz, K. N. (1979). *Theory of International Politics.* Reading, MA: Addison Wesley Publishing Company.

Weiner, A. (2001). *Making Sense of War: The Second World War and the Fate of the Bolshevik Revolution.* Princeton, NJ: Princeton University Press.

Wendt, A. (1998). *Social Theory of International Politics.* Cambridge: Cambridge University Press.

Wendt, A. (2001). Driving with the rearview mirror: On the Rational Science of Institutiona Design. *International Organization, 55,* 1019–1049.

Wight, C. (2006). *Agents, Structures and International Relations. Politics as Ontology.* Cambridge: Cambridge University Press.

Wilshire, B. (1997). Pragmatism, neopragmatism, and phenomenology: The richard rorty phenomenon. *Human Studies, 20*(1), 95–108.

Winarso, S. (2014). *Relative Deprivation and Resource Mobilization in Southern Thailand.* Helsinki: Draft Doctoral Dissertation at the University of Helsinki.

Wodak, R. (2001). A Discourse-historical approach. In *R. Wodak and M. Meyer, eds., Methods of Critical Discourse Analysis,* pp. 63–94. London: Sage.

Von Wright, G. H. (1971). *Explanation and Understanding.* London: Routledge.

Wright, Q. (1965). *A Study of War.* (2nd edition). Chicago: Chicago University Press.

Wyn Jones, R. (1999). *Security, Strategy and Critical Theory.* Boulder, CO: Lynne Rienner.

Xi, J. (2013). Let the Sense of Community of Common Destiny Take Deep Root in Neighbouring Countries, Speech by the President of the Peoples Republic of China, October 25, 2013. Retrieved from http://www.fmprc.gov.cn/mfa_eng/wjb_663304/wjbz_663308/activities_663312/t1093870.shtml.

YD, A. informant. (2001). Malay fighter. Interview, based on a questionnaire by the author, by Syarif I. Alqadrie.

Young, M. (1991a). *The Vietnam Wars* 1945–1990. New York: HarperPerennial.

Young, O. (1991b). *Bargaining: Formal Theories of Negotiation.* Urbana, Ill: Illinois Press.

Young, M. (2000). The mad bombers. *Diplomatic History, 24*(2), 365–370.

Yue, J. (2008). Peaceful Rise of China: Myth or reality? *International Politics, 45*(4), 439–456.

Zartman, I. W. (1977). *Negotiation Process: Theory and Applications.* London: Sage.

Zartman, I. W. & Berman, M. (1982). *The Practical Negotiator.* New Haven: Yale University Press.

Zeuthen, F. (1930). *Problems of Monopoly and Economic Warfare.* London: Pinter.

Zoellick, R. B. (2005). Whither China: From Membership to Responsibility? Department of State. The Office of Electronic Information. Bureau of Public Affairs. Retrieved from http://2001-2009.state.gov/s/d/former/zoellick/rem/53682.htm.

Zuhur, S. (2009). Gaza, Israel, Hamas and the lost calm of operation cast lead. *Middle East Policy, XVI*(1), 40–52.

Index

H

Habermas, Jürgen, 12, 172
hegemonic interpretations, 159
Hitler, Adolf, 57, 115, 147–148
Hume, David, 20, 44

I

India, 87
individual rationality, 129–134
Indonesia, 9, 29–30, 59, 103, 111,
    117–118, 136–137, 139, 144,
    163–164, 213
        Indonesian, 67, 83, 100
institutional facts, 5, 66, 125–126,
    143, 145
interpretation(s), 12–13, 22–23,
    29, 46, 50, 60, 68, 71, 80, 83,
    85, 88, 95, 102–103, 110, 112,
    119–121, 143–144, 147–148,
    152, 155–156, 162, 164–165,
    172, 174–178, 180–182,
    184–185, 188, 211, 214–215,
    223
        hegemonic interpretation,
        155
interpretationism, 4–5, 10, 47, 141
interpretative bargaining leverage,
    179
interpretative hermeneutical, 224
Iran, 59–60, 76, 84–89, 129,
    205–206
Iraq, 58, 84–85, 87–89, 187, 194,
    201–203, 205, 212
        Iraqi, 214
ISIS, 223
Israel, 56, 59–60, 87, 196,
    206–207
        Israeli, 83

J

James, William, 3, 8

K

Kalimantan, West, 56, 59, 78,
    100–101, 103, 123–125, 131,
    136, 138, 144, 148
Kalla, Jusuf, 111
Kant, Immanuel, 11–12, 55
Kekkonen, Urho K., 55
Kissinger, Henry, 55, 104, 119
Korea, 201

L

leverage, 92, 94, 98, 118–119,
    152, 175
liberal democratic peace, 19
Libya, 89, 133, 167, 187, 201

M

Mali, 167
Marx, Karl, 62, 111, 139
Marxist, 64–65
masculinity, 102, 138–139,
    156–157, 165, 167–169, 188
material, 17, 20
material dependence on BATNA,
    184
material realities, 46, 66, 68, 70,
    122, 126, 149–150, 153, 156,
    188, 218
material structures, 66–67
Mead, Georg H., 10
metaphor, 22, 47, 134
meta-theory, 1–3, 17, 46–47,
    172
methodology, 21, 23, 43, 69–70,
    72